GOOD TO TALK?

1/23/61

GOOD TO TALK?

living and working
in a communication culture

Deborah Cameron

SAGE Publications
London • Thousand Oaks • New Delhi

First published 2000

 SAGE Publications Ltd
6 Bonhill Street
London EC2A 4PU

SAGE Publications Inc
2455 Teller Road
Thousand Oaks, California 91320

SAGE Publications India Pvt Ltd
32, M-Block Market
Greater Kailash - I
New Delhi 110 048

British Library Cataloguing in Publication data

A catalogue record for this book is
available from the British Library

ISBN 0 7619 5770 7
ISBN 0 7619 5771 5 (pbk)

Library of Congress catalog card number available

Typeset by SIVA Math Setters, Chennai, India.
Printed in Great Britain by Biddles Ltd, Guildford, Surrey

CONTENTS

PROLOGUE

'It's how we plan and organize our lives. It's how we build friendships and get close to people. It's how we get to understand how other people feel – and sometimes discover important things about ourselves. It's how we influence people and allow them to influence us. It's how we sort out problems, co-operate with each other and create new opportunities'

– TalkWorks: How to Get More Out of Life through Better Conversations,
British Telecom, 1997.

The quotation above comes from an advice booklet produced on behalf of the UK's largest phone company, British Telecommunications plc (BT, 1997); the 'it' that begins each sentence is 'communication', or more exactly, *talk*.[1] TalkWorks is a registered trademark, the name of 'a major BT initiative to help people become more effective communicators, by providing a range of publications and learning materials'. This particular publication, available free of charge to any UK resident, announces itself on page one as 'a book that can help change your life'. The text explains: 'a lot of the anxiety, frustration and "people problems" we encounter as we go through life have their roots in poor communication. By getting better at how we understand and deal with other people, life can improve in many different ways'.

Also on my desk as I write is a book whose title is *Family Violence from a Communication Perspective* (Cahn and Lloyd, 1996). This is a very different kind of text, addressed to researchers and professional practitioners in the fields of health and social services. It is considerably less bright and breezy in tone than the BT booklet, for after all it is dealing with the darker side of human relationships: prominent among its concerns are date rape, wife beating and child abuse. Its starting point, however, is very similar to BT's. According to the jacket blurb, 'the chapters examine…emotional, psychological, verbal and sexual abuse and show how they all stem from basic communication problems'.

These texts, one upbeat and popular, the other soberly academic, are striking examples of the phenomenon I set out to investigate in this book, and they are by no means isolated cases. In recent years it has become commonplace to find all sorts of problems being described as 'communication problems' – problems arising from the ways in which people talk, or do not talk, to one another. The perception that 'poor communication' is at the root of many problems prompts various interventions aimed at getting people to communicate better. Programmes of education and training have been instituted with the goal of improving 'communication skills'; in workplaces, schools and colleges, more and more people are receiving formal instruction in how to talk to one another, and in some cases their performance is being formally assessed. Some of the most spectacular publishing successes of the 1990s were popular psychology and self-help books concerned with issues of communication, including Deborah Tannen's *You Just Don't Understand* (1991), John Gray's *Men are from Mars, Women are from Venus* (1992), and Daniel Goleman's *Emotional Intelligence* (1995). Communication is one of the themes of Britain's national celebrations to mark the year 2000: the centrepiece of those celebrations, the 'Millennium Experience', a sort of exposition-cum-theme park housed in a purpose-built dome in Greenwich, features an entire 'zone' dedicated to 'the importance of communication in our lives'. These examples illustrate that we live in what might be called a 'communication culture'. By that I do not mean merely a culture that communicates, nor one that regulates communicative behaviour (all cultures do both those things). Rather I mean a culture that is particularly self-conscious and reflexive about communication, and that generates large quantities of metadiscourse about it. For the members of such a culture it is axiomatically 'good to talk' – but at the same time it is natural to make judgements about which kinds of talk are good and which are less good. People aspire, or think they ought to aspire, to communicate 'better'; and they are highly receptive to expert advice. The *TalkWorks* booklet was requested by two million people in the first 18 months of its existence; evaluations carried out on behalf of BT were almost embarrassingly positive; many people whose opinions were not solicited contacted the company independently to express appreciation and ask for more. The booklet's author, evidently surprised as well as pleased by the extent of the demand, told me: 'we're pushing at an open door'.[2]

Practices like teaching and assessing communication skills or offering advice on 'better conversations' fall into the category of what I have elsewhere labelled 'verbal hygiene' (Cameron, 1995), meaning attempts to 'clean up' language-use so it conforms to particular standards of correctness, clarity, efficiency, beauty or morality. Verbal hygiene harnesses our propensity for making value-judgements on language to our more general desire for order and meaning; setting language to rights becomes a surrogate for setting the world to rights. Thus complaints about the misuse of the apostrophe or the ubiquity of profane language on television may express deeper, more amorphous anxieties about the loss of standards in an increasingly permissive society, while efforts to keep a language 'pure' may spring not only from concern about the language itself, but also from a feeling that its speakers' distinctive racial, ethnic or national identity is under threat. Whenever some aspect of language becomes a matter of widespread concern, and new regimes of verbal hygiene spring up to deal with it, it is always pertinent to ask: what else might lie behind this?

In the chapters that follow I consider what might lie behind the current obsession with 'communication'. I examine the discourse and the practices in which concerns about communication are manifested in contemporary English-speaking societies; and I argue that many of these concerns can be linked to the economic, social and cultural changes that are often discussed under the heading of 'globalization'.[3] Those developments have implications for our experience and understanding of ourselves as workers, as consumers, as citizens of nation states, as members of communities and actors in the wider world. They also have implications for the way we talk, and the way we perceive the significance of talk. As the linguistic anthropologist Susan Gal has observed, ideas about what is desirable in the sphere of language-using are always 'systematically related to other areas of cultural discourse such as the nature of persons, of power, and of a desirable moral order' (Gal, 1995: 171). Regimes of verbal hygiene that centre on 'communication' are inseparable from changing concepts of identity, agency and society. They are both a reflex of cultural change and one means for bringing it about. It is with that in mind that I set out in this book to discover their motivations, describe their mechanisms and assess their implications. In what ways and for what purposes is it believed to be 'good to talk'?

ACKNOWLEDGEMENTS

This list of acknowledgements would be considerably longer had not the majority of those who helped me preferred not to be identified by name. Although I regret this, since it means I must withhold from readers information which, they might well think, has a bearing on their ability to assess what I say in these pages, I owe a great debt to my anonymous informants and I acknowledge it here with thanks. It is also my pleasure to thank Emmanuel Akele, Andrew Bailey, the Bank of Scotland, BIFU, Raymond Bell, BT, Dianne Butterworth, Gordon Graham, Samantha Houten, Johanna Jameson, Karen MacGowan, Mark Sims and USDAW.

For supplying additional references, data, contacts and/or expert advice, I am grateful to Kristina Bennert, Kristine Fitch, Karen Grainger, Roxy Harris, Caroline Henton, Scott Kiesling, Bethan Marshall, David Meaden, Keith Nightenhelser, Hermine Scheeres, Stuart Tannock, Steve Taylor, Jack Whalen, Mel Wininger, Anne Witz and Anne-Marie Cullen. Also and especially, I am grateful to Simon Frith and Don Kulick, whose intelligent criticism has done so much to improve the finished text.

I thank Strathclyde University, which granted me research leave, and New York University's international visiting scholar program, which enabled me to spend some of it in the US (many thanks to John Singler and Bambi Schieffelin). Warmest thanks, too, to my editor Julia Hall for her support, and to Meryl Altman, Tom and Beryl Markus for their friendship and hospitality. Since the completion of this project coincides with my departure from Strathclyde, I will end by acknowledging the professional and personal debt I owe to my closest colleagues there: Nigel Fabb, Martin Montgomery and Margaret Philips.

1

INTRODUCTION:
GOOD TO TALK?

'I think a lot of people tend to take communication for granted in some way...it's something they don't have to think about...if they perhaps learned to do it better it would improve everything else – all other aspects of their life'.
– Anonymous respondent, National Communication Survey, 1996.

Throughout the 1990s, 'it's good to talk' was the advertising slogan used by the phone company British Telecom (BT).[1] I imagine the advertising agency chose it for much the same reason that I am recycling it: not because it is original or witty, but because it is a truism – indeed, it is one of the great clichés of our time.

In its advertising, BT uses the everyday word, 'talk'. Elsewhere, it prefers the more formal and technical term 'communication'. In 1996, the BT Forum (a BT-funded body that sponsors research on 'the role of communication in society') commissioned the first in a promised series of National Communication Surveys, *Listening to the Nation*. Researchers interviewed a random sample of almost 1000 people. Among the 'headline findings' they reported were that 83% of respondents agreed with the statement 'good communicators lead happier lives', and 73% agreed that 'making the effort to communicate is the key to happy relationships with people'. At the same time, only half considered themselves to be good communicators, and 60% expressed a desire to be better. One respondent commented: 'I think a lot of people take communication for granted in some way...it's something they don't have to think about...if they perhaps learned to do it better, it would improve everything else – all other aspects of their life'.[2]

It seems then that people attach considerable importance to 'communication'. Good communication is said to be the key to a better and happier life; improving communication 'would improve everything else'. But that in itself surely casts doubt on the idea that communication is something people 'take for granted' and 'don't have to think about'. The very fact that it is apparently so important might suggest that, on the contrary, we think about it a great deal. There is certainly no shortage of people exhorting us to think about it: employers and the various consultants they bring into our workplaces, experts who write self-help books and appear on TV talk shows, bodies that commission and publicize surveys like *Listening to the Nation*. When these people remind us how important communication is, the idea that we should 'learn to do it better' is seldom far away.

It is significant that people like the survey respondent quoted above use the term 'communication' when what they actually mean is 'talking' (*Listening to the Nation* found that 86% of all reported communication was face-to-face, while a further 12% was on the telephone). A common-place social activity has been transformed into a technical skill, with its own professional experts and its own technical jargon. It is because I am interested in this transformation that I have chosen to focus on spoken interaction in this book. Equating 'communication' with 'talk' may seem perverse or naive; this after all is the much-hyped 'information age', and we are constantly reminded that the global citizen of the 21st century will need not merely to be literate, but to be literate in a range of media. Yet in a great deal of current rhetoric about 'communication' it is clear that the object of concern is spoken language used for interactive purposes. Where 'communication' refers to writing, or to the use of electronic media, or even to very formal modes of public speaking, that will usually be spelt out. In the unmarked case, 'communication' means *talk*: it means the spoken interactions we engage in routinely at home, at work or school, and in the course of our other everyday activities. This covers a range of social settings and relationships, and encompasses a spectrum from very casual to fairly formal talk, but still it is basically 'ordinary' talk: sponta-neous as opposed to planned, interactive rather than monologic. And what interests me is precisely the novelty of approaching this sort of talk in the way we have traditionally approached writing, and more recently other 'literacies'. The norms of written language have been codified and taught for centuries; literacy has always been an acquired skill – albeit in modern times one that is expected of almost everyone. In the case of spoken language, by contrast, only the most formal and ritual-ized instances have been extensively codified and their rules explicitly taught. Judgements of skill have undoubtedly been made, but the criteria have been variable and largely implicit. Now it seems that things are changing.

Changing attitudes to and practices of talk are the subject of this book, and I will ask two main questions about them. One is, *how* are people being exhorted or required to talk in contemporary society? What lin-guistic and social norms define 'good' and 'bad' communication? By whom, and for whom, are the norms constructed, and how are they enforced? The other question is *why*. Why is there a perceived need to regulate, codify and make judgements on even the most banal forms of spoken communication? What motivates the contemporary belief that communication is both the cause of all problems and the cure for all ills? Detailed answers to these questions must wait until later chapters. Here, though, I want to sketch out the broader context in which I have found it useful to locate my questions.

I have found it enlightening to think about the phenomenon of 'communication' (by which I mean not 'the phenomenon of people talking' but 'the phenomenon of widespread concern about the skills people bring to the activity of talking') in connection with the economic and social developments of the historical period that is sometimes termed 'high' or 'late' modernity. In particular, I find it pertinent to locate 'communication' in relation to recent shifts which are often put under the heading of 'enterprise culture'. These developments affect language, and our ways of thinking about language; in many cases they also work at least partly *through* language, which is an instrument as well as an object of cultural change.

Reflexive modernity

In his book *Modernity and Self-Identity*, the social theorist Anthony Giddens is concerned with the way people in the conditions of late modernity create what he calls 'self-identity', which he glosses as 'the self as reflexively understood by the individual in terms of his or her biography' (Giddens, 1991: 244). The concept of 'reflexivity' is central to Giddens's understanding of modernity in general. Modern societies continuously generate knowledge and information about the world, which then informs the way people act in the world: as a result the world itself changes. It is also characteristic of modern societies that knowledge and information are ordered into what Giddens calls 'expert systems': 'modes of technical knowledge which have validity independent of the practitioners and clients who make use of them' (1991: 18). Pre-modern or 'traditional' cultures recognize expert knowledge, of course, but Giddens argues this is usually dependent on procedures that cannot be codified and used indifferently by anyone. (Penicillin should work no matter who prescribes it for whom, but the efficacy of a traditional healing ritual may depend crucially on who performs it and in what circumstances.)

Modernity's 'modes of technical knowledge' are not only about things like medicine and engineering. There are also acknowledged 'experts' deploying recognized 'technical knowledge' about social identity and social relationships. These experts offer specialist knowledge and guidance on sex, marriage, divorce, bringing up children, and so on, all subjects where in the past people would have acquired knowledge and skill through more informal modes of instruction and through direct initiation.

As Giddens says, the way people in contemporary societies both understand and actually 'do' sex, or parenthood, is affected significantly by their exposure to authoritative technical knowledge about it. In this book I will explore the idea that 'communication' is another area in which expert systems are asserting themselves over more traditional, informal and diffuse ways of organizing knowledge and practice; and that this has implications for the way we experience, understand and conduct spoken interaction.

The increasing systematization of knowledge and the codification of procedures for talking to other people can plausibly be linked to the developments Giddens associates with the creation of 'self-identity' in late modernity. He suggests that 'in the context of a post-traditional order, the self becomes a *reflexive project*' (1991: 32, italics in original). People no longer make pre-ordained transitions from one life-stage to another in a cultural milieu that stays the same over generations. Instead they must constantly make and remake themselves (their 'selves'), connecting their personal histories to a larger social history in which change is rapid and continual. Giddens argues that people do this by reflexively constructing autobiographical narratives: 'A person's identity is not to be found in behaviour, nor – important though this is – in the reactions of others, but in *the capacity to keep a particular narrative going*. The individual's biography...must continually integrate events that occur in the external world and sort them into the ongoing "story" about the self' (1991: 54). This account throws up the possibility – one which, again, I will explore further in the chapters that follow – that at least some current anxieties about 'communication' are anxieties about the ability to tell that 'ongoing story about the self', either to oneself or to others. If identity depends on 'keeping a narrative going', and if narrative is essentially a verbal construct, then language and communication are implicated in the success or failure of identity, and will be foregrounded in relation to anxiety about identity.

One very obvious contemporary manifestation of this sort of anxiety is the pervasiveness of therapy and self-help (much of which is therapy minus the therapist). Therapy is an institution with its own particular procedures for constructing a narrative of the self. Anthony Giddens argues that in contemporary conditions it should be understood not, as some commentators have suggested, as a secular substitute for religion or as a compensation for the alienation and dislocation of life in consumer capitalist societies, but rather as a 'methodology of life-planning' (1991: 180). In therapy the individual pursues her or his 'reflexive project of the self', striving to integrate the inherited past and the present into a coherent ongoing narrative which leads to a 'better' future. While I agree that this is one of the things therapy is for, I will suggest that it also has the function – a moral, even if not specifically religious one – of disseminating ideas about what it means to be a 'good person', and more concretely, of providing models for the behaviour of such a person towards other people. 'Communication' is significant in relation to both functions.

Giddens makes the assumption that it is reasonable to talk about individuals having a *single* 'self-identity'. It is an assumption that might be disputed, as he himself notes: for some theorists, 'an individual has as many selves as there are divergent contexts of interaction' (1991: 190). He is alluding here to certain followers of Erving Goffman, but he also remarks on the resemblance of this view to poststructuralist/ postmodernist ideas about the 'fragmentation' of identity. His own view is rather different. Given that modern societies are complex, and do demand that their members participate in 'divergent contexts of interaction', the construction of identity may involve the integration of diverse experiences and different roles; but in general there will, precisely, be *integration*, or at least an attempt at integration. Individuals do not simply treat their varied experiences as a series of disconnected fragments, but actively try to weave them into a single coherent narrative, whose protagonist is felt to be 'a *continuous* self and body' (1991: 55, my italics). 'A person with a reasonably stable sense of self-identity', Giddens maintains, 'has a feeling of biographical continuity which she is able to grasp reflexively, and, to a greater or lesser degree, communicate to other people' (1991: 54).

The demands made on their members by complex modern societies, and the resulting tensions between fragmentation and integration, have reflexes in linguistic or communicative behaviour, and in the regimes of verbal hygiene which seek to regulate, standardize or 'improve' that behaviour. Some regimes of communication training, for instance (particularly in the workplace and in vocationally oriented forms of education) are prompted by a perceived need to prepare individuals for the 'divergent contexts of interaction' they will encounter, and for which their previous experiences have not prepared them, because the contexts are either new or involve significantly reshaped expectations. For instance, as I will explain in more detail below, many regimes of workplace communication training are part of a managerial project whose overall aim is to produce an 'enterprising' or 'empowered' worker. The context – work – is not new or unfamiliar, but the expectation of enterprise/empowerment is a novel one, and people need guidance on how to meet it. Training and disciplinary regimes associated with 'empowerment' aim to change, not merely the way people behave in the context of work, but who they feel themselves to be in that context (Gee et al., 1996).

Other regimes of verbal hygiene, particularly those found in therapy and self-help, are more concerned with helping people 'make sense of their lives' – that is, to integrate the diversity of their experience into a satisfying narrative, and (crucially in the context of 'communication') to verbalize that experience more effectively and more 'authentically'.

Although this might well be seen theoretically as a process of self-*construction*, it is more commonly represented by those engaged in it as a process of self-*expression*. It does not change who people 'are' or feel themselves to be, but gives them new tools for making intelligible – to themselves as well as others – who they are. A topic that receives systematic attention in some regimes of communication training is 'talking about feelings' – the assumption being that the feelings themselves are 'there', the established property of an already-existing self, and what is lacking is only the level of communication skill needed to do them justice.

Theoretically, I understand regimes of both types as constitutive rather than merely expressive: I would not argue that one is about creating 'inauthentic' selves and the other about expressing 'authentic' ones. Nevertheless, one reason I prefer Giddens's account of self-identity to the postmodernist postulate of endlessly fragmented selves is that 'authenticity' appears to be a key issue in understanding the way people respond to regimes that seek to regulate their spoken interaction. Giddens observes (1991: 54) that 'The individual's biography, if she is to maintain regular interaction with others in the day-to-day world, cannot be wholly fictive'. He is talking about the need for an individual's story to integrate things that happen in the outside world, as opposed to being completely inward-looking and solipsistic; but in the context of 'communication' the comment takes on an additional resonance. The individual's ways of talking are part of the whole biographical package; indeed I will argue that they are commonly understood as rather direct products of innate 'character' combined with individual life experience (the sort of person someone is together with the sorts of things they have done). Consequently, people often display resistance to being made to interact with others in a linguistic persona they regard as 'wholly fictive'. Such resistance is one of the most significant problems facing those who wish to build new and comprehensive expert systems around the everyday activity of talking. Expert systems are general and impersonal: they apply without regard to the particularities of persons or contexts. In this case, they detach the skills and techniques of 'communication' from the personal histories and qualities of those engaged in it. But this approach does not meet with universal or complete acceptance, largely because it conflicts with ideas about individual 'authenticity', and about speech as an important reflex of that, which continue to have wide currency. If most people today really inhabited the multiple and fragmented subjectivities suggested by some poststructuralist and postmodernist theory, this would be difficult to account for.

In sum, then, current concerns about 'communication' provide a good example of modernity's 'reflexivity'. They exemplify the way every aspect of modern life is liable to be put under the microscope, both by experts and by laypeople. They are part of the general reflexive project of knowing how things are or should be done in order to control them and do them better. They are also part of the more specific 'reflexive project of the self', since the construction of a biographical narrative is a discursive and linguistic accomplishment. At the same time, the kind of biographical narrative that constitutes self-identity has continuity and 'authenticity' (see Giddens, 1991: 78–9) among its central concerns. The overall effect is somewhat paradoxical. As spoken interaction comes increasingly to be treated as a set of 'skills', and colonized by expert systems with their decontextualized, transferable procedures, there is a risk that its capacity to signify 'authentically' who an individual is and what s/he thinks or feels will be compromized.

Enterprise culture

The colonization of spoken interaction by expert systems has been accelerated and intensified by the recent social and economic shifts which are often glossed in the phrase 'enterprise culture'. Later I will make specific connections between 'communication' and enterprise culture, but first it is necessary to say something more about the phenomenon of enterprise culture itself. While the phrase may call to mind specific political projects, such as the propaganda initiative launched during the 1980s by Margaret Thatcher's government to encourage people to set up businesses and invest in the stock market, here it is intended to mean something much broader. It encompasses developments which have outlasted the Thatcher era (in some cases they post-date that era), which are not peculiar to Britain, and which cannot be seen as the sole preserve of the ideological Right. 'Enterprise culture' should not be taken as synonymous with 'business culture' either. It is possible to do business in ways that are not 'enterprising', and to conduct other activities (such as family life) in ways that *are* 'enterprising'.

If you look up *enterprise* in the *Concise Oxford Dictionary*, you find three senses listed: 1. An undertaking, especially a bold and difficult one. 2. (As a personal attribute) Readiness to engage in such undertakings. 3. A business firm.

The 'enterprise' in 'enterprise culture' means a set of attributes, values and behaviours – such as resourcefulness, self-discipline, openness to risk and change – that enable people to succeed in bold and difficult undertakings. These are prototypically of the business variety, but not exclusively so. As Graham Burchell notes (1993: 275), the hallmark of enterprise culture is to make business undertakings the model for all undertakings, so that there is a 'generalization of an "enterprise form" to all forms of conduct – to the conduct of organizations hitherto seen as non-economic, to the conduct of government and to the conduct of individuals themselves'.

Many illustrative examples of this 'generalizaton' come to mind (I will take mine mostly from the British context, but I have no doubt they will resonate with the experiences of readers located elsewhere). To begin with 'organizations hitherto seen as non-economic', the most obvious example of 'enterprise' in this context is the 'marketization' of public services since the 1980s. Some services that were state-run monopolies (such as the utilities and the railway network in Britain) were sold into private ownership, and are now enterprises in the 'business firm' sense. Others remained public institutions run on a non-profit basis, but were required to adopt the disciplines of business and the trappings of its culture. Schools and universities were encouraged to write mission statements and compelled to undergo quality auditing. The running of some public institutions, such as prisons, was 'outsourced' to private contractors. In the British National Health Service (NHS), an 'internal market' was created in medical services – which continued, however, to be paid for by tax revenue – in a deliberate effort to simulate features of market capitalism that were thought to make it more efficient than the welfare state.

Moving on to 'the conduct of government', it is notable that politicians now routinely compare the activity of democratic governance to managing a business. The US Vice-President Al Gore once declared: 'We have customers: the American people'. Shortly after the election that brought his 'new' Labour Party to power in 1997, the British Prime Minister Tony Blair told a BBC interviewer: 'If you are running a company nowadays, suppose you are running Marks & Spencer [a major clothing and food retailer] or Sainsbury [one of Britain's 'big four' high-street supermarkets], you will be constantly trying to work out whether your customers are satisfied with the product they are getting. ...I don't think there is anything wrong with government trying to do that'. The grounds for the analogy between politics and retailing have always been there, but it is only recently that politicians have found it appropriate to incorporate it into their rhetoric. (To see what difference that makes, we only have to put Al Gore's 'we have customers' soundbite alongside something that was said by one of his most illustrious predecessors: 'Ask not what your country can do for you...'). The comparison is not only rhetorical, either; government departments are increasingly run on business lines, and new policies, like new product lines, are tested using market research methods like focus-group discussions. It has become fashionable to discuss the nation itself – quintessentially a political entity – in terms more usually associated with marketing consumer goods. One project to which Tony Blair gave a high profile in the early days of his administration was 'rebranding Britain' – modernizing its image so it would be seen less as a heritage theme park and more as 'Cool Britannia'. It was widely reported that this project had been inspired by a report produced for the think-tank Demos, which argued that a clear national identity, like a distinctive brand image, was an economic asset that helped to sell a country's products. The Demos report was titled *Britain™* (Leonard, 1997).

When Graham Burchell asserts that enterprise values govern 'the conduct of individuals themselves', he does not mean only individuals' conduct in the public sphere of industry, commerce and politics, but also in their private lives as community and family members. For example, bringing up children has emerged as a 'bold and difficult undertaking' requiring the acquisition and exercise of quasi-managerial skills (this enterprise is now known as 'parenting'). Advice on all kinds of personal relationships urges us to treat them as if they were business projects: we are told we should 'set goals' or 'negotiate contracts' with family members and friends. We are also urged to 'work on' our individual selves with a view to becoming healthier, happier, better-adjusted and more successful. This philosophy of self-improvement is not new, of course, but it has never been more pervasive than it is now. It also acquires a certain edge as other developments within enterprise culture shift responsibilities from the state to the individual or household.

As I noted in passing earlier, though, enterprise culture is not just a matter of imposing the values and practices of one sphere, business, on other spheres like politics and family life. The values and practices in question are drawn from a particular approach to business, which is relatively recent (and not yet universal) in the business sphere itself. The new approach goes under various names, among them 'enterprise' or 'entrepreneurial' management, management for 'empowerment' or for 'excellence' (a reference to the work of the management 'guru' Tom Peters), or simply 'new wave' management. Whatever it is called, though, the important point to bear in mind about it is that it represents a culture change *within business*. Business has always been a privileged locus for enterprise, but the message of the 'new wave' is that practices which served business well enough in the past are not sufficiently enterprising to meet the particular challenges of the present and future.

If one asks what challenges those might be, the standard response focuses on economic globalization. Financial deregulation together with technological developments (such as better and faster telecommunications and computerized record-keeping) has enabled capital to move more freely across the globe. This intensifies competition: businesses can shift investment to wherever in the world they can produce goods to the necessary standard at the lowest cost. Developing economies, like the so-called Asian tigers, offer modern technology and skilled workers who do not however demand 'first world' wages. To compete, therefore, companies operating in the more affluent parts of the world must attempt both to lower their costs and to improve their standards of quality and service. It is this imperative that has been seen to require a new way of managing business organizations.[3]

Proponents of 'enterprise' usually contrast it with 'bureaucracy', a system that depends on elaborate hierarchies and rigid procedures. In a bureaucratic organization, management is a matter of 'command and control', that is, telling your subordinates what to do and making sure they do it. The 'enterprise' philosophy is different. Instead of setting tasks, the new manager sets goals, and motivates subordinates to meet those goals. The new manager is less concerned with the performance of particular actions than with the achievement of specified, measurable outcomes. Employees have more freedom to decide for themselves how best to achieve those outcomes: the expectation is that they will be 'flexible' – able to pick up new skills as the need arises. It is also assumed that employees at every level already have skills that were untapped, and so wasted, under the traditional 'command and control' regime. With the demise of that regime, their own 'enterprise' is liberated from bureaucratic constraints. This liberation is known as 'empowerment', and in theory it goes along with a flattening of the bureaucratic hierarchy (also known as 'de-layering'). The enterprising organization does not require as many layers as the command and control model did; nor does it want them, for one of its aims is to cut costs, and this is achieved by, among other things, 'downsizing'. 'Enterprise', then, is the key to achieving what on the face of it seems impossible: higher standards at lower cost. Fewer people making freer use of their entrepreneurial talents are supposed to be able to do more for less.

Another pervasive feature of 'enterprising' business is a relentless focus on serving the needs of the customer. Globalization and the associated intensification of competition can be invoked to explain this too. If you cannot compete on the price or the basic quality of the product (because it can be made just as well, and cheaper, in Mexico or Thailand) then you have to compete on service: giving the customer what s/he wants, when s/he wants it, and distinguishing yourself from your competitors through 'intangibles', such as helpfulness and friendliness. It is also notable that the most advanced economies have moved towards being 'post-industrial': the manufacturing sector contracts while the service sector expands. More and more people are working in the kinds of businesses where customer service is not just one consideration among others, but the defining purpose of the organization. And it is businesses of this service-oriented kind – companies like McDonald's or the Disney Corporation – that now tend to be held up as models for successful business in general.

If much of this sounds familiar even to readers who do not work in private businesses, that is partly because we have all encountered some of the manifestations of 'enterprise' when we are the customer, but also because the same philosophy now underpins the management of many public sector and non-profit institutions. Here, obviously, enterprise is not a response to the intensification of global competition. British schools and hospitals do not face the prospect of being undercut by rivals in Malaysia, and British government departments are not going to be subject to a hostile takeover by Germany. There *is* an economic motivation, in as much as most contemporary governments wish to reduce levels of public expenditure. But there are also ideological motives. These are not necessarily straightforward expressions of the 'business is best' philosophy that animated right-wing radicals in the Thatcher/Reagan years. One important motivation for importing elements of enterprise management into the public sector is the idea that state and local government institutions ought to be more responsive and more accountable to the people they supposedly serve. Institutions whose values are liberal or socialist (like universities and Labour councils) have proved as susceptible to this argument as capitalist organizations. But the 'customer care' approach to public service does implicitly take market relationships as paradigmatic, and this requires a change of attitude, from service users as well as providers. Many novel features of public service culture – mission statements, user charters, quality auditing accompanied by published league tables for institutions like hospitals, universities and schools – are intended not only to make public servants shape up, but also to encourage a more enterprising, consumerist approach on the part of the public itself. School league tables, for instance, are published so that parents can make informed choices about where to educate their children; charters for rail passengers or post-office users incorporate complaints procedures and promises of compensation for those who exert themselves to take underperforming institutions to task. To reap the full benefits of 'better service' it is necessary to become a 'better customer'.

Questions of empowerment

A claim often made about the managerial approach taken by 'enterprising' organizations is that this approach *empowers* people – customers, service users and in particular, employees. Commentators have evaluated this claim in a variety of ways, and since the point at issue is relevant to my analysis in later chapters, I want to examine it more closely here.

Nikolas Rose describes the positive assessment made by enthusiasts of new managerial approaches, who believe that the empowerment of workers in enterprise culture produces what negotiators call a 'win/win situation'. Because employees are respected as individuals and given scope for the exercise of their abilities, they can fulfil themselves while simultaneously advancing the interests of their employers and indeed their customers. In Rose's words:

> Employers and managers equipped with these new visions of work have
> claimed that there is no conflict between the pursuits of productivity, efficiency
> and competitiveness on the one hand, and the humanisation of work on the
> other. On the contrary, the path to business success lies in engaging the
> employee with the goals of the company at the level of his or her subjectivity…
> Through striving to fulfil their own needs and wishes at work, each employee
> will thus work for the advance of the enterprise. (1990: 56)

Other commentators take a much more negative view. For the eco-
nomics writers Larry Elliott and Dan Atkinson, for example, the new
managerial approach both arises from and contributes to increasing economic and social inequality. In their book *The Age of Insecurity* (Elliott
and Atkinson, 1998), these writers argue that the removal of restrictions
on the global movement of capital and the near-universal adoption of
low-inflation policies by governments over the past two decades have
shifted the balance of risk from capitalists to workers (by which they
mean not just proletarians, but anyone who relies on selling their labour
to earn a living). If costs rise or sales fall, the response is not to cut the
dividends paid to investors, but to demand more 'flexibility' from the
workforce. But the capitalist's 'flexibility' is the worker's insecurity. In
practice it means de-layering and downsizing – that is, people losing their
jobs; it means cuts in pay and changes to working conditions which are
disadvantageous to the workers. Hourly paid workers may be asked to
come in only when there is work and to stay at home, unpaid, when there
is none; full-time jobs may become part-time, and permanent contracts
fixed-term; certain types of work once done 'in-house' may be outsourced
to independent contractors who employ fewer people and pay them less;
salaried employees may be asked to do the same work on a self-employed
basis. All these arrangements are commoner than they used to be, and
they affect middle-class professionals as well as the less skilled and lower-
paid. The results have been much commented on: not only un- and under-
employment, but also large numbers of working people who suffer from
overwork, stress and anxiety because they are insecure, and who find it
difficult to take on long-term commitments because they are uncertain
whether they will have a job or an adequate income in future. People in
this position, Elliott and Atkinson argue, have little choice but to submit
to demands they might otherwise consider unreasonable: they are not so
much fulfilled by new ways of working as fearful of the consequences if
they do not go along with them.

Elliott and Atkinson also discuss the effect of new economic developments on the activities of governments, which affect citizens regardless of
what kind of work they do. It has come to be accepted by politicians
across the ideological spectrum that national governments cannot and
should not try to clip the wings of global capital, and this implies that
politicians can no longer control national economies in the same way they

could in the past. Government's role is instead to make the nation a place in which capitalists will want to invest, by offering tax breaks and subsidies, adopting low-inflation policies and employment policies which are conducive to labour market 'flexibility' (for instance, curbing the costs of employing people and restricting the power of organized labour), and delivering through the state education system the skills and dispositions companies want their workers to have. The other project that increasingly engages governments, according to Elliott and Atkinson, is a kind of social engineering. As control over capital decreases, so control over individuals intensifies. In its first year of office, for example, the British Labour government proposed a whole raft of measures that might once have been thought too trivial to preoccupy the nation's leaders, from imposing curfews on schoolchildren to making bicycle bells compulsory.

In a book titled *The Corrosion of Character: the Personal Consequences of Work in the New Capitalism* (1998), the sociologist Richard Sennett argues that 'flexibility' is a serious obstacle to the development of long-term social identities and relationships. In Giddens's terms, it interferes with people's ability to sustain a continuous narrative over the course of a lifetime. The new order 'does not offer much, economically or socially, in the way of narrative': it idealizes an entrepreneurial individual who is comfortable with not knowing what comes next, but 'most people...are not at ease with change in this nonchalant, negligent way' (Sennett, 1998: 30). Like Elliott and Atkinson, Sennett distrusts the rhetoric according to which flexibility gives workers more autonomy and freedom. 'In fact, the new order substitutes new controls rather than simply abolishing the rules of the past – but these new controls are also hard to understand. The new capitalism is an often illegible regime of power' (1998: 10).

There are positions in between the rosy picture drawn by enterprise enthusiasts and the unremittingly bleak one drawn by critics like Elliott and Atkinson or Sennett. One kind of 'intermediate' position is taken, for instance, in Paul du Gay's study of cultural change in the UK retail industry, *Consumption and Identity at Work* (1996). Du Gay finds it simplistic to read enterprise culture as either unambiguously liberating or monolithically oppressive. Rather he suggests that culture change has produced 'new ways for people to be at work', and that these are not necessarily 'better' or 'worse', they are simply different – they bring new costs and benefits which different people negotiate in different ways.

Du Gay conducted field research in four companies, and his account of what went on in them supports his call for a complex approach to the phenomenon overall. Some of his informants had, indeed, used the opportunity offered by the rhetoric of empowerment to 'take ownership' of their work, finding new possibilities and pleasures in it; others were more exercised by what they saw as petty restrictions on their personal autonomy. In many instances, du Gay found that the aims of management were partly accepted and partly resisted by subordinates. He discusses, for instance, a 'Quality Team' (QT) meeting where staff in one shop were supposed to take the initiative and produce what management called 'three *hows*', that is, three possible solutions to a particular problem. The staff did produce the desired 'hows', but they pointedly refused to take on their prescribed roles as active initiators of suggestions. Essentially they obliged the manager in charge to drag the right answers out of them. As du Gay comments, this incident can neither be celebrated as a success for the philosophy of empowerment nor admired as a case of collective resistance to that philosophy from below: 'While staff translated the QT into a different discourse register, thus undermining the original intent, they also reproduced its basic conditions of existence by agreeing to implement three "hows"' (1996: 171).

Du Gay's use of the phrase 'discourse register', meaning a particular, institutionally sanctioned way of talking, prompts the question of what role is played by language and communication in the new culture of enterprise. Below I will suggest that their role is a crucial one: language is both an instrument *of* change and a target *for* change. To become 'enterprising', whether as an individual or as an organization, requires you both to put a higher premium on communication in theory, and to do it differently in practice.

Enterprise, language and communication

At the heart of the new management philosophy is a change in the relationship between organizations and the individuals who work in them. Instead of just doing what they are told, 'enterprising' employees are made responsible for motivating, disciplining and directing themselves. At the same time, the organization must ensure that the self-directing worker is moving in step with institutional policy. Empowering people to use their creative abilities is all very well, but their creativity could be directed to some very undesirable ends (embezzlement, sabotage and union organizing, for instance). As Paul du Gay points out (1996: 62–3), the aim is not to liberate workers unconditionally, but rather to organize things in such a way that 'all employees make the goals and objectives of their employing organization their own personal goals and objectives, thus ensuring they will deploy their "autonomy" and "creativity" correctly from the organization's point of view'. And as he also notes, this approach will depend for its success on 'the construction and promulgation of a "strong corporate culture"'. Persuading people to adopt the organization's goals as their own is an ambitious aim, especially if you are talking about the whole range of employees, and not just those with interesting jobs and relatively high status (or the prospect of attaining it). To achieve that aim, the company must endeavour to create a culture in which its goals and values are both made apparent to the workforce and presented in a way that encourages positive identification with them.

In this project, the language of internal communication will play a major part. Du Gay's informants said as much to him; he quotes many references to the idea that culture change involves, or even boils down to, linguistic change, and many more in which language is used metaphorically or metonymically to stand for organizational culture as a whole. For instance:

'You really have to learn a new language' (Regional controller, p. 128).
'You have to win hearts and minds, and it's jargon, I know, but hearts and minds, energies of every member of our staff...so that all 40,000 odd people in [company] would eventually be singing from the same hymn sheet' (Controller, p. 131).
'I don't underestimate the difficulties we have in making sure...that our managers get the right message every time and communicate the message consistently' (Personnel director, p. 132).
'[The success of staff training depends on how far] it becomes part of their everyday language...if they don't take it on board then it won't be successful' (Training manager, p. 147n).

Internal communication may be used simply as a way of 'cheerleading' for particular goals and values (this is the main purpose of the 'vision' and 'mission' statements displayed on office walls across the capitalist world). A more interventionist strategy, however, involves creating new communicative events in which employees are compelled to use a new linguistic register actively. The QT meeting at which sales assistants in one of the companies studied by Paul du Gay had to come up with 'three hows' is an example. The format of the meeting itself obliged participants to orient to certain norms of interaction and play particular communicational roles (in theory, anyway: in practice, as we saw above, the staff refused to adopt their prescribed roles as initiators of talk). In addition, the subject matter and purpose of the meeting obliged participants to make use of a new terminology – it does not seem likely that anyone previously possessed the concept of 'a how', still less that they used the expression. Another increasingly common 'new' workplace speech event is the 'appraisal interview', where the goal of assessing an employee's performance is realized using interactive conventions that resemble those of a therapy or counselling session (some organizations actually call appraisal 'counselling'). Employees may be invited to discuss their strengths and weaknesses, reflect on their past achievements and future goals, and set their own targets for improvement. Since appraisal is typically compulsory, and often consequential in terms of pay and promotion, everyone has an interest in mastering the quasi-therapeutic register associated with it.

Regulating the use of language for purposes of communication within the organization, then, is an important tool in the creation of a 'strong corporate culture'. New values, practices and implicit expectations are signalled by the adoption of new ways of talking – new genres like the mission statement, new speech events like the QT meeting and the appraisal interview, new terminologies which encode important new concepts such as the 'how' (or, to take some notorious examples from the recent history of British university teaching, the 'aim', the 'objective' and the 'learning outcome'). But language use is also regulated – often even more intensively – at the interface between the organization and the outside world, which is to say, in interactions with clients, customers, users and suppliers. This is another locale where enterprise culture requires its members to communicate differently, and to become more conscious of what they are doing when they talk.

As I noted above, the enterprising organization is likely to stress the importance of what is often labelled 'customer care'. After globalization, advanced capitalist economies are dominated by service industries, and even in the manufacturing sector it is often through its service that a company gains its competitive edge. This has implications for language and communication, because 'service' is to a significant extent accomplished by interacting with people. *How* staff interact with others when they represent the organization has become a matter of intense concern. Paul du Gay recounts a conversation with a retail manager who had been impressed, during his training, with an anecdote about the Disney Corporation firing a trainee sales assistant at one of its stores, not because she was dishonest, incompetent or slow, but because she did not make appropriate eye-contact with customers. This story had been told to the manager, and then repeated by him to Paul du Gay, as a tale about the Disney Corporation's legendary attention to detail. An acknowledged world leader in the customer-service game, Disney expected excellent communication skills, verbal and non-verbal, to be displayed by everyone from the CEO to the lowliest checkout clerk.

In the story, Disney fired the unsatisfactory employee; in other companies, or in a case judged less hopeless, an alternative solution might have been to try and fix her 'faulty' eye contact. Employees in many occupations are now routinely given training in various aspects of communication, from 'active listening' to body language. In later chapters I will discuss in more detail what they are being taught, and what they think of it. In quite a few occupations, too, the approach has been adopted of trying to *standardise* interaction between employees and customers. Rather than being trained in general strategies, staff are trained to use standard formulas, and at the extreme, to perform to a uniform script. This is one salient aspect of the phenomenon which the neo-Weberian sociologist George Ritzer calls 'McDonaldization', whereby organizations try to maximise efficiency, calculability, predictability and control in all aspects of their operating routines (Ritzer, 1996).

In relation to customer care, language is once again an instrument of cultural change – new linguistic norms are intended to function as the outward and audible sign of a new inner commitment to the interests of the customer – and at the same time, language is a key target for attitudinal and behavioural change. If it achieves nothing else, communication training impresses on people that they have to think about the way they talk, and not take for granted that their ordinary communicative competence will be adequate for the particular purposes of the workplace. Often, it is intended to achieve rather more than this. It is intended to eradicate, or at least reduce, the variation people exhibit in their ways of interacting, and to bring the communicational behaviour of individuals into conformity with norms defined by the organization.

As we saw early on in this discussion, it is a feature of enterprise culture that norms and practices elaborated first in business are subsequently diffused into other spheres. Norms and practices relating to 'communication' are no exception to this rule; and there is a particularly strong link between the sphere of work and that of education. This is not surprising: from the point of view of employers, and of many politicians, parents and students, schools and colleges are there in large part to provide an appropriately skilled workforce. Educators themselves may take a somewhat different view, but few would deny entirely that it is part of their mission to prepare students for future employment. In any case, they are subject to both political and financial pressure to take notice of what employers want. Increasingly, employers are emphasizing that they want 'communication skills'. This is not, of course, a novel demand, but it is becoming more insistent, more explicit and more systematic.

One reason for that is that more and more jobs actually require workers to communicate. This is partly because of the growth of the service sector. Service work and selling have always involved talking to people; today significant numbers of workers are employed in occupations that consist of little else but spoken interaction (one recent and rapidly spreading development of this kind, which I will consider in detail later, is working in a 'call centre'). Traditionally, manufacturing jobs made fewer demands on workers' linguistic abilities; but the advent of new managerial approaches has changed this to some extent. Even factory assembly-line workers may nowadays find themselves in an appraisal interview, a team meeting or a 'quality circle', which means that talking has become part of what is expected of them.

Another change is that job descriptions, appraisal criteria and so on now foreground the status of communication *as a skill* – not just something workers are expected to do, but something they are expected to be, or become, 'good at'. The interpersonal and linguistic aspects of many jobs often used to be mentioned in job descriptions, if they were mentioned at all, as a vague afterthought ('must enjoy working with people'). Consider, by contrast, the following 'person specification', which defined the ideal recruit for the job being advertised as someone who could

- demonstrate sound interpersonal relationships and an awareness of the individual clients' psychological and emotional needs;
- understand the need for effective verbal and non-verbal communication;
- support clients and relatives in the care environment by demonstrating empathy and understanding.

(source: *Medical Monitor*, 1994).

The language used in this specification might suggest that it is describing a skilled caring professional – a psychologist or social worker, for instance – whose job is centrally about talking to 'clients'. In fact, though, the job on offer is that of a ward orderly in an NHS hospital. Orderlies are 'ancillary' workers (the *COD* gives 'cleaner, esp. male, in a hospital' as a definition of *orderly*); the interactions they have with patients and visitors occur in the course of performing other duties, and are not part of the official clinical regime. In the past it is unlikely the routine but incidental 'communication' element of the job would have been considered worth remarking on. But in the new-style specification, the talking that orderlies do has been formalized as a professional responsibility that calls for specific skills.

The source from which I took this example cited it as a case of 'political correctness' (an attempt to be sensitive to the feelings of unskilled workers by representing hospital cleaning as a more elevated calling than it really is). Arguably however it has more to do with 'new visions of work', to use Nikolas Rose's phrase, according to which there is no such thing as an unskilled job or an unskilled worker – even the most menial job demands the exercise of multiple skills. This point is insisted on, not to spare the feelings of people who do menial jobs, but to make it easier to subject them to new kinds of discipline, such as training and appraisal. When talking to people on the job becomes a formal 'skill' instead of merely an incidental accompaniment to other activities, it becomes legitimate to regulate and assess the way employees talk. It also becomes legitimate to use people's 'communication skills' as a gatekeeping device in recruitment – a criterion for deciding whether or not to offer them employment.

It is at this point that employers' increasingly explicit and exacting requirements become a relevant consideration for the education system which prepares people to enter or re-enter the labour market. Oral communication is regarded as one of the so-called 'key skills' without which a job applicant has little hope of success in today's economy (other 'key skills' include literacy, numeracy, 'teamwork', information technology and problem-solving). In surveys, employers regularly rank communication as the single most important key skill; and they express considerable dissatisfaction with the oral communication skills of their recruits, whether they be school leavers or university graduates. One survey reported in *People Management* journal in 1997 found that 'oral communication was cited as the most important soft skill but was perceived to be sorely lacking in recruits coming straight from further or higher education. While 91% of respondents believed that this was an essential skill, only 32% said it was present among this group' (Mullen, 1997).

Surveys like this one report perceptions rather than hard facts, of course, and even when there is consensus on them it is difficult to gauge whether the employers' beliefs that their recruits are 'sorely lacking' in oral communication skills are well founded. Nevertheless, one reason why these skills might be lacking is that educational institutions have traditionally given them far less attention than the 'basics' of literacy and numeracy. In particular, oral communication has not been the object of standardized assessment and the explicit instruction that goes with it – or at least, not until recently. Schools, further education colleges and some higher education institutions are increasingly adopting a 'teach and test' approach to spoken language, either as part of the subject curriculum (oral skills are one component in the school English syllabus, for example) or as part of an initiative to equip students with a broad range of 'key', 'core' or 'transferable' skills (this approach is set to be adopted in education after the age of 16 in both England and Scotland). Communication has also become an element in courses that lead to what in Britain are called National Vocational Qualifications (NVQs). These courses are designed to be directly relevant to working life, and in some cases they teach oral skills that are specifically demanded by employers – one example is telephone communication.

Educators have not turned to teaching and assessing talk only because of pressure from employers. There has been, and still is, an independent educational agenda which advocates 'oracy' – a term coined as far back as the 1960s – as a means to help students learn more effectively and as part of their personal development. This agenda was at least as influential as the more utilitarian one in getting oral skills into the 'official' school curriculum in Britain in the first instance. But as business has discovered the key nature of these skills in the process of changing its own culture, its perspective on what communication means and why it matters has begun to exert more influence on educational practice.

Education is not only supposed to equip future workers with the skills and competencies their jobs will require, but also to socialize them in particular ways – to inculcate certain social habits, dispositions and values. This is explicitly recognized in the national curriculum for schools in England and Wales, with 'personal, social, health and citizenship education' forming a recognized part of the educational regime. According to the National Curriculum Council, 'the education system...has a duty to educate individuals to be able to think and act for themselves, with an acceptable range of personal abilities and values which must also meet the wider social demands of adult life'. I take this quotation from a report produced for the BT Forum, *Communication: a Key Skill for Education* (Phillips, 1998), which suggests that communication training could play a vital part in the process of socializing the young. Many forms of anti-social behaviour, whether directed against others (like bullying) or against oneself (like drug taking), arise, the report claims, because those who engage in them have not learned to use language to express their feelings and build good relationships with other people. Communication skills teaching offers a way to address these problems: even when remedial intervention is not called for, 'all children benefit from learning skills that will make them better friends, better employees, better life partners and better human beings' (Phillips, 1998: 7).

This sort of rhetoric may seem less obviously connected to the concerns of business than the discourse of vocational skills, but in fact businesses that have adopted new management philosophies and practices have a direct interest in the values and dispositions of the workers they recruit. 'Empowerment' calls for individuals who 'think and act for themselves', while increased emphasis on team building and customer care calls for people who have a certain ease in expressing themselves and relating to other people. The ideal recruit to an enterprising business is self-motivating, but also able and willing to fit in with the corporate culture. As the BT education report puts it (Phillips, 1998: 6), 'Management de-layering, and the need for a flexible workforce able to pick up new skills and competencies, means that businesses can no longer accommodate the genius in the corner...Employees today need to be able to pick up new skills and pass them on. They need to listen carefully and motivate themselves and others'.

But in any case, work itself is not the only domain in which 'enterprise' can be displayed. Calls to raise standards of communication in order to make 'better human beings' are part of the more general trend whereby every aspect of life becomes potentially a self-improvement project. This in turn reflects perceptions of the self as a tradable asset. Andrew Wernick argues in his book *Promotional Culture* that 'social life in every dimension has increasingly come to assume a commodity or quasi-commodity form' (1991: 185): not only jobs but social and sexual relationships have their 'markets', in which individuals must advertise themselves as desirable commodities. Language is both a medium for this kind of advertisement and one of the commodities being advertised (something that becomes overt in personal ads, which commonly specify conversational facility and a 'good sense of humour' as attributes of the desired/desirable person).

When incorporated into the school curriculum, the self-improvement project effectively becomes compulsory for people of a certain age; but there are plenty of other social locations where adults may (and do) engage in it by choice. Guidance on better communication is available even without making an institutional commitment (like signing up for therapy or counselling, or taking a course). Initiatives like the BT Forum and its 'practical' arm, TalkWorks, make some forms of communication skills training readily accessible to people in their own homes. Bookshops and libraries devote acres of shelf-space to self-help texts with titles like *Confident Conversation, Difficult Conversations, I See What You Mean, That's Not What I Meant, Words That Hurt, Words That Heal*, and so on. Entertainment media, too, especially talk radio and television, now disseminate to a mass audience the idea that being able and willing to talk about problems, feelings and relationships is inherently desirable. Some popular media formats – notably the confessional talk-show – not only provide continual reinforcement for the basic idea that 'it's good to talk', but also model the 'correct' way of talking about personal experience in some detail.

Hybridity and technologization

The main part of this book is devoted to investigating 'communication' in the three major social domains discussed in the previous section, namely work (Chapters 3 and 4), education (Chapter 5) and social/personal life (Chapter 6). (Details of the methods used in each case are given in the notes to the relevant chapter; a more general discussion of method appears in the Appendix.) Though I have separated them in order to make the material manageable, it needs to be borne in mind that the three domains are interconnected. For example, as we saw above, communication skills teaching in schools and colleges is advocated not only for its specific value in educational contexts ('oracy' enhances learning), but also on the grounds that employers demand the skills in question (a 'work' consideration) and that possessing those skills makes people 'better friends...better life-partners and better human beings' (a 'personal life' consideration).

Work is also, perhaps surprisingly, a 'mixed' domain. It might seem logical to treat business as a privileged source of ideas relating to 'enterprise', but in the case of ideas about language and communication that would be an oversimplification. Earlier I remarked on the tendency to compare the enterprises of private or personal life, like 'parenting' and 'relationships', to business projects. The analogy also works the other way, as people are advised to solve business problems using approaches developed by therapists and counsellors to sort out troubled marriages and dysfunctional families. This cross-fertilization between the corporate and the clinical is in fact much older than 'new wave' management. Communication is among the 'human factors' which were and are the province of occupational psychology – a discipline that had already established itself well before World War II (Hollway, 1991).

Workplace training frequently claims educational and personal development objectives as well as more narrowly instrumental ones to do with on-the-job performance. Many workplace training initiatives now involve close collaboration with educational institutions, and result in trainees acquiring nationally recognized credentials. It is not only at the point of entry to the labour market that workers need to acquire knowledge, skills and credentials – 'lifelong learning' and 'continuing professional development' are buzz-phrases for politicians as well as businesses. Employers are encouraged to regard themselves as 'Investors in People' (the name of a (British) national scheme recognizing organizations that institute high-quality programmes of staff development through training and appraisal). The rhetoric of 'new age' management is full of claims about caring for the whole person, as in the following extract from a financial services company's 'vision statement':

> Our work environment will value our ideas and entire life experience. We will be treated with fairness and dignity, and recognized for excellence. We will be challenged to learn, to continuously improve, and to aspire to the highest standards. We will draw on the broadest base of expertise to ensure that we achieve our goals. Our work and personal lives will complement and enrich one another.[4]

I am suggesting, then, that the notions of 'communication' found in each of the three domains this book will consider are not 'pure' but 'hybrid', products of cross-fertilization. Ideas, theoretical frameworks and even specific pieces of practical advice on language-use circulate freely from one domain to another. This movement of ideas across different social and linguistic domains is characteristic of the process that the linguist Norman Fairclough dubs 'discourse technologization'. Fairclough explains:

> We can usefully refer to 'discourse technologies' and to a 'technologization of discourse'...Examples of discourse technologies are interviewing, teaching, counselling and advertising. ...[I]n modern society they have taken on, and are taking on, the character of transcontextual techniques, which are seen as resources or toolkits that can be used to pursue a wide variety of strategies in many diverse contexts. Discourse technologies...are coming to have their own specialist technologists: researchers who look into their efficiency, designers

who work out refinements in the light of research and changing institutional requirements, and trainers who pass on the techniques. (1992: 215)

'Communication' is, admittedly, less well-defined and specific than Fairclough's examples of 'discourse technologies': it could perhaps be considered a higher-level discourse whose subject is discourse technologies in general. But teaching or discussing 'communication skills' surely qualifies as a 'transcontextual technique', with the skills themselves seen as appropriate, not to say indispensable, for all kinds of purposes in all kinds of situations. It is also the case that 'communication' has acquired its own 'technologists' – its specialist researchers, consultants and trainers. From these people's activities emerges a body of expert knowledge and practice. But this new body of knowledge and practice does not emerge fully formed out of nothing. In the next chapter I consider its sources and its antecedents.

2

CODIFYING 'COMMUNICATION': KNOWLEDGE, AUTHORITY AND STANDARDS

There is a lack of common understanding about communication skills
– Communication: a key skill for education, *1998 report.*

In Chapter 1 I suggested that talking to others ('communication') is an area of modern life in which expert systems are asserting themselves over more traditional, informal and diffuse ways of organizing knowledge and practice. I also referred to Norman Fairclough's proposal that discourse is being 'technologized', acquiring in the process its own specialist technologists – researchers, designers and trainers (Fairclough, 1992: 215). Such observations are suggestive, but they lack concrete detail. Among the questions I will address in this chapter are: what are the relevant 'modes of technical knowledge', and where do they come from? What 'traditional' kinds of knowledge are they replacing, if indeed that is what is happening? How different is today's expert knowledge from yesterday's? Who are the relevant 'experts'?

The kind of expert knowledge I want to discuss is not necessarily *academic* knowledge, though it may draw on academic sources among others. There are, of course, academic disciplines that include the word *communication* in their titles (such as 'speech communication' and 'communication studies'[1]), but I will be concerned with the knowledge produced within those disciplines only to the extent that it is appropriated for another purpose. That purpose, briefly stated, is to provide a coherent, structured framework for the practice of teaching people how to communicate 'better'. Those engaged in the practice, whether as trainers or trainees, need to be able to refer to some collection of relevant principles, definitions, facts, recommendations, and so on. What I mean by 'codifying communication' is essentially a process of gathering relevant knowledge from a variety of sources, arranging it in a more or less systematic way, and (re)-presenting it in a form which practitioners can access. Inevitably (if perhaps ironically), that means presenting it in *written* form. In modern conditions, all educational and training enterprises depend on the availability of written texts, and communication training is no exception. Speech may be the medium in which communication skills are displayed, but it is not the main medium through which they are defined and transmitted. Writing is not just an incidental support for the kinds of training and regulation I will later describe; it is an essential precondition for their existence.

Although communication skills training is a (relatively) new practice, and I will argue later on that its central preoccupations fit well with Anthony Giddens's observations on the nature of late modern cultures, there are nevertheless objections to the simple thesis that it is a case of modern expert knowledge taking over a domain where before there were only pre-modern, uncodified folk beliefs and traditional practices. One objection is that the production and dissemination of expert knowledge in this field, or something like it, is by no means a novel phenomenon: it cannot be assumed that pre-modern knowledge about talk was necessarily uncodified. Some bodies of expert knowledge – classical rhetoric is an obvious example – were set down systematically many centuries ago. Historians and ethnographers have shown that notions of skill in speaking and practices designed to develop that skill have been present in some form in all periods of known history and across a wide range of cultures. In this chapter I concern myself only with those bodies of (Western) knowledge and practice that have demonstrably influenced the contemporary discourse which is my focus in this book, but a full survey of the field would have to consider a wide variety of non-Western traditions as well, including some that are unwritten, though they may be highly systematic.[2]

The second objection is the converse of the first: whereas some very ancient knowledge relating to skill in speech was highly codified and widely acknowledged as authoritative, present-day knowledge about communication does not seem as yet to have achieved a similar state. The point is encapsulated in the epigraph to this chapter, in which the author of a report on the teaching of communication in schools observes that the enterprise is currently impeded by 'a lack of common understanding about communication skills' (Phillips, 1998: 4). The present drive towards more formal instruction in spoken language-use follows a lengthy period in which oral skills were neglected by comparison with reading and writing. According to the report, many or most of those who are now called upon to teach communication skills receive virtually no guidance on how to do it; uncertainty and disagreement still surrounds issues like assessment. The implication is that at present there is no body of expert knowledge about communication skills that is recognized as definitive.

It also remains unclear what constitutes 'expertise' (and therefore, who has authority to make definitive statements). Schoolteachers need formal teaching qualifications, but they do not have to be (and typically are not) qualified to teach communication skills specifically. Outside the education system, anyone at all may set up in business as a 'communication consultant' or a 'communication trainer': there is no licence to practise and no standard curriculum practitioners must demonstrate they have mastered. The communication consultants and trainers I encountered in the course of this research had acquired their professional expertise in a variety of other fields, including advertising, counselling, journalism, management and teaching. How much and what kind of additional study they had undertaken to prepare for their new vocation varied, but in most cases it was neither extensive nor academically rigorous (one consultant told me, for instance, that his own preparation had largely consisted of reading relevant works of popular self-help literature).

I do not intend to disparage the individuals concerned; rather I am making a general observation about the way fields of expertise develop historically. Professions like medicine, nursing and social work all went through an early period when their boundaries were indistinct, regulation was non-existent and training informal or perfunctory, a matter of observing and being supervised by more experienced practitioners rather than reading standard textbooks and passing examinations. I am not suggesting that communication training will ever be professionalized in the same way as, say, medicine, but pointing out that it is still an *emergent* field of expertise. That prompts the question: what is it emerging from? What earlier traditions of knowledge, and pre-existing practices of teaching talk, are available as a resource for today's communication experts?

Teaching talk: a brief history

The oldest extant Western body of knowledge/practice concerned with effective spoken communication is classical rhetoric. Rhetoric is often glossed as 'the art of persuasive speech', but for the purposes of this account it would be better characterized as a set of principles and rules for engaging in certain kinds of *public* speech. In classical democracy citizens needed to learn public speaking skills, since they were expected to take part in collective political decision-making and also when the need arose to plead cases before the courts. Hence rhetoric was part of what we would now call the educational 'core curriculum'. But the teaching of rhetoric on the classical model outlived the civilizations whose particular social arrangements gave rise to it by many centuries. Even when formal education in Europe ceased to be conducted in or solely concerned with the classical languages, rhetoric persisted as a curriculum subject. It continued to denote a concern with skill in the use of language, and if this no longer meant spoken language only, it did not refer exclusively to written language either. In American colleges as late as the mid-nineteenth century, for instance, 'composition' often meant writing a text to be delivered orally.[3] In time, however, the written word came to stand on its own. (In some US colleges today, the word *rhetoric* is still used to refer to the teaching of composition.)

It is evident that classical rhetoric is one source for contemporary expert discourse on communication skills. One 1990s writer goes so far as to claim: 'Everything we modern scientists have learned over the past 50 years about what makes one person more persuasive than another – using our scientific designs, multivariate statistics, and mainframe computers – was taught by Aristotle' (Whalen, 1996: 138–9). The remark is followed by a discussion structured around the Aristotelian concepts of *ethos, logos and pathos*. But it is also evident that the 'communication skills' to which contemporary experts allude are not identical to the speaking skills developed by rhetorical training. The most important difference is that 'communication' does not refer solely or primarily to public speaking, and certainly not to those highly ritualized types of public speaking (like political and legal oratory) that were the mainstay of traditional rhetoric. While communication training materials may conceive talk as taking place in some kind of institutional context (a meeting, a classroom, a service encounter), they may equally conceive it as happening between family members at home or friends and acquaintances at a private social gathering. Similar 'skills' are held to be relevant in either case, and on the whole these are 'interpersonal' rather than 'rhetorical' skills. The prototypical form of talk that communication training materials advert to is not a monologue delivered by one person to a larger audience in a formal public setting, nor is it the interactive but agonistic discourse of the debate or 'disputation'. It is conversation.

Conversation may not have been part of the classical curriculum, but it has nevertheless inspired a vast corpus of instructional literature over the centuries. (The term *literature* is used advisedly: once again, it is writing that typically functions as the preferred medium for normative metadiscourse on speech, and this is not new.) The varieties of this literature that proliferated in early modern Europe have been discussed by the historian Peter Burke in a book titled *The Art of Conversation* (1993). 'The art of conversation' was, of course, a popular subject for early essayists (like Montaigne and Bacon), who reflected more or less anecdotally on the question of what makes conversation 'good'. The improvement of conversation was also one preoccupation of the literary, artistic and political 'salons' that flourished across Europe from the seventeenth to the nineteenth centuries. Conversation was an important activity of the salons, and it also seems to have been among the topics most frequently discussed in them. In France, regarded as the centre of European salon culture, Michèle Cohen remarks that 'most major seventeenth-century writers wrote about conversation', adding that 'many of the treatises on the art were themselves written in the form of conversations' (Cohen, 1996: 17). These 'treatises' were not just works of scholarship or reflection, they also had an exemplary and pedagogic function, advising their readers on how to converse in particular settings.

From the early part of the sixteenth century, conversation had been an important theme of 'conduct' literature aimed at courtiers or those who aspired to become courtiers. Authors (like Baldassare Castiglione in his *Book of the Courtier* published in 1528) took it upon themselves to explain the rules of discourse in the court milieu. Peter Burke notes the existence of a related instructional genre known as 'table talk', which purported to record the actual conversation (usually the mealtime conversation, hence the name) of individuals whose talk was considered worthy of imitation. In time, versions of this kind of literature developed that were tailored to the needs of other social classes (particularly the bourgeoisie) and settings other than the court. Historians have argued that by the eighteenth century, conversation was the most important arena for the cultivation and display of 'politeness', a quality that was ideally supposed to characterize all social intercourse among cultivated persons, whether public or private (Cohen, 1996: 42).[4]

Conduct literature is the antecedent of more recent texts on 'etiquette', meaning the conventions of acceptable behaviour, including language use, in polite society. Advice on etiquette remained popular until the mid-twentieth century and even now is not wholly extinct – witness the continuing existence of syndicated newspaper columns such as 'Miss Manners', in which correspondents often seek guidance on matters of polite usage. It might also be argued that the didactic literature whose theme is 'how to succeed in business' (and which remains, unlike etiquette, very much a going concern) is an offshoot of the conduct tradition. This genre has always incorporated advice on spoken-language use: one chapter of Dale Carnegie's classic text *How to win friends and influence people* is optimistically titled 'How to be a better conversationalist and make people like you instantly'. Though business texts draw selectively on insights allegedly provided by behavioural science, the advice they give usually has as much or more to do with the personal experiences and values of the author. Authors are important in this kind of literature, which resembles the conduct book in being an insider's guide to the rules governing behaviour in a particular community. The community in question is not, however, a royal court in renaissance Europe, but a modern business organization.

The historian Theodore Zeldin makes some interesting observations on the way guidance about conversation has changed over time to express the changing values and aspirations of the societies that produced it. He notes that the Victorians 'poured out a vast mass of books on the subject, showing that they felt a new style was needed for their new ambitions', but comments that from a late twentieth-century reader's perspective, Victorian guidance literature seems overly concerned with questions of propriety and social respectability (etiquette, in other words), and oddly unconcerned with 'the idea of personal contact, of the intimate meeting of minds and sympathies' (Zeldin, 1998: 94). Victorian authorities may not have had their predecessors' obsession with 'politeness' in the special sense that term had in the eighteenth century, but they treated conversation essentially as 'social intercourse', an activity whose chief ends were the diversion and improvement of the assembled company. Today, by contrast, probably the most important purpose people accord to conversation is, as Zeldin puts it, 'personal contact', and especially the creation of intimacy with 'significant' others. Genres concerned with issues of propriety in speech, like etiquette and elocution, are now in decline, whereas the popular psychology texts that focus on intimacy, honesty and openness are in the ascendant.

This change can be interpreted with reference to Anthony Giddens's observations on the nature of late modernity (Giddens, 1991, and see Chapter 1). Seeking guidance on how to talk more effectively to others has become a key element in the late modern quest to perfect what Giddens calls the 'pure relationship', an intimate tie with another person that is contracted and valued entirely for its own sake. The classic case of a pure relationship is the form of marriage, or quasi-marriage, that is now commonplace in many Western societies. As Wendy Langford observes (1998), the English word *relationship* is coming to have this type of relationship as its commonest referent: when people say they are 'not in a relationship' they do not mean they have no relations with other people at all, they mean they are not part of a couple. The word *communicate* has a comparable specialized sense (a point I will examine in detail in Chapter 6): to say of a person or persons that they 'can't communicate' implies not that they do not converse or that their conversation is unintelligible, but that it lacks intimacy and emotional depth. Giddens observes that pure relationships are heavily dependent on communication in the 'deep' sense, because trust between the parties 'can be mobilized only by mutual self-disclosure. [It] can…no longer be anchored in criteria outside the relationship itself – such as criteria of kinship, social duty or traditional obligation' (Giddens, 1991: 6). If trust depends on mutual self-disclosure, it also depends on the parties being able to use spoken language to self-disclose (the kind of ritualized courtship talk that preoccupied earlier writers on the art of conversation does not pass the modern test of being 'honest' and 'authentic'). Thus guidance on talk in the age of pure relationships is far more concerned than earlier traditions with the techniques of mutual self-disclosure – being open, being honest, talking about your feelings, listening 'actively' and sensitively, understanding and making allowances for communication differences, particularly between men and women (since the prototypical pure relationship involves one person of each sex). Some qualities that were once presented as virtues – reticence, for instance – have now become communication *problems*, obstacles standing in the way of personal fulfilment.

The shift from talk as 'social intercourse' to talk as the primary means for creating intimacy has affected what kinds of expertise on spoken communication we recognize as most valuable. When conversation was an 'art' displayed in public by cultured people, the obvious experts were socialites, scholars and literati, who could claim authority as arbiters of taste and/or skilled practitioners of the verbal arts. Now that talk is thought of more as the glue holding personal relationships together, people turn for guidance to the professionals who are thought to have specialist knowledge about human behaviour, emotions and relationships: psychologists, therapists and counsellors.

Here it might be objected that psychology and therapy[5] are by no means the only disciplines that have produced potentially relevant knowledge. Readers of this book may well consider the knowledge produced by conversation and discourse analysts, working within linguistics or sociology, to be at least as significant. But it is striking that knowledge from those sources is rarely alluded to in pedagogic texts or popular advice literature on communication. Linguists are regularly cited as authorities only in the area of 'intercultural' communication between people of different nationalities, ethnicities or genders. Not coincidentally, this is an area where the researchers themselves have often had practical problem-solving and the production of teaching materials as an integral goal (see for instance Gumperz, 1982a, 1982b; Roberts, Davies and Jupp, 1992; Clyne, 1996). Otherwise, linguists tend to adopt a descriptive rather than prescriptive or pedagogical approach; they are concerned to describe the minutiae of naturally occurring spoken interaction, to formulate its general rules and principles, to explain what social or cognitive factors might motivate those principles, and – in the case of 'critical' discourse analysis – to relate what is observed in interaction to the power structures of a given context. They are not interested in telling people how to talk 'better', and this may be one reason why their work is seen as having limited relevance for an enterprise that aims to *improve* communication.

Therapy, by contrast, is a kind of expert discourse in which the experts are more willing to prescribe. For many therapists it is axiomatic that clients' problems may be caused by their inability to communicate effectively with others, and it is not uncommon, therefore, for therapeutic regimes to include training in different and allegedly more effective communication strategies. (A case in point is assertiveness training, which seeks to put 'honest and direct' communication in place of passive, aggressive or manipulative behaviour. Though it is often associated now with feminism and with business 'leadership' courses, assertiveness originated as a clinical technique and continues to be used by clinicians.) Therapy as a practice is also based on the more general assumption that problems can be addressed, precisely, by talking about them in particular ways: what the word *therapy* most readily brings to mind is captured in that well-known Freudian formula, the 'talking cure'. Given the extent to which therapeutic assumptions about the efficacy of talking have permeated popular consciousness, it is not surprising that therapists should have come to be regarded as important authorities on the subject of how to talk.

There is another sense in which therapeutic models of talk are prescriptive whereas the models produced by linguists (and indeed, empirically or positivistically inclined psychologists) are less so. As I will discuss in more detail below (Chapter 6), therapy tends to incorporate a moral agenda, a value system with consequences for what is taken to be acceptable or desirable behaviour. The discourse norms recommended in various therapeutic sources do not bear only (sometimes, arguably, they do not bear at all) on how to be a good speaker, but also on how to be a good person. Yet far from being a peculiar feature of modern therapeutic approaches, this moralizing tendency places them in the historical mainstream. The connection between being a good communicator and being a good person is as old as the tradition of commentary and advice I have been surveying. Aristotle, for instance, defined 'possessing a good reputation and personality' as a criterion for being able to speak effectively. A controversial issue in ancient Greece concerned the activities of the sophists, skilled practitioners and teachers of rhetoric who were prepared to use their persuasive powers to advance arguments without regard to their moral implications. Critics of the sophists found it repellent that wrong should defeat right just because it was more eloquently expressed.

The same dispute between moral and technical excellence runs through the whole history of guidance on how to talk. In modern communication training the issue surfaces in arguments about whether or not instruction in communication skills should be, in today's jargon, 'values-based'. Many contemporary experts insist that good communication cannot be regarded merely as a neutral matter of technique. Angela Phillips's report on the teaching of communication in schools highlights the views of an organization called the National Forum for Values in Education, which believes the teaching of communication should be designed to promote pupils' 'spiritual, moral, cultural and social development' (Phillips, 1998: 9). This report is enthusiastic about the potential of communication training to bring about morally and socially desirable outcomes like conflict resolution and enhanced self-esteem. Meanwhile, a latter-day sophist approach continues to flourish in the teaching of communication techniques to, for example, salespeople (some good examples are given by Leidner, 1993).

From this discussion it appears that the history of instruction in how to use spoken language encompasses two main traditions: one concerned with public speaking and the rhetorical skills it requires, and one concerned with conversation or 'social intercourse'. The first tradition was institutionalized in educational curricula from classical antiquity onwards, and although it was eventually downgraded relative to the teaching of reading and writing, it still has a vestigial presence in certain kinds of professional training (for instance, of courtroom advocates and preachers) and in extra-curricular activities (like debating and public speaking contests) pursued in many schools and colleges, especially élite ones. The second tradition was largely non-institutional; it was part of a more general culture of self-improvement, in which people participated voluntarily and, on the whole, privately. This self-improvement tradition continues, and advice on spoken interaction continues to play a part in it. However, there has been an important change during the latter part of the twentieth century: guidance on talk has become markedly 'psychologized', while the 'polite social intercourse' tradition has steadily declined.

Communication skills training as it exists for the most part today is unmistakably a product of the 'psychologizing' process. But the change did not happen overnight, and there are still continuities with past practice. At this point I want to illustrate more concretely just what has changed, by comparing two texts produced almost 50 years apart. One is a correspondence course in *Effective Speaking and Writing* first produced in 1951, and the other is a book titled *How to be a Better...Communicator*, written by Sandy McMillan and published in 1996. McMillan's book is a good example of contemporary self-improvement literature about 'communication', but while the correspondence course also belongs to the genre of self-improvement literature, it differs strikingly from the later text. By comparing them we can see, not only how new bodies of knowledge have displaced older ones, but also how the contemporary idea of 'communication skills' has emerged out of what used to be a more diffuse set of concerns addressed by this sort of instructional literature.

Continuity and change: from effective speaking to better communication

The bulk of the material in *Effective Speaking and Writing* appears to have been produced in the US in the early 1950s, though it was only in the late 1970s that it was first offered to the British public.[6] The company responsible for publishing it in Britain is still in business and as far as I can tell, still offering the same material. (British readers may well have seen this company's quaintly old-fashioned advertisements, which continue to appear in national newspapers under headings like 'Shamed by your mistakes in English?' and – more intriguingly – 'I said two simple words...and we were escorted to the finest table in the restaurant!') The fact that this course remains in circulation might well invite criticism; certainly in today's market it is an unrepresentative and arguably rather unsatisfactory product. But for my purposes here that objection is irrelevant, for there is no reason to think it would have been anything but unremarkable of its kind in 1951. It consists of 12 lessons: one on preparing speeches, two on conversation, two on vocabulary, four on written composition, and one each on letter writing, speed reading and spelling. There is also a book of 'model speeches' giving specimens of set-pieces such as wedding toasts and presentations to retiring colleagues. In addition, readers are invited to set down any questions they may have as they work through the materials in a letter and send it to the publisher, who will post back a suitable response in due course. The materials make little explicit reference to any particular kind of reader, but their content implies someone who has occasion to make public speeches, write business letters and converse with 'business, professional, church, club and lodge associates'. The attention devoted to spelling and vocabulary-building might also suggest that the target reader, though middle class in occupational terms, has not had extensive formal education.

The later text, *How to be a Better...Communicator*, is one in a series of *How to be a Better...*titles produced under the auspices of the Industrial Society, a nonprofit organization providing skills training and consultancy services to businesses. Addressed to a 'professional' but otherwise vaguely specified audience, this text differs from *Effective Speaking and Writing* in being a book rather than a correspondence course – an obvious point, but worth making because it is in itself a sign of changing times. With the advent of new technologies the traditional 'correspondence' course has given way to other forms of 'distance learning', using multimedia materials and sometimes providing tutorial support by electronic mail. There is also strong competition for the self-improvement market from the mainstream publishing industry. In the 1990s, inexpensive mass-market paperbacks are the commonest vehicle for all kinds of self-improvement advice, and the more serious texts are designed to fulfil the same educational functions that correspondence courses had in the past. *How to be a Better...Communicator* is a case in point: it may not offer personalized tutorial support, but it has clearly been designed for systematic self-study, addressing questions directly to readers in the text, and providing space for them to write their own notes and comments.

There is a considerable difference in the way the two items define and organize their subject matter. *Effective Speaking and Writing* addresses a broad range of concerns about the use of language. Despite the fact that 'speaking' comes before 'writing' in the course title, face-to-face spoken communication is the subject of only three lessons out of 12, whereas reading and writing skills of various sorts occupy seven lessons, and a further two are given over to vocabulary-building. Apart from the fact that they are all to do with language, what ties these concerns together is arguably little more than the compilers' perception that the target audience is likely to need guidance on each of them. In *How to be a Better...Communicator* by contrast, spoken language is the subject of five chapters out of seven; writing gets just one chapter, while reading and vocabulary-building are not addressed at all. This text defines its subject explicitly as 'communication', and has a clear sense of which aspects of language-use properly belong under that heading. It is not only that more emphasis is placed on speech as opposed to writing: whether the topic is spoken or written language, the focus is always on 'communicating' in the sense of 'getting your message across to the intended audience'. It is particularly striking that the issue of 'effective' communication has been severed from concerns about *correctness*, historically the dominant motif in all linguistic advice literature. In Sandy McMillan's text vocabulary, grammar and spelling – matters of correct usage rather than communication – are hardly touched upon.

The emergence of 'effective communication' as a distinct object of verbal hygiene, separable from 'correct usage', is a point of some historical interest. It is therefore worth digressing for a moment to observe that in terms of the attention given to matters of 'communication' as distinct from matters of correctness, *Effective Speaking and Writing* itself can be seen to represent a shift away from older instructional traditions. This becomes clear if one compares it with Estelle B. Hunter's *New Self Teaching Course in Practical English and Effective Speech*, a text produced only around 15 years earlier for what seems to be a comparable audience (Hunter, 1935).[7] The content of this course is exhaustively summarized in its subtitle: *Comprising Vocabulary Development, Grammar, Pronunciation, Enunciation and the Principles of Effective Oral Expression*. Only the last of the items on this list is concerned with spoken discourse as such – the others all pertain to 'correctness'. Furthermore, the guidance given regarding 'effective oral expression' has a strongly literary flavour, suggesting that effectiveness in speaking is a matter of avoiding the commonplace by using figurative language and other kinds of elevated diction. By the 1950s, 'effectiveness' is much more clearly defined in the terms of behavioural science – a source of authoritative knowledge that is hardly ever invoked by Hunter (unsurprisingly, since much of the scientific research that came to underpin what is still standard advice on effective communication was published in the 1940s and 1950s). *Effective Speaking and Writing* appears to represent an intermediate stage between the 'belle-lettristic' approach of Estelle Hunter in the 1930s and the fully 'psychologized' approach taken by Sandy McMillan in the 1990s.

If we examine what our two exemplary texts have to say about spoken interaction, again there are striking differences. The two lessons on conversation (2 and 3) that appear in *Effective Speaking and Writing* have many of the hallmarks of the 'polite social intercourse' tradition. Lesson 2 deals with 'elementary principles': talking with a purpose, adapting yourself to the demands of your audience, finding ideas to talk about and arranging them in a systematic manner. Lesson 3 describes what are referred to as 'advanced techniques': for starting conversations, keeping them going by asking questions, 'cutting in' to build on others' contributions or to forestall embarrassing developments, injecting humour, and changing the topic. Really, the division between the two chapters is less one of 'elementary' versus 'advanced' techniques and more one of matter versus manner. Lesson 2 concentrates on what to talk about, whereas lesson 3 is more concerned with managing the mechanics of interaction.

The discussion of 'matter' seems particularly dated. Students are counselled that before they embark on a conversation it is necessary to have a clear idea why they are talking and about what: 'our conversation, even in many purely social situations, is pleasanter and more effective if we have in our minds, before we start, a definitely formulated purpose' (L2: 5). The default purpose is 'to be friendly and agreeable' (L2: 6), and for that purpose some subjects are particularly suitable: suggested ones include your and your interlocutor's personal interests and hobbies, or if you are talking to a total stranger, more generic topics such as 'your surroundings', or 'seasons, holidays and modes of travel'. For use in more extended conversation, the author advises keeping a notebook and jotting down ideas and opinions on topics of general interest – she suggests making it a habit to read magazines like *Life* and *Reader's Digest* in order to keep abreast of current affairs and glean interesting ideas for talk. Male students are advised to know something about fashion, and female students to make a study of sport, so that they can engage members of the opposite sex in conversation on topics of interest to them. All of this is reminiscent of the advice on conversation given by Emily Post in her classic *Etiquette: the Blue Book of Social Usage*, a bestseller in 1922. And there is nothing like it in *How to be a Better…Communicator*. Admittedly, the latter text is more narrowly concerned with communicating in professional contexts, where presumably it is less often necessary to cast about for conversational topics. But other contemporary texts that *are* concerned with 'social' conversation (BT's *How to get more out of life through better conversations* (1997), for example, which I discuss in detail in Chapter 6) do not address the issue of matter either. It is assumed that people generally know what they want to talk about; what they need guidance on is the mechanics of putting their thoughts across. Anxieties about matter belong to the age of etiquette: they are about finding 'safe' ground, avoiding potentially offensive subjects and displaying oneself publicly as an informed and 'cultured' person.

How to be a Better...Communicator suggests that people in the 1990s have a different set of anxieties. It devotes a whole section, for instance, to the subject of 'tricky situations', inviting the reader to rate the potential 'trickiness' of 'being praised or complimented', 'handling complaints', 'disagreeing', 'criticizing', 'asking for something I want', 'refusing things I don't want to do', 'broaching sensitive subjects' and 'talking about my feelings' (McMillan, 1996: 35–6). Sociolinguists will readily recognize what makes these situations 'tricky': they all put the hypothetical communicator in a position where s/he may have to perform what politeness theorists call a 'face threatening act' (Brown and Levinson, 1987). Speakers may either lose face themselves (as with 'asking for something I want', which calls for a degree of self-abasement and carries a risk that the request will be denied) or cause the interlocutor to lose face (as with criticizing somebody), or both. The attitude of *Effective Speaking and Writing* to speech acts of this type is basically that they have no place in polite social intercourse. An accomplished conversationalist will be skilled in the art of avoiding them, and in performing repair-work if they do happen to crop up. Thus if someone broaches a 'sensitive subject' or makes a potentially offensive remark, the author advises: 'break into the conversation with a remark that may be partly mild reproof and partly a change of subject' (L3: 16). The author of *How to be a Better...Communicator* in contrast is guided by the principles of 'assertive' communication. He assumes that effective communication in 'tricky situations' does not mean avoiding the issue, but rather confronting it honestly and dealing with it skilfully.

Turning to what the two experts say about mechanics, it is evident that the more recent text is also the more systematic and elaborate. McMillan organizes his advice around what he calls 'three sets of basic face-to-face communication skills' (1996: 22–34). First is 'getting a hearing' – how to behave so that others respect you, listen to you and understand what you say. Under this heading, readers learn that the way others respond to them is determined by (in this order) body language, tone of voice, and words. It is claimed that body language accounts for 50–80% of the message and prosodic/paralinguistic features for 15–30%. The main advice given, not surprisingly, is to pay closer attention to body language and tone of voice. The second set of skills is concerned with 'getting the information you need' – how to listen. The author asserts that 'improving communication skills really means improving listening' (p. 26). Advice on listening makes reference, again, to body language (you should smile, have an 'open' posture (arms not folded), lean towards the speaker, maintain eye contact and be relaxed). It also deals with the use of questions (open questions are distinguished from closed ones and the former are recommended, except where the purpose is simply to check you have heard accurately; 'encouraging questions', meaning back-channel utterances, are also discussed). The third set of skills involves 'getting a workable agreement' – how to get consent for something everyone agrees to, so that the interaction can move forward. Readers are told to establish rapport, solicit other participants' views using questions, summarize the points people agree on, and repeat the process until a joint solution has been established.

No such taxonomy of skills informs the advice in lesson 3 of *Effective Speaking and Writing*. Instead, much of the lesson is organized on a kind of chronological principle: it begins by discussing ways of 'breaking the ice', then proceeds to consider methods for keeping talk going. At this point, the author digresses into a section called 'understanding people' (there is a list of difficult characters one might encounter in conversation, including 'the know-alls', 'the morbid ones', 'the risqué story tellers' and 'certain elderly people'). The text then returns to issues of interactional mechanics, such as how you change the subject, and how you inject humour into conversation. This is followed by a section on 'active listening', and then finally by a section on how to close conversational encounters.

Some of the differences here probably reflect the fact that one text is primarily about 'purely social' conversation, while the other is primarily about talk at work, a more explicitly goal-oriented activity. (It is rarely necessary – or appropriate – to 'get a workable agreement' from your fellow guests at a cocktail party.) But other differences have less to do with the imagined context. There is, for instance, a considerable difference in how concretely and specifically the advice itself is formulated, and in what sort of information is given to justify or explain it. Sandy McMillan tends to support his advice by adducing generalizations and statistics ('body language accounts for 50–80% of the message'), whereas the author of the lessons in *Effective Speaking and Writing* is more apt to support hers by producing an exemplary anecdote ('I remember being in a group of professional women one night when the subject of women lawyers came up...' (L3: 17)). McMillan makes use of abstract conceptual categories and technical distinctions (like 'open' versus 'closed' questions), whereas the correspondence course makes use of examples and formulae: readers are advised to memorize lists of phrases that might be useful for keeping a conversation going, like 'I agree, but', 'That reminds me', or 'As you were saying'. One way to describe the difference would be to say that the later text is more 'scientific': information is presented in a more systematic way, more impersonally, more technically, with more generalizations and more reference to formal canons of knowledge (as opposed to experience and commonsense).

There are, then, two especially significant differences between the 1951 course material and the 1996 text. One, as just noted, is the more 'scientific' orientation of the later text. The other is the overarching framework in which the two authors think about speaking and what constitutes 'skill' in it. The earlier text conceives of conversation as polite social intercourse, harking back to the tradition of conduct and etiquette writing. 'Skill' in this paradigm means essentially the ability to be interesting and entertaining while remaining always within the bounds of propriety, which is why the author devotes as much attention to the matter as to the manner of talk. The later text on the other hand subscribes to a more contemporary view of talk as the medium in which people relate to one another, solve problems and pursue joint ventures. 'Skill' means being able to interact in such a way that your purposes – exchanging information, solving problems, securing group consent to a course of action – are accomplished; the most valued qualities of a communicator are honesty, openness and flexibility rather than, say, politeness, eloquence and wit. These differences, however, should not prevent us from seeing that the two texts also have things in common. Some topics, such as 'active listening', the importance of body language, the use of questions, and the need to be 'sensitive' to your interlocutors, are emphasized by both authors. Some specific pieces of advice (for instance, to make sure that the meaning of your words is not undercut by the message your body language conveys) are identical in both texts.

This comparison of two texts points to important differences between contemporary guidance on communication and guidance produced 40 or 50 years ago, and the observations made about *How to be a Better... Communicator* give something of the flavour of the contemporary genre. I want to broaden the discussion, however, by considering a wider range of contemporary materials. What are the recurrent preoccupations of current instructional literature about communication, and what is the substance of the guidance it offers?

Reading communication training materials

The following discussion is based on examining 15 sets of instructional materials.[8] All were obtained in Britain, and all date from the 1990s. Eight were produced – in most cases by outside consultants – for use in training the employees of a particular organization. Some of these materials are generic 'communication training', but others are tailored to more specific needs, such as 'telephone training' or 'customer care training'. Whatever they are called, communication skills and the use of spoken language are prime concerns in all of them. The other seven are addressed to a wider, more general audience. Essentially they fall into the category of 'self-improvement' texts, a category that encompasses self-study, correspondence and distance-learning courses, self-help books and tapes which are advertised in the press, or sold in high street bookshops and newsagents.

It might be asked why I chose these types of material – workplace training materials and self-improvement texts – as opposed to materials designed in and for institutions centrally concerned with the production and transmission of knowledge (that is, educational institutions). The answer is relevant to the general theme of this chapter. Because of the long neglect (and arguably the continuing marginality) of spoken language skills in educational contexts, the production of instructional material has typically been undertaken in and for the commercial sector, which has therefore established a commanding position. Though communication is becoming a more explicit concern in the education system (a point I elaborate in Chapter 5 below), its status continues to be contested. Consequently, it may be argued that the types of material I examine here are the ones from which people are most likely to be getting specific knowledge about communication and the skills it involves.

Although no sample of this size can make claims to be 'representative', I tried to avoid materials that might be considered idiosyncratic or 'fringe' products, choosing self-improvement texts produced by reputable publishers and workplace materials used by companies that are in most cases household names. (Though I cannot reveal their identities, three of the eight are multinationals with hundreds of outlets and thousands of employees, three are leading British firms in their sectors, and the remaining two are important players in their regional economies.) One obvious bias that results from my selection is towards materials intended for use in professional rather than personal contexts. But comparing the professional materials with those personal examples I do have suggests that the similarities are greater than the differences ('personal life' materials will be discussed in more detail in Chapter 6).

My examination of the materials here will be selective, in the sense that I will not consider concerns that are particular to one item or class of items (such as 'telephone training'). All the materials do include sections that relate specifically to their purpose and audience, focusing on skills like chairing a meeting, taking a phone message, dealing with a complaint, or communicating with elderly people who have some degree of language impairment. In later chapters I will return to these specifics. Here, though, I concentrate on topics that recur across materials designed for different audiences and purposes. That recurrence suggests that certain communication skills are considered both 'generic' and basic: as essential in professional as personal life, as fundamental in an office as in a residential care home. The skills of this sort which receive attention most consistently are – in no special order – (1) the effective use of 'visual' (body language) and 'vocal' (prosodic and paralinguistic) components of communication; (2) the ability to identify and label emotional states conveyed in speech; (3) the ability to assess and 'type' other people's behaviour in order to communicate effectively with them; (4) the acquisition of an 'assertive' rather than 'passive' or 'aggressive' way of communicating; (5) the selection of appropriate question forms; (6) the ability to listen 'actively'.

Before I turn to the details of what is said about each of these skills, it is worth noting that in all cases (that is, for each skill and in all materials in the sample), there is at least as much 'theoretical' discussion as there is practical advice on how to talk. It is of course possible that this balance is altered in actual training contexts, where trainees spend time practising skills in, for instance, role-play exercises, receiving feedback from the trainer and from each other. But it is clear that the ambitions of communication training usually go beyond the purely practical: its designers want trainees to 'know *about*' as well as 'know *how*'. Those texts which are study guides make this clear by including quiz questions that require the reader to reproduce the definitions, typologies, reasons, advantages and disadvantages that have been set out in the relevant section of the text.

I. Defining 'communication': verbal, vocal and visual

As one might expect, many items in the sample contain a definition of 'communication'. Almost invariably, this definition does not say what communication is or accomplishes (presumably that is taken to be obvious) but rather explains what its constituents are, dividing it into three elements. Terminology varies, but a variant that has the merit of being easy to remember is the alliterative 'verbal, vocal and visual'. 'Verbal' means the actual words; 'vocal' means, in linguists' terms, prosodic and paralinguistic features; and 'visual' means gaze, posture and other aspects of body language. And wherever this division is made, the materials go on to stress (as we saw earlier in the discussion of *How to be a Better...Communicator*) that the verbal element of an utterance is the *least* important in terms of meaning, while the visual element is the *most* important. Statistics may be cited in support of this claim (though they vary: different materials assert that body language carries anything from 55% to 80% of the message). There are warnings against 'incongruent' or 'inconsistent' messages – where your words are inconsistent with the tone in which you say them or with your body language – and it is often suggested that consistency among the three elements is a precondition for 'the message to get through'.

The concern about consistency, as well as the statistical claim about how much of a message is carried by its verbal, vocal and visual elements, seems to be based on the findings of experiments in which subjects were presented with 'inconsistent' messages (for instance, someone professing interest verbally but looking bored), and then asked what they actually believed.[9] The main finding was that they were more likely to believe what someone's body language told them than what that person actually said, if the two were in conflict. To translate such findings into general statements like 'body language accounts for 50–80% of the message' is problematic – particularly if you subscribe to an inferential rather than purely code model of communication[10] – but the main purpose of these statements may be less to teach scientific 'facts' than to motivate a strong focus, which is common to most of these materials, on vocal and visual communication, which are thought to be neglected by comparison with the verbal element.

In the area of body language, materials make recommendations about gaze and posture (Sandy McMillan's advice, quoted earlier, is typical), and explain the concept of 'mirroring', which means aligning your verbal/kinetic behaviour with an interlocutor's ('accommodating' to them, in social psychologists' or sociolinguists' terms). In telephone-training materials it is pointed out that since the crucial visual channel is unavailable, the vocal channel must be used to compensate. Especially in materials with a customer care emphasis, there are reminders that smiling can be heard as well as seen.

2. Emotion

The treatment of 'vocal' communication overlaps with a significant concern in many materials, namely the expression/recognition of emotions. Sometimes this crops up under the heading of 'talking about feelings'. I have already made some observations that bear on why this skill might be considered salient. Talking about feelings is one of the techniques of self-disclosure which are emphasized in a culture of self-reflexivity and pure relationships. More specifically, though, it seems to be assumed that this technique of self-disclosure is poorly developed in many people. As we will see in more detail in Chapters 5 and 6, there is concern that widespread inability to put feelings into words is an important contributory factor in all kinds of serious social problems, including disruptive behaviour at school, rising teenage suicide rates, marital breakdown and subsequent acrimonious divorce and custody disputes, and premature death among middle-aged men. If angry and unhappy people could communicate their feelings better, they would thereby be prevented from acting them out in ways that damage themselves and others.

Concern about emotional inarticulacy is addressed in training materials, first by telling people explicitly that it is acceptable and desirable to talk about feelings (this counters what is felt to be a widespread perception of such behaviour as inappropriate and embarrassing), and then by explaining how emotional states are or should be communicated. On the latter point, a surprising amount of the guidance offered relates to vocabulary, the assumption being that many people simply do not know the words to describe feelings explicitly and precisely. BT's *How to get more out of life through better conversations* (1997) offers a tape on which the same monologue is performed in three different ways, and listeners are asked to name the attitude or emotion expressed by each speaker. This task tests both listeners' own emotional vocabulary and their ability to identify emotional states accurately from prosodic and paralinguistic features. The same skills are also emphasized in workplace materials about communicating with customers. It is not uncommon to find long lists of positive and negative emotion words which trainees are urged to study: the idea seems to be that a more elaborate emotional vocabulary will help them to become aware of fine distinctions in the emotions they and others convey in speech. One set of workplace materials, after listing 25 emotion terms, counsels: 'These emotions will alter a contact's mood. You can use this knowledge [knowledge of what emotion you are expressing] to help or hinder your transactions'.

3. Classifying, understanding and dealing with people

If communication training as represented in these materials has one over-arching thesis statement, it might be the following, as impressed on the recipients of one workplace training pack: 'Our behaviour largely dictates how clients/customers behave towards us'. For 'clients/customers' read 'other people' more generally. The point about emotions 'altering a contact's mood' is only one illustration of this general principle. Although communication is by definition interactive, the idea behind a lot of training is that by making the correct choices about what to say and how, the skilled communicator can control the response of the person s/he is interacting with.

This control is enhanced, however, by understanding that there are different kinds of people, who will respond best to different communicative choices. Thus materials on communication skills often digress into what might seem the only marginally relevant issue of what kinds of people there are. The typology of conversational characters encountered in *Effective Speaking and Writing* – know-alls, morbid ones, and so on – turns out to be the precursor of many similar, though more elaborate and more sophisticated, classifications.

Some materials provide checklists to help readers divide people into types or styles, and some also include quizzes to help them identify their own type or style. The classifications used are quite variable, and it is of interest to ask where they come from. One source is the literature of organizational behaviour, though frequently filtered through more popular management materials. For example, one set of materials suggests that people can be classified by 'mind-set': they are 'systems-oriented logical thinkers', 'friends/helpers' or 'strong fighters'. The immediate source for this is the writing of the management 'guru', Charles Handy. Two sets of materials divide people into 'visual', 'auditory' and 'kinesthetic', suggesting that every individual has a preference for one of these 'sensory systems', and will respond better if you choose your metaphors with their preference in mind (say 'I hear you' rather than 'I see what you mean' to an 'auditory' person, for instance). The source of this idea is the rather arcane wisdom of Neurolinguistic Programming (Dimmick, 1995).

A more sophisticated approach is to classify the *behaviour* of people at a given moment, rather than the people themselves. In this connection, two systems turn up very regularly: transactional analysis (Berne, 1966, 1975; Harris, 1969) and the principles of assertiveness (see Rakos, 1991). These are both therapeutic models: assertiveness belongs to the tradition of behaviour therapy, while transactional analysis has more links with the traditional 'talking cure', and in particular with the practice of group therapy. Both have been taken up enthusiastically in popular psychology and self-help literature, whence they have filtered into the training materials of many business organizations. Robin Leidner reports in her sociological study of service work, *Fast Food, Fast Talk* (1993), that both transactional analysis and assertiveness are taught to managers undergoing training at McDonald's 'Hamburger University'. Their adoption by a highly successful and much-imitated company like McDonald's may help to explain why they have become so ubiquitous.

In transactional analysis, the classification is of 'ego states', and the categories are 'parent', 'adult' and 'child'. Any individual 'contains' all three, but their behaviour at a given moment comes from one rather than the others. Attention focuses on the 'transaction' – an exchange between two people – and the main consideration emphasized in communication training materials is that transactions should be 'complementary' (that is, between similar ego states) rather than 'crossed', if communication is not to break down. Transactional analysis also elaborates a series of 'life positions' ('I'm OK, you're OK' and so on). 'Good' communication is often defined by materials that use the model as an exchange that brings the parties to the 'healthy' OK/OK position. I will discuss the use made of this model in more detail in Chapter 3. In the case of assertiveness, the classification divides ways of behaving into three basic types: aggressive, submissive/passive, and (the ideal) assertive – a typical definition of which is 'standing up for your own rights while acknowledging those of other people'.

4. Being assertive

Whether or not it is explicitly acknowledged, the influence of assertiveness training is observable to some degree in every item in my sample. Although assertiveness is often used as the basis for a behavioural typology, as noted above, the point of presenting its principles is not just to enable trainees to classify where other people are 'coming from'. Assertive behaviour is unambiguously recommended as the norm which they themselves should adopt, regardless of how others behave. Accordingly, specific verbal techniques for being assertive are often laid out in detail. Classic 'assertive' speech involves, for instance, making 'I' statements, preferring directness to indirectness in the performance of speech acts (including ones which are face-threatening, such as refusals), acknowledging what another says or feels explicitly, repeating a point until it is 'heard'. This way of speaking has been criticised as sociolinguistically bizarre, and it has been claimed on the basis of evaluation studies that people do not always respond positively to 'assertive' behaviour (Gervasio and Crawford, 1989). Nevertheless this sample testifies to its continuing influence on materials designed to improve communication skills.

5. Questions

One of the ways in which training texts suggest a skilled communicator can exert control over the behaviour of interlocutors is by asking the right kinds of questions. Accordingly, a common feature in many materials is some kind of taxonomy of questions, with a listing of the purposes, advantages and disadvantages of each type. A distinction is invariably made between 'closed' and 'open' questions, which are typically equated with yes/no and WH- types respectively. Some materials use a more elaborate classification, including disjuncts like 'would you prefer A or B?' (often called 'alternative questions') and tags like 'so that's the larger model, is it?' (often called 'leading questions'). The advice most often given is to prefer open questions in almost all circumstances because they encourage people to talk freely and at length; the exception is when you are trying to stop someone rambling, where a closed question will have the effect of bringing them back to the point by eliciting a one-word answer.

This advice on questions is a good illustration of the point I made earlier, that communication experts typically do not make use of knowledge produced by linguistics, discourse and conversation analysis. The analysis of question-types in English is inaccurate, and some of what is said about their effects is contradicted by a large body of empirical work. Clearly, some WH- questions can be answered in the 'curt', one-word manner which the use of open questions is said to discourage ('when are you coming?' 'Tomorrow'). Merely saying to someone 'how may I help you' rather than 'can I help you' (something customer care materials often advise because the former is open and the latter closed) does not in itself prevent a customer giving you the brush-off. It just prevents them from doing it with the formula 'no thanks'. Conversely, it is relatively rare for yes/no questions to elicit unelaborated one-word answers, and an unelaborated 'no' is particularly unusual. The advice in other words is based on an over-simple understanding of the relation of form and function in discourse, coupled with a disregard for the principles of politeness which inhibit speakers from 'just saying no'.

6. 'Active listening'

Throughout my sample of materials, training in listening skills, or 'active listening', is repeatedly proclaimed to be essential, not just because listening is important (a platitudinous observation from which one imagines few would dissent), but also because of a firm conviction that in the absence of explicit training, many or most people are woefully inadequate at it. I have already quoted Sandy McMillan's assertion in *How to be a Better...Communicator* that 'improving communication skills really means improving listening' (McMillan, 1996: 26). An advertisement for the Sperry Corporation concurs, claiming that on average, people 'listen at a 25% level of efficiency', which may be because 'as difficult as listening is, it's the one communication skill we're never really taught'. The Sperry Corporation teaches all its employees what it calls 'expanded listening', and its advertisement presents this fact to prospective customers as a selling point. The company's approach has been adopted as a model by other organizations: my copy of the advertisement comes not from any of the publications in which the company placed it, but from a set of training materials produced by a supermarket chain for its checkout operators. In the supermarket materials it was reproduced under the heading 'Listening skills can be improved'.

The Sperry course (and the supermarket course based upon it) understands the 'best' way of listening in terms of a theoretical account of what listening 'really' is. Rather than being an undifferentiated process, listening is said to consist of four discrete stages: 'hearing', 'understanding', 'evaluating' and 'responding'. If any of these stages are neglected, the quality of interaction will suffer; it is therefore a cause for concern that many people allegedly do not get beyond 'hearing'. In the Sperry advertisement, which is headed 'There's a lot more to listening than hearing', the four stages are illustrated with a series of cartoons. They show a woman (1) hearing the bawling of two small children; (2) looking up something in a weighty volume labelled 'Dictionary' (understanding); (3) in the posture of 'Justice', blindfolded and holding a scale while the children wait quietly beside her (evaluating); and (4) holding a judge's gavel in one hand and hugging a child with the other arm, while the second child smiles happily (responding).

It happens that I interviewed a number of people who had encountered the four-stage model in training. While some had just been presented with the model as a piece of theoretical information, a couple had engaged in role-play exercises where they were given a prompt to listen to and called on to verbalize each stage of the listening process. It is hard to say what trainers think they are achieving in exercises of this kind. Presumably no one supposes that in real situations a person would have time to run through the four stages consciously. Possibly the idea is that what is done slowly and deliberately in the classroom will eventually be performed rapidly and without conscious reflection in everyday routines. This would make listening similar to driving or playing a musical instrument, skills which are also broken down into discrete procedures for the purpose of instructing beginners, though in time they become integrated and automatic. But if that is the analogy, it is surely a rather odd one. Whereas driving instructors and music teachers regularly encounter people who have never previously been behind the wheel or blown into a flute, no one undergoing workplace training can reasonably be thought of as a 'beginner' in listening.

The four-stage model is not universally encountered, though the assertion that 'there's more to listening than hearing' is very common. One set of materials in my sample explains the difference thus: 'Hearing is passive. It involves picking up the sound waves and discounting them. Listening is active and is a multifunctional activity'. Other approaches to 'active listening' focus less on what is going on inside the trainee's head, and more on how s/he can demonstrate outwardly to an interlocutor that s/he is listening actively: they concentrate on the techniques of, for instance, back-channelling, asking for clarification, paraphrasing and summarizing. On some of these points, such as back-channelling, it is assumed that people already possess the skill itself, but need to be exhorted to use it more consciously and more frequently. In other cases, such as paraphrasing, it is common to find the skill being taught using structured exercises (I discuss an example of this in Chapter 3).

In this discussion I have focused on issues that recur in my sample often enough, and with enough consistency in what is said about them, for me to feel confident that they are not merely the idiosyncratic concerns of an individual materials designer. If that is accepted, some general observations might be made. It appears to be true that communication skills training materials draw on expert knowledge produced mainly within the fields of psychology and therapy, and not on knowledge whose source is linguistics, discourse or conversation analysis. Though in this sense selective, the use of expert sources is also rather undiscriminating. Sources that might be considered academically 'respectable' (such as the literature on assertiveness, which has its critics, but is generally recognized as being framed within the normal conventions of science) are mixed with sources no academic community considers reputable (such as Neurolinguistic Programming). There is also a tendency to rely on relatively old research frameworks and findings. Many texts published in the 1990s still belong, theoretically speaking, to the golden age of social scientific behaviourism, and draw on the model of communication as a 'chain' which derives from the work of mid-century information theorists such as Shannon and Weaver (1949). A simple 'encoding–decoding' model of communication continues to be presented as unchallenged fact. The reporting of research findings – which are only sometimes attributed to a source at all – tends to take them out of context, and one result is statistics like 'people listen on average at a 25% level of efficiency' or 'body language accounts for 80% of the message', which are more or less meaningless in the absence of any information on how they were arrived at, and can be used to license all kinds of conclusions the original research might not support. To the extent that they are not concerned exclusively with the practical minutiae of how to talk, but also require trainees to assimilate theoretical and factual knowledge *about* communication, it is difficult not to be critical of communication training materials for disseminating information of questionable provenance and value.

Another thing that invites criticism is the tendency to resort to explicit or implicit 'deficit' models, according to which some language-users, or possibly even most of them, are seriously deficient in basic and essential communication skills, such as being assertive, expressing emotion, and – most startling of all, since no one could dispute its status as basic and essential – listening. The claims made about listening highlight some of the problems with deficit models in general. One might ask, for instance, how convincing the evidence is for the existence of the alleged problem. What is the Sperry Corporation's warrant for saying that most people listen at a 25% level of efficiency (a statistic from which, as I have already noted, it is difficult to extract any clear meaning)? One might also ask whether the problem has been diagnosed correctly. Are workers who seem to listen poorly really deficient in 'listening skills', or might they be bored, distracted, unmotivated? Then there are questions about the model in relation to which people are being defined as deficient (is listening, in point of fact, a four-stage process?), and about the value of the remedy being prescribed (what is actually accomplished by exercises in 'active' or 'expanded' listening such as the one described above?). Sociolinguists who remember earlier controversies about alleged linguistic 'deficits' might well be struck by the potential for discourse on poor communication skills to produce some of the same unfortunate effects as did discourse on 'semilingualism', non-standard varieties and 'restricted codes' in the past. There is always a risk that a supposed deficit will be attributed selectively to social groups who already suffer from stigmatization; there is also a risk that those people will be subjected to ill-founded, time-wasting 'remedial' intervention.

The primary objective of communication training is to improve trainees' *practical* skills: to help them to use spoken language 'better'. This sample of materials suggests that certain specific recommendations on what constitutes 'better' communication are repeated very frequently. For sociolinguists and historians of language, that might raise an interesting question. Is this codification of norms for spoken discourse in any sense comparable to the codification of norms for grammar, spelling and pronunciation which is undertaken as part of the process of constructing and maintaining a standard language?

A standard for spoken discourse?

It should be said at once that in many respects the analogy is a poor one. James and Lesley Milroy suggest that the central mechanism of the standardizing process is 'the suppression of optional variability' (Milroy and Milroy, 1991). In other words, where the language system offers a range of options for 'saying the same thing' – more than one way of pronouncing a word, or forming plurals or negative sentences – standardization requires that one of the options be prescribed as 'correct' while the others become 'incorrect'. The aim is to make language-use as nearly as possible uniform, since the purpose of having a standard language is to transcend linguistic differences within the relevant community. Discourse phenomena, however, resist this treatment. Whereas choices about syntax, morphology and phonetic realization are usually made from a small number of possibilities, in discourse it is typically the case that a given function may be realized by a wide range of linguistic forms, and these are not just ways of 'saying the same thing'. Many commentators have found it reasonable to propose that we only need one rule for negation or one way of pronouncing word-final /t/, but few would propose that we only need one way of making requests or expressing agreement, since it is obvious that varying strategies are needed in different situations. The idea that one could define a 'standard discourse', on the model of 'standard grammar' or 'standard pronunciation', is inherently implausible.

There are cases in which communication training, and other regulatory practices, do have the goal of reducing or even eliminating variation in spoken discourse performance. This invariably applies, however, to particular interactional routines performed by particular language-users in a particular context: it produces a 'local' rather than 'global' standard. The most extreme case of this kind is requiring employees to perform a pre-written script in certain types of service encounters – an increasingly common practice, as we will see in later chapters. In theory, scripting reduces variation to zero; every employee speaks the same words in the same way in every encounter of the same type. Whether the result can be called a 'standard conversation' is doubtful, since the customer is not following a script (though it has been suggested that people on the receiving end of scripted utterances tend to routinize their own verbal behaviour too (Leidner, 1993)). But in any case, to the extent that such attempts to produce uniformity are effective, they are so only on the institutional site(s) where the script is in use.

Another common standardizing strategy is to make categorical rules in relation to highly predictable and formulaic areas of discourse performance: address terms, salutations and conventional politeness formulas all lend themselves to this treatment. Once again, though, such rules are contextually restricted. They take the form: 'say good morning rather than hello *when you answer the phone'*, or 'never use the address term "love" *when talking to customers'*. It is not suggested that the same norms should apply in every situation – that saying hello or calling someone 'love' is on a par with using double negatives and glottal stops, which is to say, just 'bad English'. Standardizing performance to make it uniform, then, is a goal of some prescriptive guidance on communication, but it is a fairly marginal one with limited, localized effects. On that criterion, an analogy between the codification of discourse norms and codification of norms for grammar, spelling and pronunciation is not particularly persuasive.

Yet the activity of norm-making is never without effects, particularly when undertaken institutionally and on a large scale. Standardization in the sense of 'uniform performance' is always an ideal rather than an achieved reality; but if the codification of linguistic standards does not necessarily succeed in changing people's behaviour it usually does succeed in altering their attitudes, so that they subscribe to what the Milroys dub the 'ideology of standardization'. In other words they accept that there is a right way of doing things, even if their own behaviour does not exemplify it. In this regard, arguably, communication training materials may be performing some of the same functions as texts that offer guidance on grammar, usage and (writing) style. Whether or not specific prescriptions are being followed, a general message is being disseminated that talking, like writing, is a skill; it can be learned and it can be judged. Aspects of behaviour that normally escape conscious and critical scrutiny – gaze, posture, listening – are subject to explicit and detailed examination, with a view to improving performance. In short, there may not be *a* standard, but there are nevertheless *standards* for spoken discourse.

To the degree that this idea is accepted, and exerts influence over what happens in key domains like work and schooling, I think it marks a real change. When I went to school in the 1960s and 1970s, 'oral assessment' was something you occasionally confronted in foreign-language classes, where it largely consisted of reading prose aloud. Except to correct our 'vulgar' pronunciation and deplore certain items of 'slang', no one paid the slightest attention to the way we spoke our own language. Speech was incidental, and the way you interacted was just an expression of your personality: some people were 'naturally' shy and quiet, others outgoing and garrulous. When I went to work in a bank in 1977, not a minute of formal training time was devoted to the subject of how to talk to customers, face-to-face or on the phone. On one hand it was taken for granted that everyone was in some sense a 'good enough' communicator, with the wit to pick up the conventions of workplace talk by observing and imitating others. On the other hand it was believed that there was no point trying to make silk purses out of sows' ears: you just kept your sows' ears (the unintelligible, charmless, painfully shy or easily flustered) in the back office and away from the customers. There has evidently been some change in the course of 20 years, for these assumptions now seem archaic, rejected by teachers and 'human resources' managers everywhere. But the extent to which attitudes have changed should not be exaggerated. We will see in later chapters that old assumptions persist, and for the moment at least they are the source of a certain amount of private (and indeed, not so private) scepticism about the utility and effectiveness of communication training.

Conclusion

In this chapter I set out to consider what kind of expert knowledge underpins the practice of communication skills training. What has emerged from the discussion is an apparent contradiction. On one hand, Angela Phillips draws attention to a problematic 'lack of common understanding about communication skills' (Phillips, 1998: 4). On the other hand, my examination of a sample of actual training materials, in use by real and reputable organizations, or available to the general public through mainstream sales outlets, suggests that the experts who write these materials have quite a high degree of 'common understanding' about what they are doing and what knowledge is relevant to the task. The same definitions, conceptual frameworks, classification systems, facts, statistics, rules and recommendations reappear with only minor variations in sets of materials designed by different experts for different clients in different settings. It does not seem wholly unreasonable to talk about communication training having a – that is, one – body of knowledge that serves as a common reference point for practitioners.

At the same time it is evident that this body of knowledge has been synthesized from many sources. It is unified only by virtue of being contained within texts whose subject is communication skills – as *knowledge* it is lacking in unity and coherence. Among its most important sources are the behavioural sciences (though it is more likely to draw on their 'back catalogues' than on their current research output) and certain types of therapeutic practice (the key ones being transactional analysis and assertiveness training). But it also shows the influence of other traditions. It is not uncommon to encounter (though the encounter is usually rather brief and banal) Quintilian or Emily Post. Another seam that is clearly being mined in many texts is the tradition of anecdotal lore produced by and for salespeople. This is a much older tradition, in which certain strategies that are now widely diffused were originally pioneered (for instance, the use of invariant scripts, which until recently were most likely to be used by salespeople making 'cold calls'). Sales lore is the most likely source for such oft-repeated superstitions as '*but* is a negative word; avoid it at all costs', and 'use your interlocutor's name at every opportunity' (a strategy recommended by Dale Carnegie, which, as we will see in Chapter 3, survives to irritate customers today). Eclecticism has its limits, however: there is a rather consistent disregard for those bodies of knowledge that derive from the empirical investigation of naturally occurring talk.

Angela Phillips's report is, of course, specifically about the issue of teaching communication as part of the school curriculum. One wonders whether the problem she glosses as a 'lack of common understanding' might be better described as a doubt entertained by some professional educators about the authority, validity or usefulness of the knowledge that currently grounds communication skills training in the non-academic contexts where much of it now goes on. One section of Phillips's report is devoted to the issue of *evaluation*, and it argues that communication teaching should not be introduced into schools without a firm commitment to 'benchmarking', that is, measuring effectiveness against clear and explicit criteria:

> Teachers need help to accept an evaluation culture in which they are not expected to know what works simply by instinct but to actively seek evidence. Fear of evaluation has dogged attempts to understand how best to teach reading – for years the subject of a slanging-match between professionals each defending what, on closer examination, often turned out to be a set of beliefs, based on anecdotes and ideas [*sic*] rather than on serious study. (Phillips, 1998: 16)

However consistently they appear in training materials, it seems clear that some of the assertions about communication I have cited in this chapter are 'based on anecdotes and ideas' and would not withstand a challenge based on 'serious study'. Unfortunately most of those who design and deliver the training are not in a position to mount such a challenge; their claims to expertise are not dependent on exposure to any discipline in which the serious study of spoken language-use is undertaken.

It is also evident that the effectiveness of training materials is rarely evaluated in any rigorous way. In the case of self-improvement literature, it is obviously impossible to assess outcomes. In the case of workplace training, trainees themselves may be asked to evaluate the course, and their own individual performance may be evaluated regularly by their employers, but I did not come across any organization that monitored whether average appraisal scores typically improved following exposure to formal training in the relevant skills.[11] In the case of publicly funded training intended to prevent 'anti-social' behaviour such as substance abuse or early sexual activity among young people, the charge has been made that evaluation is unsystematic, and that where it has been carried out it has shown disappointing results.[12]

The dearth of evidence about effectiveness could be addressed, if the will were there, by defining clearer aims and objectives, and monitoring outcomes. But this would not allay all concerns, since questions might still be asked about the value of particular aims, objectives and outcomes. A list derived from the materials I have examined might well include a number which were trivial ('know the difference between open and closed questions'), misguided ('be able to go through the four stages of listening') or eccentric ('classify people you encounter as logical thinkers, helpers or fighters'). To solve that problem it would be necessary to change the knowledge-base practitioners have at their disposal. It might also be necessary to have in place some kind of institutional framework for training and accreditation of 'experts'. Without one it is difficult to ensure that people who claim expertise about communication are equipped to judge ideas and their sources – or, putting it more bluntly, to discriminate between knowledge and nonsense.

This chapter has focused mainly on the content of various instructional texts about communication. Texts, however, have contexts, not only of production but also of use. Many of the communication training materials in my sample were produced to be used in specific institutions, and they need to be analysed in relation to their local institutional contexts. The institutional contexts I will turn to first are those of *work*. In Chapters 3 and 4 I examine the verbal hygiene practices that are, for a large and growing number of employees, an integral part of working life.

3

TALK AS ENTERPRISE: COMMUNICATION AND CULTURE CHANGE AT WORK

The softer words of leadership and vision and common purpose will replace the tougher words of control and authority because the tough words won't bite any more

— Charles Handy, Beyond Certainty, 1996.

Every time a customer comes within ten feet of me, I will smile, look him in the eye and greet him. So help me Sam

— Oath sworn by new recruits to Wal-Mart[1]

A smartly dressed young man walks up to a slightly younger woman. He asks: 'how are you feeling today?'. 'Fine', she replies. 'That's good', says the young man, 'but when I ask you how you're feeling I want you to say *"outstanding!"'*. As he utters the last word, his voice rises in pitch and volume; he punches the air with both hands. The young woman looks surprised – evidently she had assumed that 'how are you' was the opening move in an ordinary exchange of greetings – and then uncomfortable. She repeats 'outstanding', but without much enthusiasm. The young man is dissatisfied. He demonstrates what he wants again, emphasizing the air-punching gesture. Then he starts the routine from the beginning: 'how are you feeling today?'. This time she produces a better imitation of his 'outstanding', though her facial expression and a certain bodily stiffness betray her continuing discomfort. They go through the whole thing again. And again. Her performance passes muster. The young man smiles and moves on.

What is going on in this little scene? Is it some kind of political rally, or a religious revival meeting, or a session from one of those 'inspirational' courses about the power of positive thinking? Maybe the young woman is an athlete and the young man is her coach, psyching her up for an important event. Or maybe he is an entertainer, and she a member of the audience reluctantly dragged up on stage. In fact, the scene took place in a McDonald's restaurant at the beginning of a shift. The young man was the shift supervisor, and the young woman a member of his 'crew'. Their encounter was recorded for an Open University television programme about new management practices in British industry.[2] The programme also showed the young man on the receiving end of the same technique, which he learnt on a course at the company's training centre, 'Hamburger University'.

This motivational routine is not the only case in which McDonald's employees are instructed in how to talk. McDonald's is among the organizations that pioneered 'routinized' customer service interactions (Leidner, 1993). In this respect as in many others, McDonald's has attracted legions of imitators; George Ritzer, the author of a book whose self-explanatory title is *The McDonaldization of Society* (1996), suggests that 'pseudo-interaction' is a widespread and striking feature of present-day consumer culture. But why do employers find it necessary to regulate such small linguistic details as what words their employees utter, and in what tone of voice? How does this kind of regulatory practice square with the philosophy of 'empowerment', which is supposed to involve *less* control over the minutiae of employees' behaviour than the traditional model? And what about the employees themselves – how do they feel about being told what to say, and taught how to talk?

Talk at work

There is already an extensive literature on talk in professional or 'institutional' settings (see for instance Boden, 1994; Drew and Heritage, 1992; Drew and Sorjonen, 1997; Gunnarsson, Linell and Nordberg, 1997; Mumby and Clair, 1997; Wodak and Iedema, 1999). Some of the most notable contributions to this literature have been made by scholars in the research tradition of conversation analysis (CA). Before I proceed further, I should clarify the relationship of my own analysis of workplace 'communication' with this body of research; for although I hope I have learned from it, I do not see myself as directly contributing to it.

CA, which has roots in ethnomethodological sociology, regards talk as an important locus for the organization of social life generally. In institutional settings, as Paul Drew and John Heritage observe in their editors' introduction to the influential collection *Talk at Work*, 'Talk-in-interaction is the principal means through which lay persons pursue various practical goals and the central medium through which the daily working activities of many professionals and organizational representatives are conducted' (1992: 3). Studying institutional talk is thus a way of studying the workings of institutions themselves. In addition to this sociological significance, however, institutional talk is of interest more specifically to analysts of language and discourse. Because it is designed to accomplish particular goals, institutional talk has features that distinguish it from 'ordinary' talk. Drew and Heritage characterize them as follows (1992: 22):

1. Institutional interaction involves an orientation by at least one of the participants to some core goal, task or activity (or set of them) conventionally associated with the institution in question. In short, institutional talk is normally informed by *goal orientations* of a relatively restricted conventional form.
2. Institutional interaction may often involve *special and particular constraints* on what one or both of the participants will treat as allowable contributions to the business at hand.
3. Institutional talk may be associated with *inferential frameworks* and procedures that are particular to specific institutional contexts.

Later on, they identify five major 'foci of research into institutional talk' (1992: 28 *et seq.*). These are *lexical choice* – for example the selection of technical or lay vocabulary in institutional encounters; *turn design* – the way turn-taking rules may differ as between institutional and other talk; *sequential organization* – for example the tightly constrained use of question-answer sequences in institutional contexts such as clinics, classrooms and courtrooms; *overall structural organization* – the way many institutional interactions have a pre-determined 'shape'; and *social relations* – which are more apt to be asymmetrical in institutional contexts.

The framework set out by Drew and Heritage is useful, and many of my own observations in this and the next chapter will relate to one or more of their 'research foci'. However, I will be approaching the phenomenon of institutional talk at work from a different angle – one suggested by the McDonald's vignette with which I began this chapter. For a conversation analyst, the 'institutional' nature of talk is not something given in advance, but something accomplished by participants in the course of talking. Ian Hutchby summarizes this position succinctly: 'institutions do not define the kind of talk produced within them: rather participants' ways of designing their talk actually constructs the "institutionality" of such settings' (1999: 41). 'Interaction', say Drew and Heritage, 'is institutional insofar as participants' institutional or professional identities are somehow made relevant to the work activities in which they are engaged' (1992: 4). But without disputing that anything that goes on in talk has in the final analysis to be accomplished by the participants, I think there are cases where institutions (or to be more exact, people with certain kinds of authority in institutions) *do* define the kinds of talk produced within them to a greater extent than the CA formulation suggests. I am especially interested in professional identities and ways of talking that are not so much negotiated by participants 'on the ground' as imposed on them from above by training, scripting and surveillance. It is my contention that many kinds of 'talk at work' are increasingly subject to this explicit codification. Today it is not always left to workers to construct a suitable professional identity and 'somehow' make it relevant in talk; instead, approved forms of interactive discourse are prescribed in advance, and often in detail.

This development has a bearing on how we understand the 'special and particular constraints' mentioned by Drew and Heritage as distinctive features of institutional talk. When institutional interaction becomes subject to detailed codification, it is not only the participants in talk who decide what will count as 'allowable contributions to the business at hand'. Certain decisions on what is 'allowable' (and what is compulsory) are pre-empted by the codifiers, while the agency of the participants is correspondingly curtailed. Prescriptive interventions constrain interaction in two respects particularly, one of which Drew and Heritage mention and one of which they do not.

The one they mention comes under the heading of 'overall structural organization'. Here I will quote more fully from their remarks on this point:

> Many kinds of institutional encounters are characteristically organized into a standard 'shape' or order of phases. Conversations, by contrast, are not. With the exception of the opening and closing stages…it does not appear that conversations ordinarily progress through some overarching set of stages. The locally contingent management of 'next moves' in conversation, and the options speakers have even within particular sequences or activities, ensure that there is no 'standard pattern' for the overall organization of conversations. The activities conducted in many kinds of institutional interactions, by contrast, are often implemented through a task-related standard shape. In some instances that order may be prescribed, for instance, by a written schedule or formal agenda of points which an inquirer may be required to answer when requesting a service…But equally the order may be the product of locally managed routines. (Drew and Heritage, 1992: 43)

Prototypical instances of institutional interactions with a 'task-related standard shape' might include examining witnesses in court, taking a patient's history in a medical consultation or eliciting information on the location and nature of an incident when answering a call to the emergency services. Drew and Heritage are obviously right to point out that this sort of 'shaping' marks a significant difference between institutional talk and ordinary conversation. But I would also argue that *within* the 'institutional' category, 'locally managed routines' seem increasingly to be giving way to 'prescribed schedules' and 'formal agendas'. More and more institutional interactions – supermarket checkout transactions, customer enquiries made to a bank or utility company via one of its 'call centres', unsolicited telesales calls, and so on – have not merely a standard 'shape' but a standard *script* covering the sequencing, the content and function, and not uncommonly the actual wording, of every move the institutional participant makes.

This tendency has not been much discussed in the 'talk at work' literature, though it has attracted some attention from critical discourse analysts and sociologists of work (Fairclough, 1992; Goodman, 1996; Leidner, 1993). This relative neglect may partly reflect the fact that so much research on institutional talk has focused on interactions involving professionals like doctors, therapists, lawyers and business executives, whose status protects them from the degree of linguistic regimentation to which many other workers are now commonly subjected. It is also fair to say that the kind and degree of regimentation that interests me has become progressively more salient during the late 1980s and 1990s. The rapid diffusion and intensification of linguistic control strategies (which may have existed before but were less widespread and less efficient than they have since become) has occurred for two interrelated reasons. One is technological change (a point to be explored further in Chapter 4, which deals with call centres), and the other is the increasing influence of new management approaches. The overall effect of these developments has been to place not just linguistic behaviour but many other kinds of on-the-job behaviour under much closer scrutiny and surveillance.

The constraint which Drew and Heritage do not mention, but which will be an important topic in my own analysis, concerns the *manner* in which workers may be required to talk, whether or not the 'shape' and content of their talk has been scripted in advance. Particularly in customer service contexts, politeness phenomena, prosodic, paralinguistic and nonverbal (body language) behaviours, and sometimes lexical choices, are strictly regulated in a process I will refer to later on as *styling*. For instance, announcers at one British rail terminus are expected to perform announcements at a certain rate of words per minute and in 'smiley voice' (an effect which results from holding the lips in the posture of a smile whilst speaking). Assistants at a designer clothes shop are forbidden to approach customers with the conventional salutation 'can I help you' and instructed instead to 'strike up a conversation', resorting if necessary to remarks about the weather. At the same shop, there is a list of words that may be used to describe an outfit: it includes *exquisite* and *glamorous*, but *lovely* and *nice* are proscribed.[3] In the rather less exclusive retail environment that is Wal-Mart, meanwhile, employees swear an 'oath' to smile, make eye contact and utter a greeting 'every time a customer comes within ten feet of me'.

In sum, then, the kinds of observations made here on 'talk at work' will overlap in some respects with the tradition of research on that topic represented by contributors to Drew and Heritage's collection, while departing from that tradition in other respects. The most important difference is that I am interested less in 'locally managed routines' than in the codified and 'styled' forms of talk which, I argue, are increasingly overriding or disrupting the locally managed character of interaction. Since my primary interest is in the phenomenon of codification, and the practices of training and surveillance which are needed to make it 'bite', my primary data here will not be examples of naturally occurring workplace talk, nor will I be undertaking the kind of microanalysis favoured by conversation analysts. Instead I will examine prescriptive texts (including manuals, memoranda, training materials and lists of appraisal criteria) whose function is to spell out what kinds of talk people are expected to produce at work.[4] Of course, my use of these data invites the question: 'but is that what happens in practice?' The short answer is, 'yes and no'. I do not intend to suggest that workers are the 'cultural dopes' whose existence ethnomethodology has famously denied – that they simply follow the rules handed down to them in a passive, unquestioning way. Codification does not in practice eliminate the necessity for talk to be locally managed; what it does do, however, is change what participants have to manage. Workers who are given a script they find unsatisfactory may deviate from it, but in that case the institutional definition of what they are doing as deviant and 'accountable' behaviour becomes one of the factors they must take into consideration. Where codification is backed up by surveillance, institutional interactions begin to resemble 'mediated' discourse – that is, talk has to be designed not only for its immediate recipient, but also for an eavesdropping third party, namely the manager or supervisor who monitors workers' compliance with the rules.

I will return below to the issues raised in this section. First, though, it is necessary to say something about the broader context in which institutional interaction has become subject to increased codification and regimentation, which means returning to one of this book's main themes, the relationship between 'communication' and enterprise culture.

Everybody's business: corporate speak and cultural change

In discussions of the 'new' economy whose character I described in the introduction, much rhetoric centres on so-called 'human capital' – a reference not to people themselves, the innumerable willing 'hands' of the industrial age, but to the skills and knowledge that are today's most valuable assets, and are embodied (or en-minded) in human beings. Governments worry about the level of *technical* knowledge and skill possessed by today's workforce (hence election pledges like 'a computer in every classroom' and ideas like 'the university of industry'). Yet many employers – particularly in the burgeoning service sector – seem more interested in the so-called 'soft skills': they want recruits to be team players, 'good with people', and not least, 'good communicators'. Language, then, looms large among the attributes employers pay attention to when recruiting, training and managing workers. But in addition, it is an *instrument* for managing both individuals and organizations as they struggle with the process of 'culture change' that global competition is believed to necessitate. The point is summed up by management guru Charles Handy in the observation that appears as an epigraph to this chapter: to succeed in new worlds, businesses must adopt new words.

In a book titled *Corporate Speak: the Use of Language in Business*, Fiona Czerniawska, a management consultant, elaborates this point. She argues that given the new emphasis on 'human capital', language, with its power to win hearts and minds, is more important in organizations now than it has ever been before. She suggests that language can be 'a weapon of competitive advantage' for companies who are willing and able to exploit its potential (1998: 13). In business, she says,

> ...[O]ur preferred mode of communication has been figures...[but] more and more companies are finding that some of their most important assets – people, knowledge, commitment – are non-quantifiable. And they are realising that if they cannot express these assets in terms of figures, then they cannot use financial metrics to manage them. It is therefore not surprising that they are turning to something other than figures to fill the gap – words: mission statements, commitments to quality, customer charters, corporate advertising – the list is growing exponentially. (1998: 2)

'Corporate speak' might seem an odd choice of title for a book whose aim is to make managers appreciate the potential of language as 'a weapon of competitive advantage'. Describing any linguistic register as X-*speak* tends to imply a perception of it as meaningless jargon, at best baffling and at worst sinister – perhaps because the '-*speak*' formulation so readily recalls Orwell's 'Newspeak'. But Fiona Czerniawska's mission is to rehabilitate something she regards as having been misunderstood and unfairly maligned by businesspeople who pride themselves on being doers rather than talkers. She does warn against Orwellian excesses: 'No sane business today would want a workforce of automatons: after all, anything an automaton can do, we can automate. People are needed for dealing with customers, for communication, and for lateral thinking, none of which businesses will get if they attempt to regiment the way people talk too rigidly' (1998: 27). But that does not mean businesses should not attempt to manage the use of words at all. If used judiciously, 'corporate speak' (a phrase that might be glossed as 'managed language-use') is a valuable 'new tool by which to influence collective culture and individual behaviour' (1998: 26). In this chapter I will focus particularly on two features of 'enterprising' corporate cultures which are thought to require the application of this 'new tool': the shift to 'teamwork' and the systematic adoption of 'customer care' policies.

'Teamwork' is one of the buzzwords of the enterprise approach, and the thought behind it is summarized in the aphorism 'None of us is as smart as all of us'. What it usually involves in practice is forms of workplace organization where people, often drawn from different levels of the corporate hierarchy, have to work together in groups to achieve particular outcomes. In a presentation of work she did with a group of colleagues in an Australian food manufacturing plant (Joyce et al., 1995), Hermine Scheeres (1998) provides a table listing the 'spoken and written language demands of the restructured workplace'. Under the heading of 'teamwork' she notes the following spoken language demands:

- Solve problems and negotiate solutions and outcomes
- Initiate and participate in team discussions
- Know how to challenge
- Know how to ask for advice
- Argue for and against a proposition
- Ask a speaker to clarify or explain a point.

Under the heading 'changing role of the manager' Scheeres also lists the new spoken language responsibilities managers acquire in a teamwork culture, as follows:

- Explain and discuss changes in workplace practices
- Explain and negotiate team membership
- Negotiate allocation of tasks
- Listen and discuss openly problems and issues that arise
- Explain section interests and needs to others.

These demands are the linguistic instantiations of the shift away from a 'command and control' culture in which managers give instructions and workers follow them, towards an 'empowerment' culture. Managers are encouraged to 'explain', 'discuss', 'negotiate' and 'listen', while workers are permitted to 'question', 'challenge' and 'argue', and expected to 'solve problems'. Training may be needed to enable both managers and workers to master the more egalitarian and co-operative forms of spoken discourse that constitute 'teamwork'. Another important issue, not explicitly mentioned on Scheeres's list but possibly implied by 'explain and discuss changes in workplace practices', is *motivation*. Motivation matters, because in theory, at least, the 'teamwork' approach puts peer support (and peer pressure) in place of 'external' sticks and carrots. A good team-member is both highly motivated and able to motivate others, which inevitably involves communicating with them. Below I will consider how far the 'ideal' model outlined by Scheeres is reflected in actual practice; and I will look more closely at the particular forms of spoken communication recommended in training for teamwork.

'Customer care' is an approach to service in which an organization systematically sets out to manage the customer's whole experience. A set of training materials in my corpus (developed for a non-profit making arts organization to which I will give the pseudonym 'City Arts') explains the concept by quoting the chief executive of the Scandinavian airline SAS, who once said: 'coffee stains on the flip-down trays mean to the passenger that we do our engine maintenance wrong'.[5] The idea is that the customer's view of the organization is conditioned by a large number of small, and possibly quite trivial, details. 'Customer care' means getting employees to focus consistently on all the details that make a difference to the customer. It is also common for the approach to be extended to employees' dealings with one another: co-workers within the organization are defined as 'internal customers'. Customer care policies overlap here with the philosophy of teamwork, for the point is that everyone should work together for the ultimate good of the customer (and thus, of course, the company). Even those employees who have no contact with 'external' or 'end' customers – the people who actually consume goods and services – are materially affecting those customers' experience through the quality of support they give to colleagues down the line.

The City Arts materials sum up customer care – whether the customers are 'external' or 'internal' – as a matter of 'having the right attitudes and behaviours in place within an organization. In general terms, these attitudes and behaviours can be summarized as *caring, co-operating and communicating*'.[6] In fact, the discussion that follows makes clear that 'communication' in the sense of 'spoken interaction' is relevant to all three of these 'attitudes and behaviours'. What is placed under the heading of 'communicating' is essentially the use of language to convey information ('transmitting information accurately and speedily'). But language is not just a medium for transmitting information, it is also a medium for constructing and maintaining interpersonal relationships. Thus 'caring' and 'co-operating' also turn out to be ways of 'communicating'. 'Caring', for instance, is explained by breaking it down into several more specific behaviours:

- Treating [customers] with courtesy and consideration
- Responding reasonably to their requests and demands
- Showing an interest in them
- Taking time to find out what they feel
- Accepting responsibility, i.e. avoiding blame and helping out when problems occur
- Being aware of how what you do affects them

It is evident that at least the first four of these requirements will depend for their fulfilment largely on the way the employee talks to customers.

Some of the most noticeable reflexes of customer care policies in language-use are aptly described by Norman Fairclough's phrase 'synthetic personalization'. As Fairclough explains:

> One finds techniques for efficiently and nonchalantly 'handling' people wherever one looks in the public institutions of the modern world. Equally, one finds what I shall refer to as *synthetic personalization*, a compensatory tendency to give the impression of treating each of the people 'handled' *en masse* as an individual. Examples would be air travel (*have a nice day!*), restaurants (*Welcome to Wimpy!*) and the simulated conversation (for example, chat shows) and *bonhomie* which litter the media. (1989: 62)

The City Arts customer care training materials warn against saying things like 'sorry, that's our policy' and 'I don't make the rules' when a customer complains about something. These utterances imply (not inaccurately, in most cases) that the organization has routine procedures that it follows with every customer. The customer care ideal, by contrast, is to give the impression of attending to the needs of each customer as an individual. (A training manager at McDonald's told Robin Leidner: 'we want to treat every customer as an individual in 60 seconds or less' (Leidner, 1993: 221), while according to George Ritzer (1996: 82) some organizations even have 'subscripts' for customers who object to the normal routine as depersonalizing; employees may be told, for instance, to say they will 'bend the rules just this once'.) The City Arts materials ask: 'can you imagine how differently your customers would react if…an employee smiled and said, "I'm sorry you've had a problem. I'll take care of it immediately"'.

The behaviour being recommended here has several features of 'synthetic personalization'. The hypothetical employee smiles, apologizes to the customer (using a formula that incorporates both first and second person pronouns – 'I'm sorry *you*'ve had a problem') and takes personal responsibility for putting things right. One difference between this approach and traditional notions of 'polite' service is the greater attention paid to what politeness theorists like Brown and Levinson (1987) term 'positive face', the desire people have to be liked or approved of by others (in contrast to 'negative face', the desire not to be imposed upon by others). Employees who have internalized the customer care philosophy are supposed to 'show an interest' and 'take time to find out how [customers] feel'. They must communicate not simply respect for the customer as a customer, but a friendly, empathetic attitude towards the customer as a person. Below, I will consider how this expansive definition of 'good service' has been codified in rules and procedures for what employees should say to customers, and how they should say it. I will also consider how employees negotiate, and in some cases resist, the positioning imposed on them by linguistic prescriptions relating to customer care.

The examples I will use in my analysis come from the commercial service sector: not from manufacturing, or 'caring' work, or the work of public institutions like universities and the civil service. That is not because enterprise, empowerment, teamwork and customer care are confined to the service sector. On the contrary, these innovations are by now very widely diffused across different types of workplaces. I have chosen to examine them in the commercial service context because, arguably, the form they take there is their prototypical form. Attempts to integrate ideas borrowed from commerce with the traditional structures and values of other sectors, especially public service and caring, cause complications, including linguistic ones (are sick, disabled and elderly people 'customers'?). These issues are interesting, but beyond my scope here. It is also worth recalling that approximately two thirds of all workers in the economies I've used in my examples are employed in the service sector, and the proportion is expected to grow. That in itself is a reason to be interested in what goes on in their workplaces.

The formal introduction of teamwork or customer care policies into an organization is an example of 'culture change'. Not only do such initiatives change actual work routines – they involve employees in new forms of training and appraisal, new events such as team meetings, and so forth – their effectiveness is thought to depend on whether the organization can bring about a more profound shift in employees' *attitudes*. Reorganizing your workforce into teams, for instance, will succeed only to the extent that people embrace the concept of teamwork and strive to become 'team players'. It is this 'deeper' kind of change that Fiona Czerniawska (1998) has in mind when she characterizes language as a 'tool with which to influence collective culture and individual behaviour' and a means for 'instilling a common outlook and ideology'.

The idea of using language deliberately for the purposes Fiona Czerniawska mentions inevitably raises the issue of Orwellian 'thought control'. I commented above that Czerniawska's phrase 'corporate speak' tends to recall 'Newspeak', the language invented by George Orwell in his novel *Nineteen Eighty-four* (1989 [1949]). Newspeak was deliberately created by the ruling party of a totalitarian state to ensure that only orthodox thoughts could be given expression in words. Indeed, it was intended to abolish not only the words, but also, ultimately, the subversive thoughts themselves. Writing just after World War II, Orwell took his inspiration from the linguistic abuses of fascism and Stalinism. Today, these ideologies are marginal, while another 'ism' – capitalism – has gone from strength to strength. We might be tempted to ask, then, if big business has taken over where Big Brother left off.

In fact, I think this is the wrong way to frame the question. Most linguists would probably agree that the notion of thought control through language is a myth: even those who accept language may influence the way we think acknowledge that this is a complex and variable matter (for one recent discussion of the issue, see Stubbs, 1997). Controlling thought, however, is by no means the only way to achieve certain objectives. It may not be possible to control what goes on in people's minds by prescribing what language they may speak, hear, read or write, but enforcing that prescription is itself a way of controlling people's behaviour. That it falls short of 'brainwashing' does not automatically make it unobjectionable.

Fiona Czerniawska gives a number of examples where companies have set to convey an official 'collective outlook' to employees, using the simple linguistic strategy of renaming things. The Disney Corporation, for instance, renamed its personnel department 'Central Casting' and its employees 'cast members'. The areas where employees can be seen by customers are known as 'on stage'. All this conveys that Disney's business is showbusiness. At one of Britain's leading supermarkets, staff were renamed 'colleagues'. A financial institution renamed meetings 'events'. This strategy underlines the symbolic importance accorded to language, but as Czerniawska herself points out, in isolation it accomplishes very little. Just calling something an 'event' without doing anything else to make it less dull than the 'meetings' it replaces is more likely to engender derision than excitement. Renaming people 'colleagues' without otherwise modifying the previous hierarchical relations among them will provoke cynicism, not enthusiasm. However, it is unusual to find a company using the renaming strategy in isolation. More commonly, the introduction of new vocabulary is part of a more comprehensive strategy for culture change within the organization. At this point it is useful to turn to an example – one which, as it happens, has some strikingly Orwellian features.

'The changes' at John Stephenson Ltd

John Stephenson Ltd is one of the organizations discussed in this book whose language practices were studied by a participant observer, an employee who was also a student in one of my classes (see note 4 and Appendix). The student in question, Gordon Graham, had worked for several years as a member of the company's sales staff (during university vacations he worked full time, otherwise part time). As well as drawing on his observations as a participant in training and work routines, he collected relevant internal documents and carried out interviews. I am indebted to him for the information and some of the analysis presented here.

John Stephenson Ltd is a regionally based retail business selling electrical appliances through a network of shops: founded by John Stephenson, it is still owned and run by the Stephenson family, whose members continue to dominate the board of directors. Until recently, the company had the paternalistic values and culture traditionally associated with family businesses. Relations between managers and staff were not egalitarian but they were 'easy going', in the words of one employee. Workers did not feel they were under undue pressure, and generally 'enjoyed their jobs'. In the mid-1990s, however, the company found itself struggling; turnover and profits declined steadily. Afraid that the business might not survive in an increasingly competitive environment, the board decided to implement major restructuring. This began with 'downsizing' – a significant number of employees lost their jobs – and continued with the involvement of management consultants and the adoption of a more 'enterprising' managerial approach.

In 1997 the Managing Director sent a memo to every department in the company, part of which read:

> This is year one; from this point onward, all that has happened before in the company is to be forgotten. This may take some time, but it is hoped that in five or ten years' time, no one will remember back beyond this year and our new beginning.

It is hardly surprising if this prompts comparisons with Orwell's *Nineteen Eighty-four*. The memo tells its recipients – many of them people who have been with the organization for years – that history is to be abolished ('All that has happened before in the company is to be forgotten'). The developments which led up to this memo and gathered pace after it are now referred to within the company simply as 'the changes'.

Rather like the society depicted in Orwell's novel, John Stephenson contains three major groups: the Management Team (analogous to Orwell's 'Inner Party'), which consists of the directors, the service manager and seven area managers known as 'team leaders'; the office staff, individual shop managers and salespeople (who are rather like Orwell's 'Outer Party'), and the behind-the-scenes workers, such as van-drivers and 'store-boys' who oversee the storage and movement of goods (parallel to the 'proles' in *Nineteen Eighty-four*). 'The changes' directly affected only the first two groups. Managers, office staff and salespeople, but not drivers or storeroom workers, were required to adopt new working routines, and to undergo programmes of training intended to inculcate the skills, attitudes and dispositions associated with 'teamwork'. (Asked about the exclusion of drivers and store-boys, one manager commented that involving them would have been pointless, since they were 'too stupid to realize what's going on, [and] even if they did they're too stupid to do anything about it'. Ben Pimlott remarks in his editor's introduction to the Penguin edition of *Nineteen Eighty-four* (1989: xv) that 'in Oceania the relative freedom of working-class people is merely a symptom of the contempt in which they are held'.)

The architects of 'the changes' believed that language was an important tool for getting employees to consent to new arrangements; in particular, they believed that certain communication practices would be crucial in motivating employees and persuading them to adopt new attitudes and beliefs. In 1997 members of the Management Team attended a training course which was intended to teach this lesson. Those who were interviewed subsequently were invited to talk about their reactions to the course, and particularly to the way the trainer used language. This question elicited the following narrative from one participant:

Manager:	Everyone had to do a presentation, including [the trainer], he did his first. He started by asking: 'who is the company?'. We all had to reply: 'We are'. His reply was: 'I can't hear you'. It was like something from an American show.
Interviewer:	Were you embarrassed by this?
Manager:	At first. But before I knew where I was, I was shouting and screaming the answers back at him, everybody was. By the time he'd gone on for about five minutes, he asked the question again, 'Who is the company?'. It was like I wasn't in control any more. I'd say it was a mixture of him controlling us using language and gestures and probably wanting to fit in with everyone else.
Interviewer:	How do you feel about this now?
Manager:	Obviously I can see how we were controlled but I don't think it did me or anyone else any harm. I think it brought us together, made us feel part of a team.

Interestingly, most interviewees who were questioned about this event both agreed that they were being 'controlled' by the techniques the trainer used, and at the same time explicitly denied (in some cases with considerable emphasis) that they were being 'brainwashed'. 'Brainwashing' was seen as a disreputable practice, and it was also seen as a sign of personal weakness to be vulnerable to such an extreme form of manipulation. If 'brainwashing' is taken to imply a permanent suspension of one's critical faculties, then clearly the managers' denial that they had been 'brainwashed' was justified: all were able to reflect critically on what had happened after the event. None, however, was willing to express resentment about being 'controlled'.

Another quasi-Orwellian feature of 'the changes' was a requirement that sales staff and managers should write regular reports detailing what they had achieved, and also what their workmates had achieved. The reports would be passed up the line and ultimately analysed at a meeting of the

Management Team. This measure was considered controversial, and some people resented it – less because of the time it consumed than because it was seen as a way of getting employees to spy and inform on one another. One team leader commented: 'only the gullible believe anything good can come from these reports, it is all about noting down the negative to use against an individual'. This is a good example of the way 'empowerment' approaches may in practice intensify rather than lessen the surveillance associated with 'command and control' methods. It is also, however, a good illustration of the fact that few employees swallow the rhetoric of empowerment uncritically. If that rhetoric is intended as 'brainwashing', it clearly does not work. But arguably it does not need to: whatever they may think of new practices, employees are in no position to refuse to comply with them. At the time of the interviews, everyone at the company was conscious that 'the changes' had been precipitated in the first place by a crisis in John Stephenson's fortunes, as a result of which many jobs had been lost. Nobody wanted to be first on the list in any new round of layoffs.

A key aspect of 'the changes' was the reorganization of personnel into teams. This required explicit attention to be given to the way employees used interactive spoken language. An internal document, 'Our Five Year Plan', proclaimed: 'We shall make the teaching of good communication, assertiveness and listening skills a priority as these are essential to effective teamwork'. To that end, a programme of communication skills training was designed and delivered by an outside consultancy. I want to look in some detail at what was taught, referring to the training materials given out to participants. (These materials have much in common with other workplace materials in my sample (see Chapter 2), and where appropriate I will compare them with other examples.)

One respect in which the John Stephenson materials are typical is in their eclecticism: they do not adopt a unified approach but draw on various bodies of knowledge or expertise. These range from the clinical/therapeutic precepts of assertiveness training to the anecdotalism of popular how-to-succeed-in-business books like Stephen Covey's *The Seven Habits of Highly Effective People* (1989). Consequently, there is some incoherence in the materials; for instance, two somewhat different accounts may be given of the same phenomenon, or principles may be adduced which conflict with one another. It is seldom explained where the accounts and principles come from – in most cases they are presented as obvious and indisputable pieces of common wisdom. Appeals to experience are more prominent than appeals to scientific authority ('if you're like most of us, positive reinforcement probably increased your desire to participate' rather than, say, 'research has found that...'). This kind of training is meant to be practical rather than 'academic'.

It is therefore interesting that one of the first documents in this set of training materials is a lengthy presentation of Eric Berne's Transactional

Analysis (TA), which is glossed as 'an important technique in the search for improved communications'. (The materials justify this unusual excursion into theoretical territory by saying: 'The main advantage of TA is that it avoids the usual psychological jargon and so is very easily learned and understood'.) It is explained that TA categorizes every communicative act according to whether it is 'parent', 'adult' or 'child' behaviour. The key to good communication is judging whether a particular utterance ('stimulus') is coming from your interlocutor's 'parent', 'adult' or 'child' and then either designing your own response to complement the stimulus or else responding in such a way as to invite the interlocutor to shift to a more appropriate mode. A sample analysis is provided, using the utterance pair

> *Fred:* John, have you seen the report on the new machinery?
> *John:* Yes, it's here on my desk.

The analysis is: 'Fred asked a straightforward question from his Adult aimed at John's Adult and John responded as expected, from his Adult to Fred's'.

A less straightforward exchange is then illustrated:

> *Jim:* Call yourself a manager, this whole office is in chaos thanks to your new system.
> *Boss:* Look, I'm the boss around here. If you don't like the system you'll just have to lump it.

Jim has adopted the position of the Critical Parent, and his boss has refused the complementary position of the Child, taking an even more markedly parental role himself. What he should have done, however, was to direct his response to Jim's Adult, by saying something like

> *Boss:* What exactly is causing the problems within the system, perhaps we could modify it to solve them.

This strategy would put pressure on Jim to 'discuss the situation logically' in his Adult persona, and in this way the incipient conflict would be resolved without the boss needing to invoke his status as Jim's superior.

I noted in Chapter 2 that transactional analysis crops up quite frequently in my sample of training materials. Although it is usually presented as a means for avoiding *communication* problems – 'complementary' transactions are less likely to lead to misunderstanding than 'crossed' ones – the examples given make clear that in practice, TA is seen as particularly useful for avoiding or defusing *conflicts*. These may be expressed or manifested linguistically, but their underlying cause is not linguistic. In the 'call yourself a manager' exchange quoted above, for instance, Jim and his boss are not having trouble because one has misunderstood what the other is saying, but because of a difference of opinion – firstly about the system which Jim alleges is causing chaos, and secondly about Jim's right to challenge a superior in the way he does. The account TA gives of conflict (or perhaps it would be fairer to say the account training materials give of TA's account of conflict) does not dwell on its causes nor consider its legitimacy in a given situation. Instead it treats conflict as the undesirable result of a failure to act in the appropriate, 'adult' manner. It suggests that conflict can and should be defused, and that this is simply a technical matter. It also suggests that good leadership is about rational persuasion and teamwork: 'how can we solve the problem' rather than 'I'm the boss, so do as I tell you'. In other words, TA is not simply a tool for understanding what is going on in interaction, but has an ideological agenda – one that fits particularly well with the goals and values of the enterprising organization. This may help to explain the otherwise puzzling phenomenon of time being spent training domestic appliance salespeople to grasp the conceptual apparatus of TA and even draw diagrams of interactions. They are not being instructed only in techniques for effective 'communication', but also, and probably more importantly, in the conduct expected of a mature, responsible, well-balanced person.

In contrast to transactional analysis, which is more about the roles speakers take up than the minutiae of their conversational behaviour, the parts of the John Stephenson training materials devoted to 'active listening' offer more specific guidance. As I noted in Chapter 2, 'active listening' is a common preoccupation in training materials and there are several different approaches to it. The one which appears in these materials focuses on four kinds of behaviour:

1. Non-verbal behaviours, for example, posture, eye contact, gestures, utterances like 'uh-huh'.
2. Paraphrasing – to check accuracy of hearing.
3. Verbal encouragement, for example, 'tell me more', 'mm-hmm', etc.
4. Summarizing.

Advice on non-verbal behaviour or 'body language' is relatively sparse in these materials – other examples in my corpus make much more of it – but what there is, is typical of most guidance on this subject. Essentially trainees are encouraged to do more consciously what they would normally do without reflection, and given a metalanguage with which to reflect on common behaviours. They are also presented with generalizations about what is 'normal' behaviour – for instance, one should make eye contact with an interlocutor for 'about 60–70% of the time'. Here, what is presumably a statistical average derived from research on naturally occurring gaze behaviour is made into a benchmark or standard: the 'normal' becomes the normative. Behaviours which in a descriptive framework would be points on a continuum or normal distribution curve are redefined in a prescriptive framework as 'wrong' and in need of remediation.

As well as making sure that there is some eye contact rather than none, trainees are counselled to avoid a 'fixed stare'. They are told that their posture should be 'relaxed' rather than 'tense' and that their gestures should be natural rather than 'stiff and artificial'. At the same time, it is emphasized that they should 'smile'. (We will see later on that this injunction is ubiquitous, even in materials telling people how to conduct telephone interaction.) It would seem, then, that trainees are being urged to simulate naturalness. They are told to think consciously about gaze, posture, gesture and so forth rather than doing what comes naturally, but at the same time warned that the resulting behaviour should not display any evidence of self-consciousness.

'Paraphrasing' and 'summarizing' – giving the gist of what someone has said in order to get confirmation that you have understood them correctly – are things people sometimes do in ordinary talk, but in the context of a business or service encounter it may be necessary to do them more explicitly and more often than usual. A number of practice exercises aimed at developing these skills are included in the John Stephenson training materials. The paraphrasing task, for example, requires trainees to write out two different paraphrases of the following passage (which handily encapsulates the rationale behind 'active listening' itself):

> Inefficient listening is extraordinarily costly. Listening mistakes have severe repercussions throughout business, however it is often simple everyday occurrences multiplied by many thousand that add up to the greatest costs. Letters have to be retyped, appointments rescheduled, shipments missed, meetings cancelled.

The most obvious peculiarity of this exercise is that it has nothing to do with listening: the passage appears in written form and the paraphrases are also rendered in writing. Another oddity is the amount of space provided in which to write the paraphrases; it is large enough to suggest to the trainee that the point of this task is simply to reformulate the original in full using different words. In conversation this would be bizarre. Someone who insisted on repeating every detail of what their co-conversationalists had said, in different words but at similar length, would quickly be judged communicatively incompetent: the results would be more reminiscent of a 'Garfinkel experiment'[7] than of any normal interaction.

Guidance on 'verbal encouragement' suggests that 'reinforcement' is necessary if people are to remain motivated. Two kinds of 'verbal reinforcers' are recommended: positive ones like 'I'm glad you noticed that' and 'What an interesting thought!', which 'reinforce desirable responses' and neutral ones like 'I see, thanks for your input', which 'discourage undesirable behaviours'. Negative comments like 'no, that won't work' are to be avoided, since they undermine people's motivation. This advice is clearly informed by an old-fashioned behaviourist model of communication and indeed of human behaviour in general, in which stimulus-response chains loom large. Another way in which trainees are advised to give verbal encouragement is by asking open rather than closed questions. 'For example', the materials suggest, 'instead of asking "did you get our free sample?" ask, "what did you think of our sample?"'. The open/closed question distinction is fetishised in virtually every set of materials I have come across, and it implies a very simple and literal model of how communication works. Form and function are thought to be so intimately locked together that if you ask someone a yes/no question they can only respond with a yes or no answer. The question 'did you get our free sample?' could never elicit an answer like 'yeah, terrific, can I place an order for 400 of them?' but only 'yes, thanks'.

Attempts to prescribe 'standard' ways of performing particular communicative tasks typically take no account of the fact that spoken discourse exhibits a high degree of contextually conditioned variation, which is functional for communication rather than presenting some sort of obstacle to it. Unawareness or intolerance of variation can give rise to some strange and unnatural prescriptions. Variation is not only a question of the presence or absence of a particular variant, but also of its relative frequency and its distribution – a point that goes unacknowledged in most communication training materials, whose assumption seems to be that you can't have too much of a good thing, be it paraphrasing, verbal reinforcement or smiling. So while the materials may offer guidance on the mechanism of, say, paraphrasing, they will not discuss the equally relevant issue of where in an exchange it might be useful to paraphrase or how often it is reasonable to do so in a given context. Paraphrasing itself is not an unnatural strategy, but it can become unnatural if it is done without regard to the demands of the specific context. A service encounter may demand more frequent paraphrasing than a casual conversation between friends, but less frequent paraphrasing than, say, a counselling session.

In some cases, the behaviour prescribed in training materials is unnatural not because it is contextually inappropriate but because it flouts pragmatic principles that apply across contexts. For instance, assertiveness training (or AT, the subject of a later section in the John Stephenson materials), counsels trainees to avoid indirectness, even or especially when performing seriously face-threatening acts. AT believes indirectness to be misleading and 'manipulative'; politeness theory by contrast tells us that indirectness is one conventional strategy for mitigating face-threats (Brown and Levinson, 1987). Consistently refraining from mitigation is not just unnatural, it has considerable potential for giving offence.

The John Stephenson materials are not only eclectic in approach but also unsystematic in structure and content. There is neither an explicit nor an implicit resort to anything like Hermine Scheeres's (1998) list of 'spoken language demands in the restructured workplace', and it is never explained why the materials developer decided to focus on exactly the things he or she did. The statement in 'Our Five Year Plan' that 'good communication, assertiveness and listening skills…are essential to effective teamwork' looks at first glance like a plausible enough statement of training priorities, but on reflection its logic is obscure. For one thing, the three items on the list are not all on the same taxonomic level. 'Good communication' is a generic phrase, which might reasonably be taken to subsume 'assertiveness' and 'listening skills'. 'Assertiveness' and 'listening skills' themselves reflect the application of different subcategorizing principles to the general field of 'good communication': 'assertiveness' is an approach that may be brought to bear on all aspects of communication, whereas 'listening skills' apply to only one kind of communicative behaviour, namely listening. It is as if someone had announced their intention of listing three kinds of fruit and then come up with a list containing 'fruit, jam making and lemons'. Why 'effective teamwork', in particular, should demand assertiveness and listening skills training, and not something else, is never made clear.

This might seem an overly pedantic response to a single sentence from an internal memo, but the sentence in question is symptomatic of a very general problem. In my sample, many or most materials have a similar 'ragbag' quality. Some of the advice given on specific points is perfectly sensible, but the whole does not hang together in the way someone used to reading or writing course materials (an applied linguist such as Hermine Scheeres, for instance) might expect. Trainees are exposed, seemingly almost at random, to ideas about 'communication', systems for reflecting upon it and practical tips on how to do it which are not necessarily connected to each other, and which are not presented as interrelated parts of any larger whole.

Whatever the shortcomings of the training programme, however, 'the changes' at John Stephenson provide a good illustration of the foregrounding of language and communication in contemporary management practice. In particular, they illustrate a widespread belief among managers that linguistic regulation can be used systematically as an instrument of culture change and of control over people. Thus the consultant who designed the training package used motivational techniques to induce managers to shout and scream 'we are the company!'; managers used new report-writing formats to keep tabs on the day-to-day performance of their subordinates; those subordinates were instructed in using TA, 'active listening' and assertiveness to produce the desired outcomes in interactions with customers and with one another. From the management team's perspective, this belief in the power of language was vindicated by the outcome of 'the changes': a few months after the introduction of new practices and new training, turnover had increased significantly. Others in the company were more sceptical: they attributed the improvement not to teamwork or communication training, but to increased effort on the part of individuals whose job was to sell the company's products. What lay behind the increased effort was fear: 'the changes' were interpreted as a sign that the company was in trouble, and that unless employees took action they would soon find themselves out of a job. Gordon Graham's interviews elicited at least some negative comments on 'the changes' from every informant, but at the same time, in his words: 'Every employee knows and has been warned that any resistance to "the changes", or any anti-company feeling reported back to the Management Team will result in dismissal'.

This might suggest one final comparison with *Nineteen Eighty-four*. The novel ends with the capitulation of the hero, Winston Smith, but the reason for his capitulation sometimes gets forgotten. Winston's resistance is broken, not by the use of Newspeak to control his thinking, but by conventional torture, and particularly his dread of being eaten alive by rats in Room 101. Obviously, businesses do not use such extreme forms of coercion. Nevertheless, it seems employees' consent to and compliance with new arrangements may depend less on Charles Handy's 'softer words of vision and leadership and common purpose' than on knowing that 'tougher' words (such as, 'you're fired') are being kept in reserve.

Forcing a smile: customer care and 'superior service'

Although John Stephenson Ltd is a retail organization, the explicit rationale it gave for introducing communication training was to ensure employees worked effectively in the teams into which they had been reorganized during 'the changes'. More commonly, however, the primary focus of linguistic training and regulation in retail businesses is the way staff interact with customers. Since the perceived standard of a company's service is a function of its employees' behaviour, the 'customer care' approach means that companies are essentially selling the qualities of their staff. Consequently, they must take a close interest in the qualities staff actually display to customers: in their appearance, their demeanour and, not least, their speech.

In October 1998, the *Washington Post* reported on a controversy that had broken out on the internet[8] around a 'superior service' programme initiated by the Safeway supermarket chain in the USA. Under the title 'Service with a forced smile: Safeway's courtesy campaign also elicits some frowns' (October 18: A1), reporter Kirstin Downey Grimsley explained the background. The rules of 'superior service' required employees to 'make eye contact with the customer, smile, greet him or her, offer samples of products, make suggestions about other possible purchases that could go with the items being purchased, accompany customers to locate items they can't find…thank shoppers by name at the checkout using information from their credit, debit or Safeway card'. To monitor compliance, Safeway employed 'mystery shoppers', people who impersonated real customers but were actually in the store to grade staff on a 19-point checklist. These gradings were used in subsequent performance evaluations; good grades could attract bonuses, while poor grades might result in the employee being sent for remedial customer service skills training at what some workers interviewed by the *Post* derisively referred to as 'smile school' or 'clown school'. (A spokesperson for Safeway defended the activities of the mystery shoppers by saying: 'sometimes people won't do what you expect, but will do what you inspect' – a telling comment, one might think, on the limits, in practice, of the philosophy of 'empowerment'.) The immediate cause of the furore, which occurred when the programme was already several years old, was that several women Safeway workers in California had complained at a union conference that the company's policy exposed them to sexual harassment. Some male customers inter-preted displays of friendliness as signs of 'romantic interest' or as cues to make 'lewd comments'. These complaints sparked off a discussion of the rights and wrongs of the superior service programme.

Much of the behaviour that is regulated by the superior service programme is 'communicative' – in the jargon, verbal, vocal or visual – behaviour. In some cases, regulation takes the form of making speech acts and routines which would be expected to occur in service encounters – such as greetings, thanks and farewells – *categorical*: that is, employees do not choose whether and when to perform these acts, but are required to perform them at every opportunity, and may be 'written up' for any omis-sion. This requirement can have bizarre consequences. The *Post* report begins with a vignette in which a clerk in a Safeway store in Reston, Virginia spots a customer coming down the aisle where he is stacking shelves:

> The clerk sprang into action, making eye contact, smiling and greeting her warmly…The woman nodded briefly in return and continued shopping. The clerk moved on to another part of the store, going about his duties, and passed her again. Knowing that he might earn a poor grade on the company's 19-point friendliness report card if he failed to acknowledge her fully each time, the clerk again made eye contact and asked her how she was doing. This time she looked quizzical…But after it happened a third time, the woman's face darkened as he approached. 'That poor lady', the clerk said ruefully. 'You could see her think-ing, "what is his problem?"'.

His problem, of course, was that the rules were enforced without regard to such obvious contextual considerations as whether an employee had already greeted a particular shopper. It is only mildly unnatural to be 'warmly greeted' by a store clerk *once*, but it becomes extremely unnatural if the routine is repeated every time the same clerk comes within greeting distance.

Regulation of employees' linguistic behaviour may also take the form of instructing them to do things that would not ordinarily be expected to occur even once in the context of a supermarket. For instance, Safeway staff are exhorted to 'make suggestions about other possible purchases that could go with the items being purchased' – in other words to initiate conversations with people who are in the middle of doing their shopping. Since in context this is a 'marked' action – conversing with staff about what they are buying is not part of most customers' existing schema for visiting a supermarket – it is interactionally quite difficult to 'bring off'. A student of mine, Karen MacGowan, carried out observations in a supermarket in the UK where staff had been furnished with a set of opening gambits for initiating conversation at the checkout (such as 'are you using coupons with your shopping today?'). She noted that although the gambits themselves were perfectly straightforward, some customers appeared to have great difficulty framing a response to them, because they could not fathom the checkout operator's underlying intentions. (Ultimately, of course, the intention both in the Safeway case and in the 'coupons' case is to persuade the customer to buy *more*.)

Finally, employees' behaviour is regulated by instructions to perform all communicative acts in a prescribed manner: smiling, making eye contact, using the customer's name, greeting him or her 'warmly' and selecting personalized formulas like 'how are you doing?' which incorporate direct second person address. These linguistic and paralinguistic preferences are designed to express particular dispositions, notably friendliness and sincere concern for the customer's wellbeing, and thus to construct a particular kind of interpersonal relationship between the customer and the employee.

All these types of regulation, especially the last, exemplify 'synthetic personalization', which as I explained above (following Fairclough, 1989) is a way of designing discourse to give the impression of treating people as individuals within institutions that, in reality, are set up to handle people *en masse*. Supermarkets are obviously institutions of this type. After all, they were founded historically on the concept (novel at the time) of customers serving *themselves* rather than being served by someone else. By comparison with shopping in a traditional neighbourhood grocery, or an upmarket department store, supermarket shopping was a *de*personalized experience, one in which service was minimal and anonymous. Customers understood and accepted this as a concomitant of the advantages offered by the supermarket over other retailing operations, namely speed, convenience and value for money. But customer care programmes like Safeway's are intended to re-personalize the experience by giving the impression that staff relate to each customer as an individual.

As the term '*synthetic* personalization' implies, however, this impression is achieved by interactional sleight-of-hand. It remains a way of handling people *en masse* rather than a genuinely individualized approach: the supposed expressions of personal concern are actually standard formulae, pre-packaged at head office and produced indifferently for every customer. Even the most markedly individualizing strategy, the use of customers' names, is a piece of artifice, and it draws mixed responses from customers. Whereas one customer told the *Post*'s reporter, 'It makes you feel good when you're spending $50 to have them know your name', another said: 'it doesn't make me feel better. I know they are looking me up in the computer. It's not because they know me'. Some people judge Safeway's superior service programme the very opposite of 'personal', because they believe employees are only following a formula: their friendliness is not genuine. A contributor to the internet discussion – not a Safeway employee – suggested that the company was forcing its staff to 'act like androids'. A checkout worker who had resigned in protest after 20 years' service was quoted in the *Post* report describing the behaviour expected of employees as 'so artificial, it's unreal [*sic*]'.

If one problem with 'synthetic personalization' is that people may perceive it as more synthetic than personalized, another is that some find personalization *per se* inappropriate to the context. One customer who was interviewed by the *Post* remarked, for instance, that he was annoyed and embarrassed by staff commenting on what he had bought. He also disliked having his name used at the checkout: 'it's almost too personal, if you don't know the person'. Safeway's corporate spokesperson admitted that the use of names had attracted many complaints – especially from foreign-born customers whose names were invariably mispronounced.

These comments raise the issue of variation. The Safeway spokesperson's assertion that 'in general, people like people to be friendly to them' sounds like a statement of the obvious, but what it conceals is individual, social and cultural differences affecting what behaviours people define as 'friendly' – one person's 'friendliness' may be another's 'over-familiarity' – and what contexts they see as requiring what degree of 'friendliness'. Politeness in general is an area where national and cultural differences can be quite pronounced, even when people speak the same language. In Britain, for instance, there are hazards associated with importing signifiers of friendliness from the US – a common practice, since many US-based companies do business in Britain, and in addition there is a widespread belief that service in the US is better than in Britain. (One UK railway company's manual urges employees to 'put American-style friendliness into your voice', as if friendly service were as intrinsically American as Coca-Cola.). Many people are irritated by formulas like 'have a nice day', partly just because they are marked as 'American', and so Americanize public space in ways that offend some British sensibilities,[9] but partly also because they arise from ways of relating to others which are themselves experienced as foreign. Although there is variation in both countries, generally speaking the British have traditionally had a greater distrust of anything that smacks of effusiveness, especially between strangers. Karen MacGowan reported that an initiative whereby shoppers in the Scottish town of Coatbridge were met at the store entrance by a 'greeter' saying 'enjoy your shopping experience' had evoked varying degrees of embarrassment, puzzlement and hilarity: exhortations to 'enjoy' are more Californian than Caledonian. Another difference, crudely stated, is that in Britain polite behaviour between unacquainted equals tends to involve the reciprocal marking of social distance. For people who have internalized this norm, the (increasingly common) practice of workers being identified by their first names only may not connote what it is intended to connote, namely friendliness, but instead may seem to demean the worker by denying her or him the social distance one accords to non-intimates of equal status.

In other parts of the world, where English is not widely spoken or is spoken as a second language, the linguistic and cultural difference issues may be far more extreme. There is much to be said about the implications of the fact that 'globalization' tends to mean 'Americanization'. Though I have neither the space nor the research evidence to take up the subject in detail here, comments made to me when I have presented analyses of service styling in English-speaking countries suggest this is a rich field for future exploration.[10] I have been told, for example, that American English formulas like 'have a nice day' are being rendered by odd-sounding calques in languages like Swedish; that the importation of American-style 'friendly' service into post-communist Hungary is disrupting the complex formal system of address in Hungarian; and that Black South Africans entering service sector jobs previously reserved for white workers have been obliged to learn forms of interpersonal behaviour which are viewed in their community as alien and bizarre. It has also been pointed out to me that some societies have their own highly formalized service styles with which the 'globalized' style is in conflict. An example is Japan, where training for customer service workers has long given considerable attention to their speech and body language. The Japanese style now increasingly coexists, however, with the totally different style favoured by American-owned companies like Disney and McDonald's.

But even within one society, everyone will not necessarily share the same understanding of particular linguistic strategies, nor the same expectations of language-use in service encounters. Making and enforcing invariant rules for 'friendly' behaviour and language-use compels staff to ignore their own readings of what particular customers want or need, and to discard their understanding that, for instance, one might wish to address people differently on the basis of age or gender. An employee quoted in the *Washington Post* pointed out that often someone's body language would tell you that they wanted to be left alone. As she also said, however, if you used your own judgement in such a case and there happened to be a 'mystery shopper' around, you would be 'written up' for poor customer service skills. In this example we see how what employers describe as 'skills' may in fact be no such thing; employees may actually be penalized for making use of their learned ability to interact successfully with others.

The problems staff encounter with the superior service programme do not only arise from being deskilled and required to behave in a way both they and many customers find artificial. There is a deeper problem with the regulation of linguistic and other interpersonal behaviour, and it is essentially a problem of self-identity in the sense Anthony Giddens (1991) uses that term. Workers may be compelled by corporate *fiat* to become, for hours at a time, someone they do not want to be, someone they cannot easily integrate into their ongoing narrative of the self, because it strikes at their self-image and self-esteem.

It is interesting, for example, that some Safeway employees who spoke to the *Washington Post* complained about customers 'abusing' the practice of offering samples. They explained that some people requested an endless succession of samples at the deli counter, knowing that because of the superior service policy the staff would be unable to call a halt: 'they come for lunch. I'm not kidding'. These customers' behaviour does not 'hurt' employees in any material sense (if anything, it gives them more opportunities to gain points on the service score card), and where employees dislike the superior service programme one might expect them to take a grim pleasure in seeing customers exploit Safeway's generosity. But catering with a smile to the customer who 'comes for lunch' makes workers feel stupid. Letting shoppers get away with behaviour that offends against their sense of what is right is experienced as a sort of self-abasement.

A slightly different example of workers 'feeling stupid' comes from a story someone told me about her son's experience of working for a chain of restaurants in the US. Employees were required to send diners on their way with a formulaic 'bye, hope you enjoyed your meal, come again soon', accompanied by a cheery wave. Everyone found this routine artificial, but male employees had a particular problem with the hand gesture: they considered it 'effeminate' and to that extent at odds with an important aspect of their own identity, their (straight) masculinity. They eventually resolved the problem by rendering the wave as a sketchy salute.[11]

A more serious version of the self-abnegation problem appears in the case of the California Safeway employees who complained that their friendliness was misconstrued by male customers. Safeway's response to this complaint was that no increase in sexual harassment claims had been recorded since the inception of the superior service programme. That may be true, but it misses the point. The fundamental problem is that the philosophy and practice of 'customer care' places employees at the customer's disposal, with few well-defined limits on what the customer may expect of them. Their job is no longer just to stack shelves, operate tills and direct shoppers to the deli counter. Their job is also to make the customer feel good. Male customers who treat women staff as sexual objects are unlikely to have 'misinterpreted' friendliness as flirting. Rather they have understood and applied the basic principle of a customer care culture, which is that the staff are there to 'meet and exceed customers' needs'. Even where customers do not take this understanding to the extreme of harassment – sexual or otherwise – it places staff in a subservient position. This marks a difference between the customer service interactions I am focusing on here and the interactions most often studied under the heading of 'institutional' or 'professional' discourse, such as job interviews, medical consultations and classroom discourse. As Drew and Heritage (1992) point out, such interactions are 'asymmetrical': typically it is assumed that the institutional participant will be the more powerful party, as well as (and indeed by virtue of) having more responsibility for the conduct of the interaction. In service interactions structured by the discourse and practice of 'customer care', however, that assumption does not hold: service employees remain responsible for the conduct of talk, but customers are positioned as more powerful. The fact that workers are positioned in this way is a cause of resentment among them. As one recently retired (male) employee told the *Washington Post*: 'I believe in courteous service, but Safeway has taken it to such an extreme that it's torture for most of the employees'.

This remark gestures toward an important distinction: there is, indeed, a difference between 'courteous' service and the kind of service demanded by current philosophies of customer care. The difference is not simply that the latter is insincere and artificial. Old-style professional courtesy could equally involve a degree of artifice: a worker might feel animosity towards a particular customer, or might simply be in a bad mood, but courtesy would require that s/he refrain from showing it. In addition, as Erving Goffman noted in his classic text *The Presentation of Self in Everyday Life*:

> We know that in service occupations practitioners who may otherwise be sincere are sometimes forced to delude their customers because their customers show such a heartfelt demand for it. Doctors who are led into giving placebos, filling station attendants who resignedly check and recheck tire pressures for anxious women motorists, shoe clerks who sell a shoe that fits but tell the customer it is the size she wants to hear – these are cynical performers whose audiences will not allow them to be sincere. (Goffman, 1959: 18)

This observation, made in the late 1950s, is a useful reminder that insincerity in itself is not a novel feature of service work. In Goffman's account however it is customers who compel service workers to 'delude' them, and the workers are described as 'cynical performers', suggesting they are ultimately in control. In regimes like Safeway's, by contrast, insincerity is less a cynical response to the behaviour of customers and more a matter of complying with rules laid down by those in direct authority over workers. What is demanded, moreover, is a particular kind of insincerity. Both old-fashioned 'courtesy' and the forms of deception instanced by Goffman required workers to suppress negative feelings or judgements – to betray no irritation with people who are vain or recalcitrant or make a fuss about nothing, for example. But the hallmark of many present-day service regimes is the emphasis they place on displaying – which usually entails *simulating* – positive feelings towards customers. This, it has been argued, makes greater demands on workers, and is more likely to be resented by them.

Communication as emotional labour

In her prescient study *The Managed Heart* (1983), Arlie Hochschild elaborated the concept of 'emotional labour' to describe the kind of work that involves making others feel good. Emotional labour involves workers in managing both their own feelings and other people's: the classic example of this duality might be smiling, which signals your intention to make the person you are interacting with happy by displaying to them that you yourself feel happy. The implicit model is the way people behave in personal relationships where the parties have an equal investment – the worker acts like a friend, or a nurturing parent, or a surrogate wife – but in the workplace this behaviour is a commodity with an exchange value: it is part of what the worker gets paid for. Another important contextual feature is that the customer or client does not have reciprocal obligations to the worker.[12] The lack of reciprocity places workers in a subordinate position and compels them to look after the customer's feelings at the expense of their own. Arlie Hochschild studied flight attendants, who reported that they found this aspect of their work particularly stressful. They noted for instance what a strain they found it to smile continually for hours at a stretch, however they were feeling and however the passengers treated them; and how demeaned they felt by the image of subservience and sexual availability they were required to project. The job of a flight attendant is of course one of those 'pink collar' jobs, historically done by women, where emotional labour has always been expected: other examples are secretarial work and nursing. But the codification of 'customer care' has made emotional labour a more prominent part of all kinds of service jobs.

This point is recognized very explicitly in a popular management text titled *What Customers Like About You: Adding Emotional Value for Service Excellence and Competitive Advantage* (Freemantle, 1998). The author David Freemantle (inevitably, a management consultant) argues that:

> Given a range of comparable and competitive products to choose from, in future customers will choose the company they like. In the main this means they will be choosing the *people* they like. …Where there is little or no personal contact between the customer and the company, the brand is all important in matters of customer choice. However, competitive advantage can be better secured when a customer's emotional attachment to a brand is reinforced by an emotional attachment to the people who sell and deliver the branded product. This is the essence of added emotional value. (1998: 6)

From Freemantle's perspective, something like the Safeway superior service programme is an unsuccessful attempt to generate 'added emotional value' or 'e-value'; its rigid prescriptivism inhibits real 'emotional connectivity', which can only be achieved 'if [employees] are sensitive to each customer's individual requirements for emotional value. Sometimes a smile and enthusiasm are totally inappropriate' (Freemantle, 1998: 8). In order to add 'e-value', then, companies must move away from scripted greetings and obligatory smiles, and towards an approach in which workers are trained instead to practise a kind of amateur psychology. What they need to learn is how to 'read' customers in order to decide what kind of emotional response is appropriate for each individual.

Verbal interaction is an important site for this interpretive work, in addition to being the prime site for the actual production of 'e-value'. Thus a later chapter of Freemantle's book titled 'Everyday likeable behaviors' has sections on 'the emotional eye', 'the emotional ear' and 'the emotional voice', all of which deal with aspects of face-to-face communication – gaze, listening and speech (more specifically, the prosodic and paralinguistic aspects of speech). A sample quotation from 'the emotional voice' conveys the flavour of the advice. Readers are instructed first to develop awareness of the emotions they project in their own voices, and then to practice 'modulating' the voice 'to reflect genuine feelings for each customer and to develop their feelings for you'. For example:

- If a customer comes across as cold and diffident, convince yourself that beneath the surface is a warm, caring, loving human being. Try to reach that suppressed warmth by injecting emotional warmth into your own words.
- If a customer comes across as being overpowering and effusive, convince yourself is that beneath the surface is someone who is desperate for recognition and admiration. Therefore in responding to the customer, try to underline your words with a tone of emotional approval.

- If a customer comes across as being kind and caring then respond in the same way, ensuring that your voice is soft, rounded and undulates smoothly to reflect your own feelings of compassion.
  By drawing on your feelings and emotions to fine-tune the way you use your voice, you will be much better able to connect emotionally with customers and become someone they really like. (1998: 109)

Readers are then given a list of emotions that customers' voices might project, and told what emotion they should try to project in response: for instance, if a customer sounds 'worried' you should be 'reassuring', if they sound 'sad' you should be 'compassionate', if they sound 'angry' you should be 'soothing' and so on.

This sort of guidance gives a new meaning to the expression 'retail therapy'. It is a more sophisticated approach to customer care than simply 'writing up' staff every time they fail to smile, but the conduct being recommended nevertheless remains a form of emotional labour, accomplished linguistically through the techniques of synthetic personalization. If it really were spontaneous and natural, an expression of the employee's 'genuine feelings for each customer', presumably there would be no need to spell out the 'correct' responses and exhort workers to practise them consciously. Then again, at times Freemantle appears to be suggesting that people can be trained, not merely to *simulate* the desired emotions but actually to *feel* them. In a chapter titled 'Training people to be liked by your customers', he suggests that training must focus not on 'programmed behavior', but on 'dealing with people's innermost feelings and trying to modify them so that they feel good about the customer and the customer feels good about them' (1998: 229). He adds:

It is an incredible challenge to teach a person to like a customer as well as develop the necessary attributes to be liked by a customer. To do so you have to teach people how to manage their feelings and emotions; you have to teach them to re-examine some fundamental principles relating to integrity, openness, honesty and trust…It is pointless teaching someone to smile at customers unless that person can reach deep down inside themselves to determine the real, genuine reason why they should smile.

Freemantle does not address the possibility that someone might 'reach deep down inside themselves' and discover a real, genuine reason why they should *not* smile. Although his 'big idea' is that customers' choices are not governed exclusively by rational calculation, he does not foresee that *workers* might have some emotional resistance to the kind and degree of re-education he proposes. The hypothetical worker who appears in the pages of management texts is invariably both eager to meet changing corporate expectations and sufficiently plastic to do so easily. By contrast, the real workers whose opinions are reported in, for instance, the *Washington Post* report on Safeway's superior service programme are fully formed persons who bring a certain amount of other baggage to work with them. It would not be surprising if in reality, many workers were reluctant to take on the 'incredible challenge' of becoming a different person – 'someone [customers] really like'.

In fact, though, Freemantle has an alternative suggestion, which is discussed in his chapter 'Recruiting people your customers like'. As that title suggests, the solution is to hire people with the 'right' qualities in the first place, rather than trying to modify them through training later on. 'Too often', Freemantle observes (1998: 211–12), 'the priority in selecting people is technical skills and experience rather than their ability to relate emotionally to customers. …subjectivity is essential when selecting the right candidate'. He cites with approval a retail company in New York which recruited workers for a new store by calling applicants in, ostensibly for interview, but then simply watching how they conducted themselves in the waiting room: whether they talked to other candidates, if they offered to get coffee, how they handed the cup. The company took no account of qualifications or previous experience, but selected those whose self-presentation struck observers as most 'likeable'. Such a proceeding is of course antithetical to the current orthodoxy of 'human resources' management with its 'objective' job and person specifications (not to speak of its commitment, at least in theory, to equal opportunities).

After a decade of 'programmed behavior' inculcated by customer care training, it seems there may be something of a backlash, of which Freemantle's book is not the only expression. A 1998 advertisement for the Irish airline Aer Lingus proclaimed, for instance: 'Our people don't need to be trained on how to be nice'. Whereas it has been common for some years to make the thoroughness of your customer care training a selling point, here the selling point is that Aer Lingus staff's niceness is *not* the product of thorough training, but the genuine article. No doubt this exploits a national stereotype of the Irish as particularly friendly people, but it also suggests a more general feeling in the air that consumers have had enough of synthetically personalized service, and are looking for something more 'authentic'.

In early 1999 an industrial dispute – also within the airline industry – provided a dramatic illustration of the increasing tension between managers' wish to present customer care as a natural expression of their staff's sincere desire to please, and workers' experience of it as a form of productive labour. After Cathay Pacific airlines announced that flight attendants must work additional hours in order to qualify for a pay rise, the attendants voted to take industrial action by refusing to smile at passengers for one hour of every flight. Their union chair pointed out that this was essentially a kind of work to rule, given that 'our contracts do not say we have to smile' (Thorpe, 1999). Although the action was reported in newspapers as a humorous story, the reports made it evident that Cathay Pacific's management did not regard it as a joke; it also became evident that management attitudes to the status of smiling on the job were confused and contradictory. On one hand a company spokesman was quoted saying 'I don't think it's fair to the passengers...because they are paying good money for a good service' – a comment which suggests that smiling is a recognized part of the service and so part of the attendant's contractual duties. On the other hand, the same spokesman insisted that 'the attendants are not *told* to smile, there is sincerity and genuine meaning in it'. This supports the union's contention that smiling is not compulsory, but at the same time denies the union's implicit argument that it is work; rather it is presented as something that 'comes naturally' to these particular workers. To quote the company spokesman again: 'most Asian carriers, and the region in general, are renowned for their warmth and superior service'. Asian female subservience for Cathay Pacific has the same status as Irish friendliness for Aer Lingus, and also, of course, the same importance for the airline's brand image. The company spokesman conceded that the flight attendants' action would have 'a serious effect on the image of the airline' – presumably not just because passengers would miss the smiles during the hour they were withheld, but because afterwards it would be impossible to maintain the belief that the smiles were authentic expressions of attendants' feelings.

As Robin Leidner (1993) also notes, authenticity is an issue for all organizations that regulate communication in order to personalize service. Despite the ubiquity of synthetic personalization, the idea that a speaker's institutional persona might be wholly constructed, bearing little or no resemblance to their 'real' self, appears to cause many people considerable discomfort. Thus customer care may lose its charm for the customer if it is revealed as 'inauthentic' – coerced or, to echo Goffman, merely cynical. This is the weakness the Cathay Pacific flight attendants exploited, and which some customers pointed out in their comments on Safeway's superior service programme. The Safeway example also illustrates the other dimension of the problem: there is a point beyond which companies are likely to encounter resistance from their own employees to demands for behaviour they perceive as 'so artificial it's unreal'. Generally stated, the problem is that many or most people subscribe to the commonsense view that the way you interact with others in talk is an expression of your individual personality, which is both 'natural' and unique. Certainly, I found this to be the dominant assumption among my informants. Those who objected to the regulation of their spoken interactions at work almost always did so on the ground that it suppressed individuality. The suggestion that regulation imposed, say, a 'white' or 'middle class' or 'southern English' model – that is, that it suppressed *social* differences – was rarely broached, and when I broached it myself it did not elicit such strong reactions as the 'personality' issue. Similarly, when I asked a group of students if they thought it would be a good idea to assess their oral skills in the same way as their writing skills, a majority felt this would be 'unfair' because it would discriminate against people who were 'naturally' quiet or slow to put their thoughts into words. I pointed out that traditional ways of assessing writing might be said to discriminate against bad spellers, nonstandard dialect users and people with writer's block. The students insisted this was quite different: there was not the same close identification between writing style and the individual self.

The idea that the way you speak derives directly from the person you are also underpins a common view, expressed by both managers and workers, that *training* in interpersonal communication is only marginally useful: some people are just not good communicators, and never will be. In a focus group made up of bank employees, for instance, one informant, asked whether he had received training in dealing with complaints (in fact, a very common topic on customer care courses), replied, to general agreement, that such training would be futile. 'You either have it or you don't have it. I mean no one could tell you how to be sympathetic, it's either in your nature or it isn't'. This group made many references to sympathy, confidence, friendliness and other linguistically projected qualities that training often attempts to develop as 'not something you can train into people' and 'something you can't do on a flipchart'.

These views were not shared by everyone I spoke to. Some students saw nothing wrong with assessing oral skills, some managers placed great emphasis on customer care and communication training, and some informants talked about valuable lessons they had learned from the experience of working in service environments where systematic attention was paid to spoken interaction. But the continuing strength of the other point of view shows what the discourse of 'communication skills' is up against. One of the things the 'skills' discourse tries to do is place the ability to interact with others orally on a par with the ability to type, or compose acceptable business letters (or essays), or make arithmetical calculations. The 'skill' is learned, and is taken to be separable from the person; a deficiency of skill is not the same as a personal defect. But persuading people to approach 'communication' in this way is not as easy as persuading them to take a similar approach to numeracy or information technology. One reason why there needs to be so much propagandizing on behalf of 'communication skills' is precisely that many people still do not see the way they talk to others as a form of behaviour which is detachable from their individual personality and, as a corollary, susceptible to modification at will and without limit. This makes criticizing someone's way of talking a more sensitive proceeding than, say, criticizing the speed and accuracy of their typing: judgements on interactional style are easily apprehended as judgements of personal (in)adequacy. A general issue I will return to at various points is how far the idea of talking as artless self-expression is in the process of being displaced by new understandings of communication as a set of skills, which can be improved by the application of expert knowledge, informed constructive criticism and self-conscious practice.

But the foregoing discussion of customer care and emotional labour in service work has raised another question, one which cuts across the 'natural behaviour versus learned skill' debate. Does the sort of linguistic regulation practised by Safeway, or recommended by David Freemantle, really have anything to do with *skilling* people, or would it be better described as *styling* them?

'Skilling' and 'styling'

The term *skill* connotes *practical* expertise, the ability to *do* something, but skills training as traditionally conceived also places emphasis on knowledge, understanding and judgement. A 'skilled' person does not only know how to do certain things, but also understands *why* those things are done the way they are. S/he is acquainted with the general principles of the activity s/he is skilled in, and so is able to modify what s/he does in response to the exigencies of any specific situation. A communication training programme based on Hermine Scheeres's 'spoken language demands of the restructured workplace' (1998) would in these terms be a 'skilling' programme. No doubt it would instruct trainees in specific techniques for 'arguing a point' or 'negotiating', but it would also identify these as linguistic genres or 'activity types' (Levinson, 1992) and explain the general principles in virtue of which some interactional strategies are likely to be more effective than others. Although the execution is inept, the John Stephenson materials examined above are also at least partly about 'skilling' trainees. The advice is mostly of an 'instrumental' kind – it is about using language to do things – and specific recommendations on how to do things are commonly accompanied by reasons and principles (albeit in this case drawn from a manifestly inadequate model of human behaviour).

The word *styling*, on the other hand, connotes a kind of grooming of surface appearances. This, arguably, would be a more accurate description than 'skilling' of what goes on in many regimes of customer care, where there is little engagement with the underlying purposes and principles of verbal interaction, but rather an intense concern to manage what might be called its *aesthetics*. Perhaps the most obvious indication of this preoccupation with the aesthetic is the amount of attention paid to the *voice*, with particular emphasis on prosody and voice quality. Railway announcers are told to perform in smiley voice, Safeway employees are graded on the 'warmth' in their voices, David Freemantle's readers are given pages of instruction on 'the emotional voice'. (As we will see in Chapter 4, call centre operators are subject to a whole set of vocal performance criteria, and in some cases are recruited for the supposed qualities of their voices.) By contrast, Hermine Scheeres says nothing, and the John Stephenson materials very little, about how people should sound.

The phenomenon of 'aesthetic labour' in service economies has been discussed by Witz et al., who point out (1998: 4) that aesthetic 'sense knowledge' has traditionally been distinguished from 'intellectual knowledge', and argue that in the service sector, employers are increasingly prioritizing the former over the latter. Rather than judging people on their knowledge, experience or technical skills, employers now seek 'a supply of embodied capacities possessed by workers at the point of entry into employment' which they can 'mobilise, develop and commodify' in order to 'produce a particular "style" of service encounter' (1998: 4). This 'style' is defined in terms of aesthetics:

> ...a sensory experience through which objects appeal in a special way...or, more simply, are imbued with expressive form. The concept of aesthetic labour moves beyond the concept of emotional labour because it foregrounds the *sensible* components of the service encounter. In particular, it foregrounds the *embodied* character of service work, and the ways in which distinctive service styles depend as much upon manufactured 'styles of the flesh'...as they do upon the manufacture of 'feeling'. (1998: 4)

The notion of workplace regimes seeking to imbue the behaviour of employees with a prescribed 'expressive form' in order that service encounters should conform to a predetermined 'style' nicely captures what I mean by 'styling' communication. The 'styled' communicator uses language less to do things (negotiate, argue, solve problems) than to be, or appear to be things (warm, friendly, enthusiastic, soothing). Expressiveness is valued over instrumentality. The fact that speaking is part of 'aesthetic labour' is underlined by the intense interest taken in employees' accents, their pitch, rate of speech, intonation and voice quality, but it is not just the voice that is 'styled', or 'imbued with expressive form'. There is also an aesthetic dimension to the less obviously 'fleshly' *interactional* style which is valorized by an institution and codified in its instructions to, or scripts for, its embodied representatives. In face-to-face contexts, voice-styles and interactional styles are in addition inseparable from the styling of nonlinguistic elements of the encounter – the employee's appearance and dress, the layout and design of the site where service encounters take place, and so on. The intention is that all these elements should meld into a single, coherent aesthetic experience for the customer.

My use of the term *styling* here is related to the notion of 'linguistic style' elaborated by sociolinguistic researchers such as the California Style Collective and Penelope Eckert (who is also one of the collective's members). Eckert explains:

> Linguistic style is a way of speaking that is peculiar to a community of practice – its linguistic identity…Briefly put, style is a clustering of resources that has social meaning. The construction of a style is a process of bricolage: a stylistic agent appropriates resources from a broad sociolinguistic landscape, recombining them to make a distinctive style. (1996: 3)

Eckert and her colleagues are interested in the *self*-styling undertaken by adolescents and pre-adolescents, and particularly in the way they appropriate socially meaningful variation in, say, the pronunciation of vowel sounds. Styling in the workplace operates in a somewhat similar way: a community of practice with a distinctive way of speaking is constructed through bricolage, using resources for meaning among which prosodic, paralinguistic and politeness phenomena are especially prominent. What is different about it is that it is not the speakers themselves who are the 'stylistic agents', deciding what to appropriate from the 'broad sociolinguistic landscape' and how to put elements together. Instead the preferred style is designed by people who will not have to use it themselves, and imposed on those lower down the hierarchy. Like feeling in emotional labour, style in aesthetic labour is a commodity; although they may be encouraged to identify with it, 'styled' workers do not 'own' the style they are obliged to adopt. It is not their own 'cultural capital' but someone else's.

In this discussion of 'styling' and 'skilling' I have invoked a number of distinctions (for example, intellectual knowledge/sense knowledge, instrumental/expressive, acting/appearing) which can hardly fail to recall another culturally salient opposition, masculine/feminine. Commentators on both 'emotional' and 'aesthetic' labour point out that there is a strongly gendered dimension to these forms of work: though increasingly performed by workers of both sexes, they are culturally coded as 'feminine'. It is interesting in this connection that John Stephenson Ltd – a retail business, but one that deals in electrical goods and has traditionally employed men to sell them – emphasizes rational and instrumental aspects of language-use (for instance, problem solving) in its communication training materials, whereas 'feminized' retail environments such as supermarkets and clothes shops seem concerned almost exclusively with styling phraseology and, especially, vocal performance, to project certain attitudes and feelings. This is hardly a watertight distinction, of course: the John Stephenson materials do have an 'emotional' element (they also have some of the hallmarks of 'styling', such as the advice to smile at interlocutors). But it does raise an issue of general interest in relation to 'communication', not only at work but in all the domains to be discussed in this book. That issue is the very widespread perception that women/ girls are 'better' communicators than men/boys. In the work domain the postulate of women's superior communication skills underpins the oft-expressed view that women are naturally better suited than men to routine customer service work with its emphasis on the expressive and relational. But the same postulate also underpins a strand of management discourse on enterprise and empowerment, according to which women are well placed to dominate higher status positions too. The thesis is summarized in the title of a piece which the guru of 'excellence', Tom Peters, wrote for *Working Woman* magazine in 1990: 'The best new managers will listen, motivate, support: isn't that just like a woman?'. As the 'communication culture' tightens its grip, we hear more and more that the future is female. Conversely we hear more and more about the problem of men and 'the trouble with boys' (Phillips, 1994). I will revisit the issue of gender in later chapters.

Conclusion

As I have tried to show in this chapter, 'communication' – the use of spoken language to interact with others – is at the heart of several important developments in workplaces which have been restructured in line with new managerial approaches. It is both an instrument of organizational 'culture change' and a target for change in its own right; it is implicated, particularly, in the trend towards demanding more and more 'emotional' or 'aesthetic' labour from employees in customer service positions. Discourse about communication at work is also a locus where we may observe some of the contradictions of 'enterprise culture'. The rhetoric of 'empowerment' is in tension with a reality in which the minutiae of linguistic behaviour are obsessively regulated. There is also a contradiction between the rhetoric and the reality of 'skills'. Improving 'communication skills' is the declared aim of numerous workplace training programmes, but at the same time there is debate on whether the ability to communicate in the desired ways really is a teachable 'skill' or whether it is an innate quality of (some) individuals. It is evident, too, that what many employers want, and what they mainly train their employees in, is not communication *skills* but rather a communication *style*. As the Safeway case in particular illustrates, styling employees is not the same thing as skilling them: indeed, one might argue it is often just the opposite.

In the next chapter I will develop these points further, focusing on a kind of workplace where the importance of language and communication is foregrounded even more insistently than it is at John Stephenson or at Safeway: the 'call centre', where standards of service depend entirely on the quality of talk because all customer contact takes place via the telephone. Considering the case of the call centre also allows me to consider a pervasive feature of restructured workplaces that I have not so far mentioned, though it certainly has implications for language and communication: the incorporation of new technology into service routines. The job of the call centre operator illustrates the demands made on workers when service work, and service talk, are subjected to some of the disciplines of the factory production line.

4

COMMUNICATION FACTORIES: INSIDE THE CALL CENTRE

No sane business today would want a workforce of automatons: after all, anything an automaton can do, we can automate
— *Fiona Czerniawska*, Corporate Speak, *1998.*

You should all know by now that we intend to introduce a standard telephone speech. ...Every operator must use the speech, no exceptions!
— *Internal Memorandum, Teleprocessing Centre, 1996.*

On the fifth floor of a building in central London is a space that looks much like any other open-plan office. It also sounds like an office; as you approach you hear the soft click of computer keys and a faint hum of voices, muted by the carpet and the padded partitions dividing this space from an adjacent, more or less identical one. Around the edge of the space is a familiar office scene: amid piles of papers and folders, people read, type, make phone calls, or perch on desks chatting to one another. But the real action is going on around a large central island divided into a dozen workstations, where – since this is not a busy time – eight people are currently sitting. Collectively they form a team, one of several on this floor. They are talking, but not to each other (though they can see each other, and are close enough to talk): each person is wearing a lightweight telephone headset, and those who are talking direct their speech into its mouthpiece. Each sits in front of a computer; they watch the screen and type as they talk. Sometimes they smile. Occasionally they glance up at an object suspended from the ceiling, which looks not unlike the destination indicators at modern railway or underground stations. Wherever you sit around the island, one of these will be in your line of sight. Its red light display announces how many calls have been processed, how many are currently in progress and how many are waiting to be dealt with.

What I am describing here is a call centre, a kind of workplace where communication is not just part of the job description, in essence it *is* the job description. Workers' routine involves two main activities, both of them language-based. One is talking to customers on the telephone; the other is inputting and retrieving data by computer. Although in practice these activities are simultaneous and interdependent, it is the first – telephone interaction – which provides the institution's *raison d'être*, and which is the focus for most regulation and monitoring. Here I want to look in some detail at the linguistic regime of the call centre: what aspects of language-use it regulates, how, and why.[1]

First, some background. If you use the phone to order goods from a mail-order catalogue, check your bank balance, get an insurance quote, book a rail ticket or make an airline reservation, query a utility bill or report a fault, it is increasingly likely that you will be calling, not the nearest general office of the organization you are dealing with, but a centre many miles away where the staff are employed specifically to deal with telephone enquiries. This is the call centre: its distinctive features are *specialization/concentration of function*, and *remoteness of location*. Telephone service provision is separated from the organization's other functions and done by a dedicated workforce in a dedicated place, which may be remote both from the customers and from other parts of the organization, such as its offices, shops and warehouses. Such arrangements are made possible by advances in phone and computer technology. With a few keystrokes a worker in Leeds can check the bank account details of a customer in Worcester, or find out whether an item is in stock at a warehouse in Wolverhampton. The customer's call to Leeds need cost no more than calling the bank around the corner, and if all the lines in Leeds are busy, calls can be automatically re-routed to another centre somewhere else.

Call centres come in two varieties: 'inbound', where the customer makes the call, and 'outbound', where the organization calls actual or potential customers, usually in the hope of selling them something. In this chapter, I will be directly concerned only with the 'inbound' type. Although 'outbound' calling raises some of the same linguistic issues (such as the use of scripts and fixed routines), it also raises issues which, though interesting, are beyond my scope here. Typically, outbound call centres involve employees in sales rather than service encounters, and since the calls are often unsolicited on the customer's part, the interpersonal dynamic is also different from cases where the customer has initiated contact.

Call centres were introduced to Britain in the late 1980s. Their pioneers were 'direct' banking and insurance companies set up to do business exclusively by phone. These companies competed with the established providers on convenience ('direct' customers could make transactions outside normal office hours[2] and in the comfort of their own homes) and on cost (since overheads were lower in a telephone-only operation, savings could be passed on to the customer). But many 'non-direct' companies, in the financial services sector and elsewhere, have since seen the advantages of shifting some of their own operations to call centres. For these businesses, concentration and remote location offer scope for cutting costs and increasing efficiency. Instead of having to make staff available to deal with telephone enquiries in every local branch office, a company can centralize this function on a small number of sites, or even just one site, and either reduce staff numbers elsewhere or free staff to do other things.[3] Some organizations apply the same logic to providing customer services by phone as to catering, cleaning or security, and contract out the running of their call centres to a specialist firm. As more and more organizations have seen their potential, call centres have proliferated. By the middle of 1998 Britain had more than 5000. According to one frequently cited estimate, they employ one per cent of the nation's workforce – more than a quarter of a million people. A more conservative calculation puts the number of call centre workers in Britain at around 150,000 – still a far from negligible figure.

Since customers do not have occasion actually to visit a call centre, in principle its physical location could be anywhere. (Some US call centres are in prisons.) It has been suggested that as global telecommunications become easier and cheaper, centres serving the UK could be relocated to somewhere like India, where English is widely spoken and operating costs would be much lower. (The intercultural communication issues this might raise do not seem to have been considered as yet, though customers' responses to certain regional accents are a relevant consideration when making location decisions. The advantages of the Scots accent, for instance, are frequently mentioned in connection with the large number of centres located in central Scotland.) In Britain many centres are concentrated in regions where rental and labour costs are low,[4] and they are often on out-of-town sites such as industrial estates located on major roads. These are 'no-frills' operations – they do not need to look and feel like a bank or a shop since the customer cannot see them – and this also helps to keep running costs down.

Communication factories?

In the title of this chapter I compare call centres to 'communication factories'. This is not because of their appearance or ambience, for as I have said, they look and feel more like offices than factories. At first sight, too, the work of a call centre looks more like traditional clerical work than factory work. It is sedentary work requiring clerical skills (such as typing and telephone technique). The resemblance to clerical work is unsurprising, since the tasks in which call centres specialize are clerical tasks that would previously have been performed in offices. But what call centres do is apply to those tasks the logic of the production line.

One resemblance between production line work and call centre work is that both are extremely repetitive. To a far greater extent than most conventional office workers, call centre employees spend their working hours performing exactly the same task in exactly the same way, over and over again.[5] Along with this repetition goes a factory-like regimentation of time. Like the production workers who must match their efforts to a predetermined output target, measuring every hour in boxes packed or collars stitched, call centre operators have little control over the pace and rhythm of their work. Typically, an Automated Call Distribution (ACD) system feeds calls to the operator one after another, and operators are given targets for the time they should take to process each call. One operator told me, for example, that the centre where he worked set a target average call duration of 32 seconds or less. It is worth dwelling for a moment on the implications of this statistic. Assuming a constant flow of calls, this centre's operators would be expected to process a notional 112 calls per hour, and more than 800 calls in the course of a shift.[6] Though some days and times are busier than others, it is not rare for operators to be continuously occupied. Most systems are designed so there are more lines available to call in on than there are operators to handle the calls, and where a company has several centres, calls can often be re-routed from one to another to make use of any spare capacity.

It is characteristic of factory production that the activities of workers are largely dictated by the operations of machines. Call centre work, similarly, is driven by the operation of the ACD system; but at the same time its 'core' activity is verbal interaction, a quintessentially human function that is normally assumed to demand the uniquely human qualities of creativity and empathy. These are the qualities Fiona Czerniawska has in mind when she warns against excessive regulation of talk with the observation that 'anything an automaton can do, we can automate' (1998: 27). But in the case of the call centre, her observation begs the question. Much of the work that people do in most call centres *could* in principle be done by a machine. Some functions have already been automated. For instance, where call centres offer more than one service the initial sorting is often done mechanically: callers connect with a recorded 'menu' ('if you wish to report a fault, press 1', and so on) from which they select options using the buttons on their phone. The technology of speech recognition and synthesis has also enabled whole transactions to be automated. I can check how much I currently owe on my credit card by having a 'conversation' with a machine which is capable of recognizing a limited range of single word utterances (for example, 'yes', 'no', numbers from one to ten) and then producing a synthetic spoken rendition of my balance. In North America automation has gone further than it has as yet in Britain, and it seems likely that as better technology becomes available and affordable, fully automated systems will play a greater role everywhere – though no one I spoke to believed machines would ever totally replace human operators.[7] Meanwhile, the way to maximize efficiency in a call centre is to make human operators behave more like automated systems.

The quest to maximize efficiency encourages an approach to interaction that bears comparison with the approach to production known as 'Taylorism' after its best-known proponent, Frederick Taylor, whose *Principles of Scientific Management* was published in 1911. Taylor sought to improve productivity by analysing the production process: breaking it down into its constituent actions, using time and motion studies to ascertain what was the most efficient way to perform any given action, and then training workers in the details of efficient performance. Rather similarly, call centre managers may set out to determine exactly what sequence of interactional moves is needed to accomplish a given transaction efficiently, and then institutionalize the preferred sequence in a model or script which all workers are required to reproduce in every transaction of the same type. Here it should be acknowledged that the scripting of telephone interaction found in today's call centres is not a new phenomenon. Telephone companies were among the pioneers of scripted service routines, performed by the operators who were required, in the early days of telephone service, to connect every call.[8] In call centres, however, the approach is extended to transactions which are longer, more varied and more complex, in a context where more sophisticated technology enables stricter surveillance and more precise measurement of 'efficiency'.

I will begin by considering a rather simple example of a model call centre transaction: the shortest in my corpus, it belongs, appropriately enough, to a telephone company, and explains to phone operators the standard procedure for dealing with a directory assistance call. (The manual it comes from was obtained 'unofficially' and some minor details have been changed to ensure the source cannot be identified, but the sequence of moves is reproduced exactly).

An ideal search should be conducted as follows:

Agent:	XYZ Directories, which name please?
Caller:	Jones.
Agent:	Jones, thank you.
	Which town please?
Caller:	Cardiff.
Agent:	Cardiff, thank you.
	Which address please?
Caller:	Number 28, Acacia Avenue.
Agent:	Number 28, Acacia Avenue, thank you.
	Just searching for you. [*Pause.*]
	Sorry to keep you waiting.
	Thank you. Your number is 0123 456789.
Caller:	Thank you.
Agent:	You're welcome.
Culler:	Goodbye.
Agent:	Goodbye.

This model dialogue sets out the moves that are taken to be necessary and sufficient for the successful accomplishment of a 'standard' directory assistance call (additional/alternative moves are provided for 'nonstandard' cases, for instance where the number is unlisted). Operators are expected to do no less than is specified here, but at the same time they must try not to do more: the targets for how many calls they process in a given time will be based on the assumption that this sequence is normative.

The actual design of the model is influenced by three major considerations. The first and most basic is the need to elicit, and input to the computer, particular items of information in a particular order. The items and the preferred order of their elicitation are determined by the computer software operators are working with. In this case a number will only be retrieved from the database when three prescribed steps have been completed. Therefore the core moves needed to bring the transaction to a satisfactory conclusion are the questions 'which name', 'which town' and 'which address', together with the caller's responses. A second consideration, however, is the need to be sure that the operator is inputting the crucial information correctly: if s/he is not, the computer will produce no number, or the wrong number, and the transaction will fail. This is important enough to motivate the inclusion of an additional set of moves in which the operator repeats *verbatim* the information given by the caller. Repetition extends the duration of the call, but that disadvantage is offset by the advantage of a lower error rate. The third consideration is rather different: it has to do with the interpersonal rather than the informational aspect of the exchange. In the call centre, or any service-providing institution, 'efficiency' does not only mean providing accurate information without undue delay, it also means making the customer feel s/he has been 'served' – treated well, or at least not badly. Therefore, politeness formulas are explicitly included in the model, including a relatively extended polite closing sequence, and two polite 'filler' moves ('just searching for you', 'sorry to keep you waiting') to be produced during the part of the sequence when the operator is waiting for the computer to retrieve the number. This reflects the designer's awareness that extended silence in telephone interaction is problematic; callers need periodic reassurance that the channel remains open.

Although in the standard directory assistance call I have chosen a very straightforward example, the same considerations are relevant to virtually all call centre transactions. Even where operators are not following an invariant script, they are likely to be working from a 'prompt sheet' telling them what moves to make in what order, and the basic outline usually reflects the way the computer software is set up to accept and/or retrieve the information that is the focus of the transaction. Operators are also likely to be advised to repeat back key pieces of information given by the caller and in many cases to summarize the outcome before closing. And without exception, the operating routines set out in manuals and training materials draw explicit attention to interpersonal and politeness requirements, often (as we will see later on) specifying their linguistic correlates in detail.

The fact that call centre transactions are not purely exchanges of information, but are quasi-conversational exchanges with a customer and as such have a significant interpersonal element, ensures that the human operator will never be entirely superseded by a machine. Although the politeness formulas of the directory assistance call sequence are simple and predictable, and could doubtless be built into an automated system, not all call centre transactions make such straightforward interpersonal demands. Some calls, for instance, are complaints. One manager told me that when interviewing job applicants he always stressed that they would encounter a certain proportion of irate customers wanting someone to listen while they vented their grievances: as he put it, 'there's a certain element of just being an Aunt Sally'. Even supposing that this aspect of the operator's work could be automated (perhaps by connecting the caller to something like the famous 'Eliza' program, a kind of simulated therapist[9]), automation would defeat the customer's purpose, which is to get someone – a human representative of the organization – to acknowledge their dissatisfaction. A recorded message saying something like: 'if you wish to rant about the standard of our service, press 4' would probably leave most callers more rather than less annoyed. Defusing anger is one of the more 'creative' parts of an operator's job, though at the same time it is one of the least pleasant parts; anger is often directed at the operator personally, but s/he is not permitted to retaliate.[10] Yet although it is acknowledged that dealing with angry callers makes particular demands on operators' 'human' skills, that does not mean that no attempt is made to regulate the minutiae of their behaviour in this situation. On the contrary, the subject of 'difficult' calls generates a plethora of rules and guidelines; training materials often include instruction in specific verbal techniques for dealing with them.

It will be evident from this discussion that a pervasive feature of the call centre regime is its tendency to regulate and, where possible, standardize the performance of common interactional routines. One rationale for this (we will see in a moment that there are others) is that it maximizes efficiency. Left to themselves, operators might design routines that take more time than necessary, or conversely they might aim for speed and neglect other important considerations (such as checking for accuracy and displaying politeness). These potential problems can be averted by telling operators in detail what to do and say. But to be effective, this strategy must be backed up both by training and by regular monitoring. This is another difference between call centre work and more traditional office work: call centre workers are subjected to a particularly high degree of surveillance.

The Open University television programme about 'Empowerment', to which I referred in Chapter 3, includes a sequence filmed in a call centre in the north of England, which provides banking services. This sequence shows a new employee being taken through the routine for answering an incoming call by a manager. She is wearing a headset, and he asks her to pretend a call has just come in. She says into the headset: 'Good morning, Alliance and Leicester, can I help you?'. The manager makes a generally approving comment but then adds a proviso: the correct salutation is not 'can I help you?' but 'how can I help you?'. (Later in the programme, another manager renders it as 'how may I help you?'.) The voiceover track explains that it is not only new employees who receive this kind of feedback. All calls received at the centre are recorded, and each employee is regularly asked to come into a manager's office for her or his performance, as revealed on the tapes, to be appraised. At these 'counselling sessions', as the company calls them, employees will be pulled up on any deviation from the approved script (like saying 'can I' instead of 'how may I'), and managers will also comment on 'styling' matters like whether the employee is using the right tone of voice to project a helpful, friendly attitude.

This illustrates two important characteristics of managerial control at the call centre, and indeed in many modern workplaces: *codification* and *surveillance*. By 'codification' I mean that workers are not just told in general terms what kind of role they are expected to play, but given detailed rules for the enactment of that role, or even a fully specified script. In the 1970s, I too had a clerical job in a bank. There were certainly conventions for answering the phone (be polite, be businesslike, give the name of the bank and the branch), but you picked these up on the job rather than receiving formal training, and some of the details were left to your discretion. No one cared, for instance, whether you said 'good morning' or 'hello', 'can I help you' or 'how may I help you'. Nowadays these tiny details are codified, written down and enforced as norms. This is an example, albeit a relatively small one, of control over the worker's performance being increased and the worker's own autonomy being decreased. An analogy is the difference between specifying that employees must dress smartly (as the bank I worked for did) and requiring them to wear an actual uniform (as most banks do today, at least where staff have face-to-face contact with customers).[11]

'Surveillance' means that workers' performance is constantly being monitored and measured. At the Alliance and Leicester call centre, all calls are recorded and some are randomly selected to be the subject of 'counselling'. This is a common practice, though since it entails recording the speech of customers as well as employees, it requires (in Britain) the permission of the telecommunications regulator Oftel, and companies must announce to their customers that they are doing it. A computerized display board shows how work is being dealt with overall from moment to moment: how many calls are in progress, which employees are engaged in taking calls, how long the calls have been going on, how many customers are on hold in a queue, and so on. The phone systems are usually set up so that supervisors can listen in to any call currently in progress without the operator being aware of it (a practice known in some centres as 'silent listening'). In addition, some centres employ people (analogous to the 'mystery shoppers' we met in Chapter 3) to pose as customers and log their impressions of the management of the call.

This kind of surveillance represents an intensification of traditional kinds of supervisory control. Supervisory staff in the past would certainly have checked up on what workers were doing by watching and listening. But this sort of checking was more impressionistic: supervisors could not watch everyone at once, and they did not have the technology to engage in continuous monitoring and taping or produce precise measurements of performance (like 'average call duration') with which workers could be confronted later. Also, of course, in a traditional working environment the workers knew when supervisors were watching them and could 'mind their backs' accordingly. While some of the surveillance technology in call centres is physically obvious (this is true of the large computerized display at the Alliance and Leicester centre), the activities of 'silent listeners' and 'mystery callers' are harder to detect. In Sewell and Wilkinson's words (1992: 283–4), hi-tech surveillance can 'penetrate walls'; workers' awareness that they are constantly being monitored 'creates a climate where self-management is assured'. (Interestingly, however, Tyler and Taylor, (1997) found telephone sales and reservations staff at an airline company insisting that they *could* tell when they were being monitored. These workers reported that if they encountered a rude or 'ignorant' caller and were sure no one was listening in, they would deviate from the prescribed routine, and might even disconnect the offender.)

One straightforward target for surveillance is simply the amount of effort an operator puts in (supervisors check that workers are physically present at their work stations and that they are processing calls at an acceptable rate). But managers and supervisors also monitor the operator's *linguistic* performance, and if they deem it necessary they may intervene to provide what one memorandum in my corpus calls 'coaching', or less euphemistically, criticism. In the following section I want to look more closely at the criteria on which linguistic performance is judged, drawing on information contained in manuals, memos, training materials and forms setting out appraisal criteria.

Standardizing interaction

It is characteristic of the 'communication factory' that emphasis is placed on standardizing the output, or 'product', talk. Earlier in this discussion I related the standardizing impulse to the notion of 'efficiency': standardized interactional routines are intended to ensure that information is elicited in the order the computer software needs it to be input, that ongoing checks are made for accuracy, that the exchange is conducted with due regard to the customer's expectations of appropriate service, and that talking time is not wasted on inessentials. (This last consideration has sometimes been taken to extremes: one US centre reportedly prescribed the single-syllable salutations *hi* and *bye* in place of *good morning* and *goodbye* on the grounds that the time saved would yield a 'productivity gain' worth $22 million per annum (Kjellerup, 1998).) But there are other reasons for standardization. Efficiency might dictate the number, sequence and general content of inter-actional moves, but it need not preclude some degree of individual varia-tion in the actual words uttered. In many call centres, however, it is made clear to operators that even the most trivial variation will not be tolerated. The goal is to give customers a completely uniform and consistent experi-ence of dealing with the organization, regardless of which employee they happen to find themselves talking to.

Here we see the influence of modern managerial ideas about 'quality'. In the approach known as 'Total Quality Management', *quality* does not mean what it usually means in everyday usage, namely an especially high standard, but rather refers to the consistent achievement of a specified, measurable standard – getting something right first time, every time. In relation to mass-produced goods, it is easy to understand the logic of this idea. When a customer buys a particular brand of breakfast cereal, say, s/he is entitled to expect that the packet will always contain the same amount of cereal, and that the cereal will look and taste exactly as it did the last time s/he purchased it. Quality control is not just about ensuring every packet reaches a certain minimum standard of acceptability, but also about ensuring packets vary from one another only within narrow limits. Increasingly, however, the same notions of quality that apply to mass-produced goods are also being applied to the provision of customer service. The behaviour of employees in service encounters is regulated in an attempt to make it as predictable and invariant as a packet of cereal.

The other consideration that lies behind the demand for uniformity in operators' performance is the company's concern about its 'brand image'. Branding – creating a consistent, distinctive and easily recognizable iden-tity for your products and services – is regarded as one of the key mar-keting tools companies have at their disposal. But whereas a face-to-face operation can attend to this issue in a variety of ways – in its store layout, signage and decor, the packaging of its goods, the uniforms worn by its staff – a call centre has only one means of getting its brand image across, and that is the way operators speak to customers. Some manuals in my corpus of call centre materials explicitly remind operators that they 'are' the brand; specific instructions on how to conduct calls are prefaced by a formula such as 'remember: you are [name of company]'. 'Being' the company means behaving/speaking in accordance with the values it has chosen as central to its distinctive brand image. One centre which deals with insurance claims, for instance, encapsulates its 'brand values' in the acronym FISHES, which stands for *Fast-acting, Imaginative, Straightforward, Helpful, Expert, Self-assured.*

When the notion of 'branding' is extended to the verbal and other behaviour of employees, the result is what I referred to in Chapter 3 as 'styling', creating a uniform style of service encounter by regulating small surface details that have aesthetic value. In the case of call centre operators, this styling is exclusively linguistic: language is regulated to ensure operators function, not as individuals with their own personalities (or their own individually constructed on-the-job personae) but as embodiments of a single corporate persona whose key traits are decided by someone else. The parenthetical comment in the last sentence alludes to a distinction I take to be important: between allowing people to 'be themselves' at work and allowing them to *construct* themselves. It would be idle to criticize call centres simply for demanding that employees adopt a professional persona which is different from their non-professional self. This demand has been part of what it means to 'go out to work' since work itself became a distinct social domain: competent workers understand that they must behave in ways appropriate to the context of being at work (rather than at home or in a club, say), and this in itself is not generally seen as unreasonable – indeed, there is a certain amount of pleasure and satisfaction to be had from manipulating self-presentation in different situations. But as I noted in Chapter 3, the difference between people's everyday styling practices and workplace regimes of styling is that in the latter case, the speaker is not the 'stylistic agent' and does not 'own' the style s/he adopts. By standardizing speech performance, and particularly by requiring the expression of 'standard' personality traits ('outgoingness') and emotional states ('excitement'), the call centre regime imposes on workers the demand to present themselves in a way the company determines, down to the last detail. This carries the risk that employees may perceive the prescribed way of speaking not just as 'inauthentic' in the manner of any professional persona, but more problematically, as alien and demeaning. The call centre regime is not alone here, of course. But the extent of scripting and the intensity of surveillance in call centres make them a particularly extreme case of institutional control over individuals' self-presentation.

The verbal production of a uniform and consistent operator-persona is often justified to call centre staff by managers as something the customer expects and indeed wants. This raises the question of whether customers in fact apply the same criteria of judgement to verbal interactions with other human beings as they do to packets of cereal. There is some evidence that they do not. In the OU programme about empowerment, it was revealed that McDonald's had stopped telling its staff exactly what to say to customers when they entered and left the restaurant, after research had shown that customers disliked getting the same scripted greeting and farewell from every employee on every occasion. And in a survey of over 1000 call centre users, 'dealing with someone clearly reading from a script' was among respondents' 'pet hates'.[12] Conversely, the main factor producing customer satisfaction was a positive perception of the individual operator.

From a sociolinguistic perspective these findings are hardly surprising. However banal an interaction, the mere fact of engaging in it creates a kind of temporary social relationship; consequently, the criteria we ordinarily use to assess the quality of social relationships (as opposed to the quality of packets of cereal) are brought into play. We do not expect people to be uniform; conversely, we do expect them to be (or at least to seem) 'sincere'. In that light, it is a curious assumption that the same high degree of personal involvement, deference, enthusiasm, and so on, should ideally be manifested in every transaction. Callers are more likely to expect, subconsciously and on the basis of long experience of spontaneous interaction, that performance will be tailored to the needs of the context: that a straightforward inquiry, for instance, will be processed with less deference than a complaint. By suppressing (at least in theory) contextual variation, the call centre regime inadvertently increases the likelihood that many routine exchanges will be so excessively deferential, or enthusiastic, as to convey an impression of patent insincerity. This is ironic, given that some materials in my corpus actually specify 'sincerity' as one of the qualities operators are required to project in their speech.

Call centres do vary in how far they go in attempting to impose linguistic uniformity. At one end of the spectrum, one call centre in my sample, dealing with technical enquiries about telecommunications, hardly regulated employees' communication strategies at all, nor did it record or systematically monitor calls (a manager told me he believed that would be 'devastating for morale'). Operators at this centre must acquire a certain amount of technical knowledge (they are not themselves engineers, but are often called upon to talk to engineers), and training focuses more on this than on the minutiae of interaction. At the other end of the spectrum, I found several call centres which provided employees with a script covering more or less any interactional move that could occur in the course of a transaction, imposed detailed style rules regarding how they should speak, and monitored compliance assiduously.

Where a high degree of uniformity is demanded, managers often include in guidance to staff some explanation of what motivates that demand. For instance, a 1996 memorandum headed 'Standard Call Speech' and addressed to teleprocessing staff in a financial services centre begins: 'You should all know by now that we intend to introduce a standard telephone speech'. It goes on:

> There are a number of reasons for standardizing the speech and improving call techniques. The most important of which is *Meeting and Exceeding Customer Expectations*. If we don't, someone else will.
> Some more reasons are:
>
> • Creating a professional image
> • Improves quality of processing
> • Allows you to manage the call sequence and pace.
>
> Every operator must use the speech, no exceptions!

An interesting (and typical) feature of this explanation is that it puts 'customer expectations' first. Considerations of efficiency – that is, the idea that standardizing calls will increase the speed and accuracy of processing – are placed below 'service' considerations. There is some reason to doubt that this is the management's true order of priorities. A further memo, addressed only to supervisory staff, notes that while the introduction of a 'standard speech' may initially slow down call processing, as operators struggle with unfamiliar scripts, in the longer term 'I expect talk times to actually reduce as we better manage calls'. This particular centre processes requests for credit authorization, and the 'standard speech' is therefore quite a complicated construct, with options covering a range of eventualities: the caller's application may be accepted, declined or referred for further investigation. There is also a scripted option for cases where the operator is 'suspicious of the customer'.

Customer care training materials for the directory assistance centre whose standard routine we examined earlier include a section explaining to operators why the company insists on what it terms 'salutations'. (In this case 'salutation' does not refer only to the prescribed greeting ('XYZ Directories') but to all those moves which are motivated by considerations of politeness rather than by the main business of eliciting and providing information.)

Why Have Salutations?
Salutations give the call structure and allow it to be handled in a polite and efficient manner. It also gives a professional standard of customer service which is consistent every time they call.

In this explanation, 'professional' service is explicitly equated with being 'consistent every time [customers] call'.

Another approach to the regulation of calls is to provide operators with a checklist of things they should do, but no explicit modelling of how to do them, except in the case of the opening move (which is scripted in all cases in my corpus). Here, for instance, is the checklist provided by a call centre belonging to a utility company:

- Quick response time
- Standard greeting
- Be polite and professional
- Use listening noises
- Take control
- Ask questions – don't demand information!
- Take notes
- Obtain reason for call
- Use customer's name
- Take appropriate action to defuse anger
- Make the customer feel important
- Treat the customer as an individual
- Know our products and services – promote them!
- Summarize the call
- Offer your name and extension
- Thank the customer for calling and finish the call with goodbye.

- ALWAYS USE THE STANDARD GREETING:
- GOOD MORNING/AFTERNOON, …SPEAKING, CAN I TAKE
- YOUR REFERENCE NUMBER?

NEVER SAY…HELLO!!!

These instructions reflect the same considerations we have noted in cases where there is a script. Some are to do with the particularities of telephone interaction (for example, 'use listening noises' – while back-channelling is normal in all conversation, it is particularly important where there are no visual cues[13]). Other instructions relate to efficiency. Since time on the phone is money (and one customer's call time is another's queuing time), operators must 'take control' and 'obtain reason for call' as quickly as possible. They must also minimize errors by summarizing information given by the caller.

Many of the checkpoints on the list, however, are concerned with 'polite and professional' behaviour. This is a subject for extensive discussion and detailed prescription in all the materials I have collected. Under the heading of 'politeness' I include not just instructions to use conventional formulas like 'please', 'thank you', 'sorry', and so on, but any instructions to use language in a way that displays attention to the caller's 'face wants', that is, their desire for approbation ('positive face') and their desire not to be imposed upon ('negative face'). One obvious area where politeness is important is in mitigating potential offence to the customer. Thus workers at the credit-authorizing call centre mentioned above are given the following script for rejections: 'Unfortunately this application has been declined but thank you for calling'. The script for acceptances by contrast is just 'This application has been accepted'. This difference formalizes an intuitive understanding that what conversation analysts call a 'preference system' is in operation: acceptance is the 'preferred' response to a request for authorization and can be produced without ceremony; rejection is 'dispreferred' and requires more elaboration. As Marion Owen has argued (1983), the moves conversation analysis (CA) has identified on formal criteria as 'dispreferred' (such as declining an invitation, disagreeing with an opinion, refusing a request – all of which are typically performed with pausing, hedging and/or additional justification) are also strongly associated with threat to the addressee's face. Not only call centres but also some shops – which rarely have scripts for 'ordinary' transactions – provide scripts for use in seriously face-threatening situations (when a customer's money turns out to be counterfeit or s/he presents an invalid cheque). Such scripting reflects the emphasis placed on handling these situations sensitively; organizations do not want to take chances by leaving the details of sensitive behaviour to the individual employee's discretion. As Robin Leidner observes (1993: 230), one function of scripting is to establish a 'floor of civility', that is, a minimum level of politeness; though the effect may be to establish a 'ceiling' as well, it is more important to ensure that a minimally acceptable standard is met consistently.

Positive face is also the object of attention in guidance for call centre workers. What the utility company's checklist alludes to under the heading of 'making the customer feel important' may be realized linguistically through a number of strategies, including using the customer's name but also and importantly through prosodic and paralinguistic features. The directory assistance materials advise, for example:

> Remember voice intonation is also very important as tone, pace and clarity convey your attitude to the customer. You must never sound bored on a call. *Your telephone manner should convey the impression that you have been waiting for that individual call all day.* To assist in this try putting a smile on your face when receiving a call. We acknowledge that this can be difficult, but at the very least you *must* sound professional (my italics).

It is extremely common to find the instruction to 'smile' being given to telephone workers (and other 'invisible' workers, such as those who make public announcements at airports and railway stations). It is also common for workers to be instructed, not only in how they should *not* sound (for example, 'bored') but also in the precise attitudes they should be trying to convey in their voices. The same company's employee handbook includes, under the heading 'Standards at Work', this paragraph:

> Voice Impression – It is amazing the impression you can give a person just by the way you answer the phone. Think of the impression you get from somebody

just by the way they say 'hello' when you call them. Our commitment is to give an impression of excitement, friendliness, helpfulness and courtesy to every caller. Additionally you should speak clearly, professionally and at a proper pace.

Of course, it has to be borne in mind that 'sounding bored on a call' is a real danger where operators may be repeating their script for the 800th time that day. It is not the caller's fault that the operator has already said the same thing to 799 other people, and presumably the caller would just as soon not be made aware of the operator's *ennui*. Even so, what caller would really expect or want a directory assistance operator to sound as though s/he has been waiting for them to call all day, or to display 'excitement' at the prospect of finding a telephone number for them?

The word 'professional', which occurs in both the examples just cited, appears to cover several aspects of language-use, including politeness, consistency of response, and formality. It is noticeable that whenever operators are provided with scripts, these tend to be in a formal register. The utility company's stern injunction 'NEVER SAY HELLO!' is not simply a reminder that 'hello' happens not to be the company's standard greeting; more importantly it is a reminder that 'hello' – the salutation most people utter when they pick up their own phone at home – is not formal enough to be selected as a standard corporate greeting; the 'professional' choice is 'good morning/afternoon/evening'. In other words there is a deliberate attempt to differentiate the 'professional' from the 'personal' call (though some businesses with a young or 'counter-cultural' customer base deliberately mark themselves out as 'cool' and 'laid back' by flouting this norm and prescribing an informal greeting like 'Hi, Trendy Co'). The scripts given to operators often prescribe forms of words which seem almost perversely un-conversational, or even un-speechlike, such as 'I *am unable to* validate your PIN number', 'what ___ do you *require*?' 'I will connect you to X who will be happy to *assist* you in this *matter*'. The register these examples call to mind is that of the business letter. How far it is the result of a deliberate decision to mark the transaction as 'professional' by actually avoiding a conversational tone, and how far it just results from scripts being composed in writing, by people more used to writing letters than scripting dialogue, is difficult to say.[14] When markers of professional formality are combined (as they often are) with markers of synthetic personalization, the result can be a strange hybrid.

Assessing performance: 'It isn't what they say...'

As the instructions I have already quoted on things like 'voice impression' suggest, many call centres seek to control not only *what* operators say but also *how* they say it. The manner of operators' performance is a particular concern for supervisors or market researchers monitoring calls, and it is instructive to look at the checklists they use for that purpose. The following list belongs to the centre with the 'standard telephone speech':

- Smiling. Does the member of staff answer the phone with a smile?
- Pitch. The depth of pitch in the member of staff's voice will determine the degree of sincerity and confidence associated with the message that they are giving the caller.
- Energy. Staff must have a certain level of energy...in order to make their message attractive and interesting.
- Volume. Ensure staff are neither shouting nor hardly audible.
- Pace. Ensure the member of staff is not dragging out the sentences nor speeding through it.
- Idea. ...short sentences and simple words must be used. Pause between sentences.
- Rapport. When rapport is created...this will persuade the caller to listen, co-operate and remain loyal to the company.
- Vias [*sic*]. Vias are conveyed through the voice and will contradict what is being said, i.e. when staff say they understand or are going to do something, yet their voice says something else. There are many ways to detect vias in a voice.
- Attention. Staff need to get and retain the caller's attention.
- Understanding. Does the member of staff seem to understand what is being said?
- Acknowledge. Staff can let the caller know they have understood them by making simple acknowledgement sounds, if the caller is not acknowledged in this way they will presume they have not been understood and repeat themselves.
- Space. Staff must give [space for the caller to respond]. This can be done by pausing...and asking questions. Staff must never talk over customers, finish customers' sentences for them, this can be perceived as being very rude.
- Direction. Where the staff member and the caller have a good balance of giving and receiving ideas and information through the conversation.

It is interesting to note what is defined as a matter of concern here, and what the balance is between different kinds of concerns. Of the 13 items on the list, almost half (six) are directly to do with the vocal performance – the speed, volume, tone and quality of speech. The other items are either about the sequential management of interaction (acknowledging the caller's contributions with minimal response tokens to encourage continuation and discourage repetition, soliciting turns from the caller using questions and pausing, not interrupting or overlapping) or else they are about the management of the interpersonal relationship more generally (getting attention, creating rapport). What is being assessed here is, of course, a scripted performance, which explains why there are no items relating to the content of what is said by the operator. But many important features of spoken interaction cannot be scripted: it is obviously impossible to specify in advance where operators should insert minimal responses, for instance, or how they should attempt to create 'rapport'. It might be feasible to include some indication of the desired prosodic and paralinguistic features in a script, but in practice this is seldom attempted.[15] The importance of vocal styling is addressed instead by proliferating performance criteria relating to the manner in which operators should speak (with a smile, confidently, sincerely, energetically and so forth).

Although the list is explicitly intended as an assessment tool, only some items give a clear and unambiguous indication of the standard employees have to meet. Staff are clearly expected, for instance, to smile when they answer the phone and to make use of minimal responses; conversely they are expected to avoid talking over the caller. By contrast, the statement that 'the depth of pitch in the member of staff's voice will determine the degree of sincerity and confidence associated with the message' gives the assessor much less to go on. Just as unhelpful is the statement 'there are many ways to detect vias in a voice', since the text does not go on to describe any of them, or indeed explain what the term *via* means. Assessors are essentially being invited to make broad and subjective assessments of characteristics like 'energy', 'confidence' and 'sincerity', whose linguistic correlates are either not defined at all, or else are defined in a way that is vague and/or makes little sense (a linguist might well ask, for instance, what 'depth of pitch' refers to. The most obvious possibility is that it means something roughly equivalent to fundamental frequency, but if so it is still unclear what a satisfactory performance would be).

The list invokes explicit theoretical beliefs about how spoken interaction works which are at odds with the intuitive practical understanding that is demonstrated elsewhere. Consider the instruction to 'pause between sentences'. The list compiler evidently does not have a metalanguage for talking about units in spoken discourse, but the scripting of the 'standard speech' whose delivery is being assessed shows that the units in between which operators should pause need not be, and in most cases are not, coextensive with a sentence. Punctuation is used to make this clear in the script, as in 'This application has been accepted, your authorization number is 1234567', where the use of the comma (producing what composition teachers know as a 'run-on sentence') signals that the clause boundary is not meant to be a turn transition relevance place and the speaker should not insert a significant pause. Whatever the checklist says, supervisors would be very unlikely to regard a failure to pause after every sentence of the script as grounds for criticizing an operator.

Despite the inexplicit and confused nature of many appraisal criteria, it is clear that supervisors and managers do typically subscribe to an ethos of standardization and to the associated concept of 'correct' linguistic performance; the practice of 'counselling' is meant to inculcate a similar attitude in their subordinates. One supervisor at an airline-reservations call centre described to the sociologist Steve Taylor how operators are made to listen critically to their own speech on tape:

> A lot of the time it isn't what they say, it's the tone in which they say it…I will play something and I'll just stop it and go, 'shall we listen to that again?', rewind it and then they'll go, 'I didn't know I said it like that'. It makes them analyse themselves and really wake up to their *mistakes*. (Taylor, 1998: 93, emphasis in original.)

The use of the word *mistakes* is striking here, and it is equally striking that the hypothetical exchange is represented as proceeding on the basis of some tacit agreement between operator and supervisor about what constitutes a 'mistake'. Exactly what is 'wrong', and what would be 'right', remains vague ('the tone in which they say it…I didn't know I said it like that'). The passage just quoted is preceded by the supervisor telling Taylor 'I really do use self-tape a lot'. Evidently it is easier to get operators to 'wake up to their mistakes' by using concrete illustration than by reference to abstract rules like those that appear on checklists. This underlines the gap between the (limited) explicit knowledge about spoken discourse which is available to the designers of call centre regimes, and the communicative competence on which they and their operators implicitly draw.

So far I have mainly been examining the explicit knowledge that underpins the linguistic regime of the call centre, focusing in particular on prescriptive documents produced for instructional and/or disciplinary purposes. The regulation of spoken language in call centres depends very heavily on the use of *writing* – printed handbooks, memos, prompt sheets, scripts and assessment checklists – and written texts are, arguably, the best source of evidence about the linguistic and interpersonal norms which the call centre regime's designers are trying to promote. Yet it will already be apparent that on their own these texts provide an incomplete and in some respects misleading picture of what 'really' goes on in call centres. They do not tell us everything about the regulation of operators' speech in practice, and they tell us next to nothing about what it is actually like to work in the communication factory. Operators' own experiences and perspectives are the subject of the next section, where I will also ask whether there is cause for concern about the effects of call centre work on those who do it.

Far from paradise?

In May 1998, a Sunday newspaper carried a feature written by journalist Meg Carter under the title 'Despite the palm trees, working in a call centre can be far from paradise' (*Independent on Sunday*, May 17, 1998). This title alluded to the décor of a call centre in Falkirk, central Scotland, whose business is selling holidays. In an effort to create what the architect described as 'an un-factory-like atmosphere', this centre – a warehouse-like building located on a typical edge-of-town site – had been given murals depicting exotic holiday destinations (hence the palm trees), an 'informal' layout (workers did not sit in rows) and a 'sensorama', the designer's term for a corridor with lighting that simulates bright sunshine, through which employees would pass on their way to begin their shifts. Other centres were reported to have installed fish tanks, provided on-site gym facilities and even introduced at-desk shiatsu massage.

These innovations mark a recognition on the part of the companies concerned that working in a call centre can produce high levels of stress. As Meg Carter summarized: 'employment experts are increasingly concerned about the impact on staff of carrying out such repetitive work in a goal-obsessed work environment'. Her report quoted a source at the Banking, Insurance and Finance Union (BIFU) confirming that the organization dealt with many health-related problems reported by call centre employees in the financial services sector.[16] The managing director of the Call Centre College, which provides training for unemployed people hoping to work in the industry, also mentioned stress as a major issue, noting that 'advanced computer systems leave operators little to do other than recite the same script hundreds of times a day, which can lead to stress-related problems'.

This may help to explain why, although call centres have an impressive record of job creation, it is not always easy to recruit people to work in them, and it is even more difficult to get recruits to stay. (According to industry analysts quoted in *The Independent on Sunday*, around a third leave their jobs each year.) Of the call centre managers and supervisors I interviewed myself,[17] all but one reported moderate to severe problems in attracting and retaining staff. The worst case described to me was a centre which, for a significant period, had had a staff turnover rate of almost 50% per month. I also encountered a centre where fewer than half the employees had been in their jobs for more than six months. The 'best' case described to me, a centre with a stable and reportedly contented workforce, was located in a small town where employment opportunities were limited, and it employed mainly mothers of school-age children, working part time.

When I interviewed operators I asked them how they had come to be working in call centres and what they considered to be the good and bad things about the work. Their answers made clear that while they did not regard their workplaces as 'paradise', they did not regard them as purgatory either. For certain categories of workers,[18] call centre work offered the advantage of convenience: shifts could be chosen to fit in with other commitments like childcare and studying; the conditions were better and the pay generally higher than in other sectors (such as catering and hospitality) where work was readily available to them. Many of my informants had left jobs after a short time, confirming the general picture of high staff turnover, but their lack of loyalty to any one employer did not necessarily mean they were moving out of the industry altogether. Several had moved from one centre to another in search of better hours and/or higher pay; they had capitalized on the fact that this was a period of expansion, with new centres opening in the area all the time. They did not see call centre work as a permanent career choice, but they were prepared to do it for a few years rather than a few weeks or months. A couple of my informants had been doing it for two years at the time of our conversations.

Perhaps surprisingly, all my interviewees cited the opportunity to 'work with people' – by which they meant co-workers as well as customers – as a 'good thing' about call centre work. Although they spent the bulk of their working time on the phone to callers, they clearly did not feel isolated from one another; the operator who characterized her workplace (a centre employing 400 people) as 'lively and chatty' was not untypical. Officially there was not much time for workers to chat among themselves, but unofficially all the operators I interviewed found ways of making downtime between calls (I will not repeat the details of the methods they described.)

But while all my informants could find something to say about the advantages of call centre work, no one declined my invitation to discuss the 'bad things'. They agreed that call centre work was stressful; they often mentioned that there were high rates of sickness among operators, which they attributed to the pressures of the work. Asked what made it so stressful, they tended to cite three things in particular: the repetitive nature of the job; the pressure imposed by performance targets; and the difficulties of dealing with callers, which arose from a combination of callers' own behaviour and managerial demands limiting operators' ability to provide what they regarded as an acceptable service.

The last of these problems – what one operator referred to as the 'frustration factor' in dealing with callers – was the one most of my informants brought up first, suggesting they regarded it as the most significant. One source of frustration was that so many callers apparently did not understand the basic logic of the call centre, particularly the feature I have glossed as 'specialization/concentration of function'.[19] In many cases it is not just telephone service provision itself that has been 'concentrated';

often there are separate centres for different services provided by the same organization (travel enquiries versus ticket sales, or directory assistance versus operator-assisted calls). This division of labour is efficient from the company's perspective – it means that operators in each centre only have to be trained to do a small range of things – but many callers do not understand why they cannot get all their queries dealt with by the same operator in a single call. Some operators I interviewed said they found this problematic because it prevented them giving an acceptable level of service, and so reduced their job satisfaction. They also regretted it because where a customer was dissatisfied, it was the operator who bore the brunt.

It was generally agreed that dealing with customer dissatisfaction was an unpleasant aspect of call centre work, and informants stressed it was commonplace to encounter rudeness or even abuse. Telephone interaction with a stranger has some of the same features that lead to the much-discussed problem of 'flaming' on the internet: the physical separation and invisibility of the parties has a disinhibiting effect on impolite behaviour and the expression of strong emotions, especially anger. As one operator remarked, 'People say things on the phone they would never say to your face'. While operators usually do not have to tolerate extreme behaviours such as swearing, they are expected to tolerate callers 'raising their voices' and 'telling you what a bad job you're doing'. In many cases they are required to attempt 'defusing' and give 'verbal warnings' to even the most abusive caller before they can legitimately terminate the call. While some informants said that in time you became used to it, they made clear that being an 'Aunt Sally' is stressful. It is also stressful, after a 'difficult' call, to have to compose yourself in a matter of seconds to greet the next caller with a smile.

Regaining composure instantly is necessary because of the call-handling targets operators have to meet, and these were seen by my interviewees as another constraint on their ability to provide high standards of service. To paraphrase a comment made by one operator at the directory assistance centre, what if the customer wants something that can't be done in 32 seconds? This informant was not alone in feeling that the management spoke with a forked tongue: its rhetoric was all about customer satisfaction, but in practice supervisors were not interested in hearing why certain calls could not be handled to the customer's satisfaction without taking the operator's average duration over the target. The target was sacred, and the consequence for operators was a constant sense of being under pressure, as well as a sense of injustice, since they felt they were being expected to deliver a standard of service that was simply not achievable in the time allotted. In most centres operators were organized in teams, and there were bonuses – extra pay or perks – if a whole team met its targets for a set period. To foster a competitive spirit, statistics on teams' performances were sometimes displayed publicly. Among the people I spoke to, however, this approach cut little ice, because they felt the targets were unrealistic. One operator recalled that in 18 months, his team had met the targets precisely once.[20]

I expected operators to mention surveillance as a source of stress, but in fact few expressed concern about the monitoring of their linguistic behaviour carried out by supervisors, team leaders or market researchers, because their experience was that the monitoring procedures were less rigorous in practice than on paper. The main reason they gave for this was that supervisors had too little time to monitor: often the volume of work was such that they were required to work on the phones themselves. A supervisor at a centre where call auditing was about to be implemented reported that she was dreading the extra work it would inevitably entail. Several interviewees reported that surveillance focused primarily on the issue of targets, and secondarily on a few selected aspects of performance (such as using the right salutations and confirming details back to the caller). If you could figure out which were the important things and do those things by the book you could often get away with ignoring the rest of the book. Thus my informants reported taking liberties with their scripts and ignoring instructions to smile. At the same time, most operators reported feeling under pressure because of the looming presence of the 'boards', the computerized displays showing calls in progress, calls held in a queue, average wait time, and so on. The displays seemed to function as an effective spur to self-surveillance, reminding operators that a backlog of calls was building up, and by implication that they needed to work faster.

All interviewees mentioned repetition as a 'bad thing' about call centre work. Two informants used exactly the same words to capture the degree of boredom they experienced: 'I could do it in my sleep'. The monotony was worst during spells when calls came one after another with no gaps in between. One operator said that by the end of a busy shift she sometimes found herself 'talking nonsense'. She described a recent occasion when she had taken a call and discovered that 'I just couldn't get the words out'.

Many of the views I have cited and quoted from interviews tally with the 'expert' opinions expressed to the *Independent on Sunday*'s reporter. Taken together, these sources might well suggest that shiatsu massage and sensoramas are rather beside the point: they may palliate stress but they do not address its root causes. The features pinpointed by the newspaper report as particularly stressful – repetition and 'goal obsession', an obsession with setting targets and monitoring performance – are not incidental to the call centre regime, they are constitutive of it. Without these features, a call centre would not be what it is, and what it has to be to achieve the goals it was designed for. Yet just pointing out that the call centre regime is repetitious and 'goal obsessed' does not entirely get to the bottom of what is stressful about operators' work and why. It might well be observed that many other workers do repetitive jobs and are subject to demanding performance targets. What is special about call centres?

Most discussions of why call centre work is stressful (in, for instance, research reports produced for trades unions representing call centre workers) tend to focus mainly on the technological aspects of the regime. It is noted that automated call distribution results in 'speed-up' – workers may find themselves processing calls continuously and without a break for several hours at a time – and so exacerbates the risk of repetitive strain injury, voice-loss and damage to the vocal apparatus (BIFU, 1997). Hi-tech surveillance is also a matter of concern to the unions.[21] Another much-discussed issue is the depressing physical layout and design of call centres: the manager responsible for the 'palm trees' centre in Falkirk told the *Independent on Sunday* he was determined to get away from what he described as 'rows of people in low-ceiling environments'. (Only one of my informants even mentioned the physical environment, and he did so when explaining why he *preferred* working in a call centre to working in a factory – call centres were cleaner, quieter and more comfortable.) But whereas technology and design loom large in discussions of call centres' problems, much less attention is given to the linguistic and interpersonal aspects of the regime. In my own view, it is not possible to understand the peculiarities of call centre work – including the kinds of stress it produces – without placing more emphasis on the fact that it is essentially *language* work, and that 'language' in this instance primarily means spoken interaction. The implications of regimenting spoken interaction in the way many call centres do are somewhat different from the implications of regimenting other kinds of behaviour.

For instance, while everyone agrees that the repetitive nature of call-handling is problematic, it surely makes a difference that the repetitive task is, specifically, an *oral communication* task. My informants made comments like 'I could do it in my sleep' and 'your mind just switches off', but it could be argued that the problem is, in fact, precisely the opposite: you *cannot* 'switch off' when you are talking to someone else. The communicative tasks operators perform are less mechanically repetitive than the manual tasks of the traditional factory production line (where work cycles can be as short as 20 seconds); but at least you can think about other things while you perform manual tasks, and perhaps relieve the boredom by talking to your co-workers (in particularly noisy factories and mills, workers sometimes learnt to lip-read[22]). If you are talking, by contrast, it is impossible to distract yourself with either conversation or 'inner speech'. Operators I interviewed did make efforts to distract themselves between calls – often using ingenious methods to 'buy time' for this – but when I put the question to them they agreed that you could not distract yourself while actually on a call without losing the thread. The informant who reported 'talking nonsense' at the end of a busy shift had lost the thread because she was exhausted, and she found the experience mortifying. Her account was precisely intended to underline that although it is not intellectually demanding, but on the contrary can be almost stupefyingly dull, call-handling requires continuous concentration.

But it is also important to consider the peculiar interpersonal demands made on call centre operators: as we have seen, these demands were what most of my interviewees chose to talk about first when asked what was 'bad' about their work. Operators are subject to many of the same demands as the supermarket workers discussed in Chapter 3 (for instance, they are required to engage in synthetic personalization), but the context is different, and arguably even more demanding. For one thing, interpersonal relationships have to be managed while also trying to meet factory-like efficiency targets. For another, the operator is using a communication medium – the telephone – that imposes pressures and restrictions of its own. In sum, although the call is an interpersonal transaction, it occurs in such a context and is regulated in such a way as to offer few of the interpersonal rewards of conversation with another person, while at the same time it exposes the operator to a high degree of interpersonal risk.

One source of risk is the design of standardized routines where the sequence and content of moves is dictated by a computer program, and the operator is required to behave essentially as an extension of a machine. Programs are rarely designed with any awareness of what is 'natural' in spoken interaction, and consequently they may require operators to do unnatural and face-threatening things. The researchers Jack Whalen and Erik Vinkhuyzen (in press) spent time observing and analysing in a call centre dealing with enquiries about problems with photocopying machines. The focus of their interest was the way operators used a computer program designed to diagnose the customer's problem. The system had been developed in an effort to, as one manager put it, 'reduce dependency on people knowledge and skills'. Operators at the centre were given no technical training – managers were reluctant to invest time and money in it – and so they did not have the expertise to either diagnose copier faults or suggest procedures for fixing minor problems. Callers typically did not know how their machines worked either. Telephone transactions were therefore a case of 'the blind leading the blind'; all knowledge was vested in the computer program, which told operators what questions to ask and used the answers to decide what was wrong. But the system design took no account of interpersonal considerations. The computer would instruct operators to ask customers questions that might be perceived as implying that they were negligent and stupid: for instance, if the customer reported a fault in copy quality, operators were supposed to ask if the same fault appeared on the original they were trying to copy. Whalen and Vinkhuyzen observed that operators tended not to follow this instruction: instead they would say things like 'good, clean originals?' which were phrased as 'checks' rather than full questions, and projected an affirmative answer (whereas the computer's question, unnaturally, projected a negative as the 'preferred' answer). This strategy carried the risk that the customer would simply say 'yes' without really checking, but it minimized the risk that the customer would be offended.

Other risks are less easy for operators to manage. Under pressure to meet efficiency targets, they are aware of the need to keep calls brief and to the point. At the same time, they are expected to 'meet and exceed customer expectations' in terms of service, and may be instructed to adopt a friendly, enthusiastic conversational manner, to 'personalize' the interaction by using their own and possibly the caller's name, and so on. But this can lead to a dilemma. Inevitably, some callers respond to the operator's personalized friendliness by initiating small talk, as if they were having a real conversation with a real person. One operator told me that when this happened she was 'naturally' tempted to respond in kind, but she also felt under pressure not to do so, to avoid lengthening the duration of the call. In this situation, she said, 'sometimes you just go with it and don't bother about your call times – because it makes *you* feel better'. Operators also have to suppress their 'natural' inclination to respond in kind, or alternatively to withdraw, when they find themselves being criticized and shouted at by callers who feel free to 'say things on the phone they would never say to your face'.

The combination of high interpersonal risk and low reward is typical of jobs where workers are expected to engage in emotional labour, and as I noted in Chapter 3, that is an increasingly salient aspect of service work generally, following the widespread introduction of more systematic approaches to customer care. It will already be evident from the materials quoted earlier that making the customer feel good is a strong expectation in call centres ('your telephone manner should give the impression you have been waiting for that individual call all day'). However, this element in a call centre operator's job is complicated by the peculiar conditions of interaction in call centres. The work of establishing rapport has to be repeated with a new customer every few minutes, and the telephone medium means that the operator has only one resource available for doing it, namely her/his voice. In addition, the absence of face-to-face contact leads to an unusually high frequency of aggressive interactions, which operators are required to manage by, in the words of one of the checklists I reproduced above, 'taking appropriate action to defuse anger'.

The issue of anger brings the problems and contradictions of synthetic personalization into sharp focus. If a caller is rude or abusive, the advice typically given to operators is 'don't take it personally'.

George Ritzer (1996: 82) lists among the 'positive advantages' of interactional routines and scripts the idea that 'employees can...protect themselves from the insults and indignities that are frequently heaped upon them...[with] the view that...hostility is aimed at the scripts and those who created them'. But this attitude appears to be comparatively rare among call centre operators. In practice, managers and supervisors told me, 'taking it personally' was a common problem; some operators seemed not to grasp that they were not being attacked in their own person, but 'only' in their corporate persona. Yet the same managers who complained about this encouraged operators to 'personalize' interaction by using their own and callers' names, putting warmth and friendliness into their voices, asking questions to demonstrate interest, and otherwise 'making the customer feel important'. It is not surprising if callers respond to this by treating the conversation as 'real' and holding the operator personally accountable for what is said. (Such 'intersubjective accountability' is a powerful mechanism in all social interaction, friendly or not; the discomfort we feel interacting with machines arises partly from our knowledge that however 'human' they sound, they have no subjectivity and cannot be held accountable for what they say.) It is one of the regime's explicitly stated goals that operators should strive to create personal rapport with callers, and they are judged on their ability to do it convincingly. That being so, it hardly seems fair for managers to complain that operators identify too closely with their personae and cannot instantly disengage if a caller attacks them.

Operators themselves are aware of the contradictory demands being made upon them, and in some cases may exploit the contradiction to resist particular aspects of the regime. One of Steve Taylor's interviewees provides a good example:

> I've had loads of battles with my supervisor, cos she'll say 'change the way you say this', 'change the way you offer this', and I'll say 'but that's the way I do it', 'that's me, that's my personality, I can't change myself', and she'll say, 'well you'll have to', but I don't. They either want us to be natural when interacting with customers or they don't, they can't have it both ways. (Taylor, 1998: 95)

By contrast, Taylor quotes other operators in the same centre whose approach was more pragmatic. For instance, one woman, discussing 'things that you should say and you shouldn't say' noted that although in the final analysis employees could not be forced to use the preferred verbal style, 'if you want to make targets, earn more money and things then you are better off doing what we've been taught...otherwise you'll not get your target' (Taylor, 1998: 92).

In these interview data we see once again the recurrent tension between viewing communication as a form of natural self-expression and viewing it as an instrumentally oriented technology. Both workers and managers are divided on the issue. Like the focus group participants quoted in Chapter 3, some call centre managers felt that the ability to deal with callers successfully was not in the final analysis a learnable skill. More than one, when I asked them about the training operators received, commented that interpersonal communication was something people could only be trained in up to a point, because it was largely a matter of individual personality. They talked about trying to ensure at the recruitment stage that they were taking on people with the 'right' personality and disposition (for instance, people who were 'outgoing' rather than very reserved, and able to take a certain amount of rudeness without getting upset).

In many sectors it is clear, too, that managers associate the 'right' disposition not merely with individual personality-types but with particular social groups; age and gender are especially salient considerations. Some of my informants expressed a preference for younger workers on the basis that they were better able to cope with the pressure of call centre work than older people. Other researchers have found evidence of a gender preference (for women), which is often explained with specific reference to vocal and interactional style. Marshall and Richardson (cited in Reardon, 1996) found that call centres in the financial services sector were predisposed to recruit young women, who were said to have a more 'naturally' friendly telephone manner, exemplified by their ability to 'smile down the phone'. Sociologists Melissa Tyler and Steve Taylor elicited similar attitudes from a male manager at the airline-reservations centre:

> The vast, vast majority of the agents we select are women…it's not as if we don't get men applying for the job, up here [in north eastern England, an area of high unemployment] you tend to get applications from everybody for everything…[women] just seem to fit better, they're better at it…we are looking for people who can chat to people, interact, build rapport. What we find is that women can do this more, they're definitely more natural when they do it anyway. It doesn't sound as forced, perhaps they're used to doing it all the time anyway…women are naturally good at that sort of thing. I think they have a higher tolerance level than men…I suppose we do, yes, if we're honest about it, select women sometimes because they are women rather than because of something they've particularly shown in the interview. (Tyler and Taylor, 1997: 10)

There is, of course, a historical tradition of employing mainly women to work as telephone operators. The long distance phone company AT&T was at one time the largest single employer of women workers in the US. In a 1999 radio feature on the AT&T archives (see note 8), listeners heard part of a 1960s recruitment advertisement in which a perky jingle that included the line 'turn your work into play' was followed by a young woman saying (in a markedly 'girly' voice characterized by high pitch, breathy voice and 'swoopy' intonation): 'I love all kinds of talking, I can talk all day about nothing. So I guess the best kind of work would be being a telephone operator'. To judge by the comments of the manager quoted above, the image of the ideal operator as a young woman who is naturally disposed to 'talk all day about nothing' remains alive and well, albeit expressed nowadays in more circumspect terms. If one objectionable thing about it is its unreconstructed sex stereotyping, another is that it treats a large part of the work operators do as if it were not work at all. Without exception, my own interviewees (of both sexes) considered the verbal production of a friendly, helpful and cheery service persona – often in the face of callers' hostility and always under pressure from call handling targets – to be hard work. If employers (and in some cases, unions) do not grasp the *interpersonally* demanding nature of the work call centre operators do, it is no wonder they have an inadequate analysis of the stress that afflicts so many of them.

Helplines and sex lines

The call centre is not the only institution where services are provided by telephone. It is instructive briefly to compare and contrast the call centre regime with two other, apparently very different cases: helplines and telephone sex services.

By a 'helpline' I mean the kind of telephone service that exists, often under the aegis of a government body or a charity, to provide information, advice and sometimes counselling on subjects like HIV/AIDS, giving up smoking, bullying at work or school, rape, domestic violence, child abuse, suicide, and so on. Some helplines have a permanent existence (for instance in Britain there is a national AIDS helpline sponsored by the government). Other lines are set up to meet demand following, say, a television programme dealing with a distressing subject, or are temporary responses to some crisis.

Helplines are on the face of things very different from call centres. They do not have a business ethos: the profit motive is entirely absent, there is no question of marketplace 'competition', and although they may get paid, in many or most cases the helpline workers are not full-time employees, and their motivations for doing the work are charitable or political. Many lines were started by activists on issues like rape and HIV/AIDS who wanted to provide community services of a kind the authorities were not at the time providing. Helpline workers usually have to undergo extensive training, but it is more like counselling training than the sort of communication training call centre workers are given. While doing this research, however, I met a small number of people who had been involved in helpline work, and who described dramatic recent changes in the culture of some lines, especially those sponsored directly by a government department. The government had placed these lines under more 'professional' management, and the new regime had introduced a more 'businesslike' approach to the work. For example, some lines had been merged, in the sense that although people still called one number for, say, the AIDS line and another for, say, the giving up smoking line, both sets of calls were taken in the same office by the same pool of operators. Consequently, workers had to 'cross-train' so they could deal with more than one kind of call. Since people had often become involved on the basis of their commitment to and knowledge of a single issue, this requirement was felt as a depersonalizing and sometimes demotivating influence. Even more significantly, the new management had imposed targets for call duration. One informant reported an instruction to keep calls to three minutes. This is not the 32 seconds of the directory assistance call, but as the informant pointed out, people calling a helpline because they have seen, for instance, a television programme about rape and want to talk about their own experience of it, are often either extremely hesitant or very distressed, or both; they are not looking to 'do business', and strict timekeeping in this context seems inappropriate, if not callous. It also deskills the operators, since although they have been trained to provide advice and support, and are motivated by their wish to do so, the main task it is possible to accomplish in three minutes is to refer the caller to other agencies. All the people I spoke to about helplines expressed concern about this, less on the grounds that they themselves were being deskilled than because they feared that callers who felt they had been 'palmed off' at the very moment they had finally decided to talk would probably never contact the other agencies to which they were referred.

The example of helplines might suggest that the call centre regime with its emphasis on efficiency and quasi-automation is increasingly being used as a model for all regimes of telephone service provision, no matter how different their underlying ethos. Although my sample of helpline workers was very small, it seemed clear that the introduction of call centre-like features was demotivating and was considered to reduce the standard of service callers received. Those I spoke to also believed that the main motivation for the changes had less to do with serving the public better (by increasing the number of people the lines could deal with and reducing the time callers might have to wait to get through), than with simply keeping the cost of the service down.

Another type of telephone service that may be compared with the call centre is the sex line, information on which I take from the work of Kira Hall (1995). By 'sex line' I mean a service which customers call (and for which they pay the provider directly, usually by credit card and by the minute) to be aroused by erotic talk, produced by someone who enacts, over the phone, a fantasy sexual persona. Kira Hall interviewed a number of people providing such services in the San Francisco area, and also examined literature produced for these workers' guidance.

Telephone sex work has both similarities to and differences from working in a call centre. It shares the feature of 'remote location' – communication technology makes it possible to access services without regard to the distance between customer and provider – but it is typically done from the operator's own home. The operator is not a one-woman business, but is usually employed by an entrepreneur-manager (or in traditional sex-work terms, a pimp/madam) who is the first point of contact for callers. Having ascertained what a caller's requirements are and checked his credit card, the employer calls a home-based operator s/he deems suitable, asks if she wants to take the call, and if the answer is yes, redirects the caller to the operator. It would in principle be possible to concentrate this sort of operation in something like the call centre, a 'telephone sex factory' in an out-of-town industrial shed; but employing home-based workers also keeps overheads low, while concentration might be counterproductive in other ways. One of the things sex line operators must attempt to simulate is intimacy, to which the ambience of a factory or open-plan office is particularly unconducive. In addition, for many of the women Hall interviewed, an attraction of the job was that you did not have to go out to do it. Another difference from the call centre is that sex line workers aim for the longest possible 'average call duration', this being a pay-per-minute service. Keeping the caller on the line, using extended talk to maintain his interest and arousal, is seen as one of the most important skills an operator must develop.

Like their colleagues in call centres, sex line workers are required to adopt a telephone persona that is a mixture of corporate professionalism and 'synthetic personalization'. Consider the following extract from a manual given to operators working for 970-LIVE, a sex line service in New York City (quoted in Hall, 1995: 190–91):

Professionalism
Do not talk to anyone besides a caller when taking a call. Always be bubbly, sexy, interesting, and interested in each individual caller. Remember, you are not your character on the phone.

With the exception of one or two words – sexy and character – these instructions could have come out of any of the call centre materials quoted earlier in this chapter. The 970-LIVE manual also instructs:

Create different characters
Start with one that resembles the ideal woman. Move on to bimbo, nymphomaniac, mistress, slave, transvestite, lesbian, foreigner or virgin. If the caller

wants to speak to someone else, don't waste time being insulted. *Be* someone else. (Hall, 1995: 190)

As in call centres, the operator is reminded here not to 'take it personally' if the caller is less than positively disposed towards her. The 970-LIVE manual however is more forthright than most call centre materials in drawing attention to the inauthenticity of the operator's performance, and pointing out that it may well involve playing a stereotypically subservient role (like 'bimbo' or 'slave').

The combination of inauthenticity and subservience is one that troubles many service workers required to perform emotional labour, as we saw in Chapter 3. But to Kira Hall's informants it appeared to make a significant difference that they were permitted to use their own imagination and their skills with language to 'create different characters'. Unlike most call centre workers, they perceived their work as involving a high degree of creativity; they described themselves as 'fantasy makers' and 'storytellers', and some took very explicit pride in their linguistic skills, while simultaneously regarding their customers' level of intelligence and linguistic sophistication with contempt:

> I'm a good storyteller. A lot of what I do is wasted on these people. They're not bright enough to know some of the words I use. …I have a large vocabulary, I read a lot and I'll use other words. I don't own a television, I think that's a big part of my greater command of language than the average human being. And since I've gotten into this, I've also decided that if I'm going to be a storyteller, I'm going to study more about storytelling. ('Rachel', quoted in Hall, 1995: 205)

Hall adds that the kind of call most disliked by many of her informants involved a dominance-submission scenario in which the operator was given a very limited script by the caller (for example, she was only allowed to say 'yes sir' and 'no sir', in a markedly subservient tone). Some operators actually refused these calls, though one told Hall that 'low verbal expectations did at least allow her to get a lot of dishes done' (1995: 205).

It should be acknowledged that not all sex line operators feel as positive about their work as Hall's informants; some have talked about the negative psychological effects of participating in scenarios (involving extremes of violence, for example) that they found disturbing and abusive.[23] But while sex-line work raises some issues that are not directly relevant to the case of call centres, it could be argued that the two kinds of work have more in common than might be apparent at first glance. Both involve emotional labour, and demand that the operator adopt a stylized persona (many call centre managers too would like their operators to 'resemble the ideal woman'); both may expose the operator to abusive treatment, and both seem to inspire marked contempt towards 'ignorant' customers. On the other hand, as Kira Hall's informants pointed out to her, sex-line operators do not have to contend with the regimentation and surveillance that typify the call centre regime. They can do other things (like washing dishes) while working, they do not have to meet external targets, they can refuse calls, and although they must enact someone else's scenario, they do not have to perform to a predetermined script or be assessed continually against a checklist of corporate requirements. Though the telephone sex business is a product of the new capitalism, made possible by deregulation and technological advances in the tele-communications industry, comparing it to the call centre suggests its working practices and relations are in some respects more traditional than 'new', and that this is not irrelevant to workers' perceptions of their jobs.

Conclusion

The call centre regime is of particular interest because it represents an unusually thoroughgoing attempt to regulate many aspects of talk – indeed, to 'Taylorize' it, as if it were a kind of automated production process. The regime exemplifies to a very high degree the four rationaliz-ing characteristics Ritzer (1996) associates with 'McDonaldization' (which he views as a continuation of the Taylorist project). Not only is talk regu-lated to maximize efficiency and predictability, as is the case in many other workplaces, more unusually it is also regulated to maximize 'calcu-lability' (that is, the regime cares about *quantity* of output as measured by number and duration of calls handled) and it is also subject to control using hi-tech apparatus.

This rationalizing approach is however in conflict with one of the over-arching generalizations produced by conversation analysis: that talk is a 'locally managed' phenomenon. It has rules and procedures, but partici-pants apply their knowledge of these to shape interaction as they go along. Turn-allocation, for instance, is not predetermined at the outset ('OK, first you talk, then I'll talk, then X can have a turn') but negotiated at each potential transition point. In the call centre regime, by contrast, attempts are made to manage talk 'globally': to stipulate in advance how long an interaction will last, what moves it will consist of and what the outcome will be. As Drew and Heritage (1992) observe, some degree of global shaping is a feature of many kinds of institutional talk, but in call centres it is taken to such an extreme, it is hardly surprising that problems arise from it.

The conditions of the call centre impose particular pressures and restrictions on spoken interaction; operators negotiate these in various ways, but most still report some degree of boredom, frustration and/or stress. It remains to be seen whether the increasing incidence of stress-related illness and the continuing problem of high staff turnover will force companies to address the negative aspects of call centre work in a more concerted manner. It also remains to be seen whether future technological developments (improvements in speech recognition technology and an increase in the volume of business done via new media such as electronic mail rather than by phone) will reduce the number of people who spend their working lives reciting scripts in smiley voice into telephone headsets. Meanwhile, it is difficult not to see the 'communication factory' as a deskilling and disempowering place to work.

5

SCHOOLING SPOKEN DISCOURSE

Young people face an increasingly complex world where many old certainties have disappeared. The effects of these developments are very quickly felt in schools. They are places which often seem to bring together and focus the challenges posed by economic and social change. But the ability of schools to cope with the impact of these changes beyond their boundaries is in question
– Opening Minds: Education for the 21st Century,
Royal Society of Arts, 1999.

Experience shows that communication skills can be taught...all children benefit from learning skills which will make them better friends, better employees, better life-partners and better human beings
– Communication: A Key Skill for Education, *BT Forum, 1998.*

In the late 1980s an oral communication element was introduced into the English GCSE (General Certificate of Secondary Education) examinations that are taken by thousands of 16-year-olds in Britain every year. This innovation was welcomed on the grounds that, as Jenny Cheshire and Nancy Jenkins put it, 'it lends respectability to talk' (1991: 31). Implicit in that comment is an acknowledgement of the marginal position spoken language has occupied in the modern curriculum: the 'three Rs' that in popular wisdom constitute the educational basics include reading and writing, but not rhetoric. Today, however, talk is back on the educational agenda. In this chapter I discuss the reasons for its re-emergence and examine some of the new forms in which it is re-emerging.

One of the issues to be explored here is the relationship between the new 'respectability' of talk in various educational regimes and the demands of the new capitalism for workers equipped with 'communication skills'. As I noted in Chapter 1, oral communication ranks high among the 'key' or 'core' skills that are held to be indispensable for success in the present and future labour market. Today's increasing enthusiasm for schooling spoken discourse is part of a more general trend towards foregrounding those skills in education, a point I will discuss in more detail below. But while that trend is driven partly by perceptions of what makes people employable in current economic conditions, it would be inaccurate to portray the teaching of communication skills in educational institutions as a purely vocational exercise. Preparing students for employment is only one of the functions of education; to quote a report produced by the Royal Society of Arts (RSA) on 'Education for the 21st Century', 'Schooling must be concerned with the broad development of young people into well-adjusted, happy and contributing members of civil society' (Bayliss, 1999: 7). The educational value claimed for communication skills lies not only in their relevance to students' job prospects, but also, as we will see, in the contribution they are thought to make to students' personal, social and – for some commentators – moral development.

Later on I will consider the role of 'communication' in preparing young people for work and for life. I will begin, though, by placing what I referred to above as the 're-emergence' of talk in the context of recent educational history.

From 'oracy' to 'key skills'

The rehabilitation of spoken language as a 'respectable' object of educational interest began well before the flowering of enterprise culture, and was motivated originally by quite different concerns. In Britain, the importance of talk in the classroom began to be discussed seriously in the 1960s under the heading of *oracy*, a term coined by Andrew Wilkinson in 1965 on the model of *literacy*.[1] Just as what educators mean by 'literacy' goes beyond the minimal definition of it as the ability to decode written/ printed text, 'oracy' is more than simply the ability to speak and understand one or more languages. It implies the ability to speak effectively in a variety of settings and for a range of purposes, using talk as a means to solve problems and manipulate complex ideas.

The crucial claim made for oracy (perhaps most influentially by James Britton (1970), one of a number of educationists who were interested in the ideas of Vygotsky) was that talking in particular ways helped children to learn more effectively. Developing students' spoken language skills and encouraging the use of those skills in the classroom would enhance learning across the curriculum. At first this argument had 'only a limited effect on classroom practice' (Keiner, 1992: 248). Over time, however, professional support for it became an important factor leading to the introduction of spoken language assessment into public examinations and the incorporation of speaking and listening into the national curriculum for England and Wales alongside reading and writing.

One of the key documents of the national currriculum, the 1988 Kingman Report which set out the framework for the teaching of the English language, states that

In addition to encouraging the development of speech for communication, teachers need to encourage talk which can be exploratory, tentative, used for thinking through problems, for discussing assigned tasks and for clarifying thought: talk is not merely social and communicative, it is also a tool for learning. (DES, 1988: 43)

This passage of the report restates the key argument for oracy – that talk is 'a tool for learning' – and on that basis it makes a distinction between the kind of talk that is most valuable in the classroom ('exploratory, tentative...for clarifying thought') and 'speech for communication' or 'talk [that] is merely...communicative'. What is interesting here is that 'communication' is given no special value: it is equated with the performance of mundane linguistic tasks, like chatting with peers or exchanging practical information, and treated as distinct from the more serious business of learning through talk. This is something that has changed since the late 1980s. Today, while the view that spoken language is significant for both educational and personal development remains part of official orthodoxy, it has come to be framed within a different set of assumptions and expressed in a different language: the language of 'key', 'core' or 'transferable' *skills*. What 'lends respectability to talk' in current educational discourse is its status as a key skill – and the name of that skill is 'communication'.

Before turning specifically to the place of communication in the galaxy of skills, it is worth pausing for a moment to consider the more general ascendancy of skills in today's educational thinking. Norman Fairclough has suggested that this is a reflex of enterprise culture: in the age of enterprise, he observes, 'there is a general shift towards seeing knowledge operationally, in terms of competence...and towards seeing education as training in skills' (1995: 239). What people *know* when they leave school, college or university is seen as less important than what they can *do*. Whereas the traditional approach to designing a curriculum began with content – the body of knowledge to be transmitted in a course or programme of study – the 'enterprising' approach begins by specifying outcomes, the skills or 'competences' a student should be able to demonstrate at the end of the course.[2] In its 'Education for the 21st Century' report which I mentioned above, the RSA went so far as to recommend that the traditional school curriculum (described by one expert the report quotes as 'the study of an arbitrary collection of predominantly academic subjects') should be abandoned altogether. What the RSA proposed instead was a 'competence-led curriculum' focusing on five core areas: learning, citizenship, relating to people, managing situations and managing information (Bayliss, 1999). This, to be sure, is an unusually radical proposal; if it were implemented it would be revolutionary. But regimes of teaching and assessment already exist which are organized around skills and competences, and many new proposals are being designed on similar lines.[3]

Why has this shift occurred, and how significant is it? Education has always aimed to develop students' skills as well as to increase the sum of their knowledge; it might well be asked if there is anything particularly novel in what is happening now. My own answer would be that there is, but the novelty lies less in the concern with skills *per se* than in the extent to which the skills-training element of the curriculum is now being *formalized*. Instead of treating skills as the incidental by-products of education (supposing that students will develop their writing skills, say, in the course of acquiring knowledge about English literature or history), educators are now urged to teach (and test) skills in their own right, and to value them for their own sake; even, as in the RSA proposal, to design the whole curriculum around them.

To some extent the shift to skills reflects new educational philosophies emerging in the wake of the 'information revolution'. When knowledge changes so rapidly and becomes obsolete so quickly, it no longer makes sense, the argument runs, to conceive of education as the transmission of a fixed body of received wisdom. But the shift also reflects anxieties about whether education is preparing young people adequately for the challenges of the new global economy. As we saw in Chapter 1, when employers are asked what they look for in school leavers or university graduates, they repeatedly stress that specialized academic knowledge is not important to them. New economic conditions require 'flexible' workers, equipped with generic skills which can be applied to all kinds of tasks. The pressure is on educators to respond to this demand.

Again, one might point out that there is little novelty in the mere fact of educational institutions designing their curricula with an eye to changing economic realities – preparing people for the labour market has always been a function of the education system. What is striking, however, is the *scale* of the changes now being advocated. Just as business organizations are told by management consultants and 'gurus' that to survive in new conditions they must break radically with the past, so schools and colleges are now hearing the same message from employers and politicians. The ability of the education system to respond to economic change is seen as crucial for the future competitiveness, not just of individual companies but of whole nations. In the words of the RSA report (which was sponsored by Andersen Consulting), the new global order is 'one in which the countries with strongest educational base and the highest levels of skill will win the economic prizes' (Bayliss, 1999: 2).

Competition for economic prizes occurs not only between countries or companies, but also between individuals. Education is significant at this level too, since it is through education that individuals acquire what the social theorist Pierre Bourdieu (1991) calls 'cultural capital' in the form of knowledge, skills and qualifications. Cultural capital can be converted to other kinds of capital within a given 'market': thus élite educational qualifications give the holder access to positions that produce high levels of income (economic capital) and/or high social status (symbolic capital). Bourdieu also talks specifically about *linguistic* capital, meaning the acquired ability to speak and write in particular ways, which are more or less valued in particular markets. Mastery of a standard language, for instance, is both a qualification for many kinds of work and a marker of social prestige.

In the conditions of enterprise culture, it might be suggested that 'skills' in general represent an increasingly important form of cultural capital, while 'communication skills' represent a new, or at least newly salient, kind of linguistic capital. As we saw in Chapter 2, the ability to 'communicate' has been progressively distinguished from the ability to speak or write 'correctly'. 'Communicating' implies a particular way of relating to others using spoken discourse: this is not the same thing as speaking a standard language, but if surveys of employers are to be believed, it now has a market value in its own right.[4] There is an obvious parallel with the standard language case as discussed by Bourdieu, insofar as the possession of communication skills gives access to kinds of work from which people who lack those skills are excluded.

It is evident however that the market for communication skills is a socially differentiated one. The same criterion – 'good communication skills' – may appear in job advertisements addressed to both senior executives and hospital cleaners, but these two occupational classes are not expected to deploy the same verbal abilities for the same purposes, nor can they expect to earn the same economic and symbolic rewards. As educational institutions take more responsibility for developing (and measuring, through the examination and qualification system) the communication skills of young people, the question arises of what part classroom attitudes and practices might play in the process of social differentiation. Does the teaching of communication skills in educational settings constitute different kinds of students (for example lower and higher status ones, or male and female ones) as different kinds of communicators, who start off with differing aptitudes, are destined for different social positions, and need therefore to develop different skills?

At this point I want to turn to a more detailed examination of some educational initiatives concerned with communication. Though I am interested in the relationship between education and the workplace, I have chosen *not* to look at those cases where that relationship is most straightforward – that is, at vocational courses (like Britain's NVQs, mentioned briefly in Chapter 1), where communication skills are defined with reference to the demands of a specific occupation. Such courses are in many respects similar to the kinds of workplace training I considered in Chapters 3 and 4; I have therefore preferred to focus here on other and perhaps less obvious instances. I have also selected examples that enable me to explore issues that bear less directly (though they do bear indirectly) on the relationship of education to enterprise culture. I will consider, for example, the way communication is treated in some programmes as a 'life skill' and a vehicle for teaching values to young people. I will also return to the suggestion made above – that education plays a part in distributing the cultural/linguistic capital communication skills represent, and that it does so in ways that reflect and reproduce social differences. I will start by examining how and why communication has recently begun to figure more prominently in the curriculum of some élite educational institutions.

The importance of being articulate: cleaning up campus 'mallspeak'

In January 1999 a new initiative in several institutions in the north-eastern United States, including Mount Holyoke, Smith College and the Massachusetts Institute of Technology, was featured in the *Boston Globe* under the heading 'Talk is, like, you know, cheapened: colleges introduce classes to clean up campus "mallspeak"' (Zernike, 1999). Increasingly concerned about students' ability to express themselves well in speech, the institutions in question had introduced more stringent speaking requirements across the curriculum. Students were obliged to make more oral presentations in class, and they were also encouraged to seek guidance in 'speaking centers' – designed on the model of the 'writing centers' that are common on US campuses – where mentors and tutors would critique their spoken performance. What makes this development noteworthy is that it appears to depart from a longstanding tradition whereby the most élite forms of education were also the most dominated by the *written* word, with students' ability to express themselves orally being largely taken for granted. If prestigious institutions like MIT and Mount Holyoke are now changing tack, it appears to be largely because of anxiety about employability in an increasingly competitive market, where communication skills are considered essential to graduates' job prospects. According to the *Globe*:

> For years they [élite colleges and universities] disdained it [teaching spoken language] as too vocational...But then alumni began reporting back their horror at the way graduates spoke at job interviews, or remarking how unprepared they felt to express themselves in the working world. ...Prestigious degrees won't do students much good if they can't project professionalism and poise in a job interview...At several colleges, the new emphasis on speaking came out of discussions on how to redefine the curriculum around 'essential skills'. At Mount Holyoke and MIT, formal alumni surveys cited a demand for students with better speaking skills. (Zernike, 1999)

Interestingly, however, the colleges' concern about the way their students speak takes a form that has obvious connections with more traditional kinds of verbal hygiene – specifically, with the kind of élitist prescriptivism that runs through what Milroy and Milroy (1991) call the 'complaint tradition'. The literature of linguistic complaint in/about English began in the late medieval period and continues to the present day. Its thesis is that language is in decline, and its recurring themes include dialect variation, bad grammar, ugly 'nasal' accents, 'sloppy' pronunciation, the misuse of words, and the inability of people today to spell or punctuate correctly. The article 'Talk is, like, you know, cheapened' clearly belongs to this tradition; its point could be summarized as 'standards have fallen so much that even our most distinguished institutions of higher learning are having to teach their students how to talk properly'. But the immediate cause for complaint is less traditional. 'Mallspeak' has nothing to do with spelling and punctuation, it is not a matter of grammar or pronunciation, nor is it a class or ethnic dialect: rather it is a phenomenon of spoken discourse. The items that attract criticism are specific to speech, and found mainly in interactive speech. Two are cited in the title of the piece: *you know* and *like* used as discourse markers.[5] Also in the discourse marker category is *I mean*, which is mentioned later on. *Like* (along with *goes*) comes in for further criticism in another function, namely as a quotative introducing reported speech ('and she's like, what were you thinking?'). The expression *whatever* (meaning something like, 'I know what you're saying but I don't agree/don't care') is also cited as a recurring irritant, as is the high rising terminal intonation pattern, which is presumably what is meant by a reference to 'declaratives [that] often end in a question mark'.

The main criticism made of the features defining mallspeak is not that they are 'incorrect' in the manner of grammatical solecisms, but that they are 'inarticulate'. The president of Smith College is quoted in the *Globe* saying that mallspeak is 'minimalist, it's reductionist, it's repetitive, it's imprecise, it's inarticulate, it's vernacular…it drives me crazy'. A sophomore at Mount Holyoke offers one explanation for the fall into inarticulacy: 'School has become less formal over the years, so people don't feel as pressured to be articulate as they were in the olden days'. MIT Professor Steven Pinker ascribes the problem to the recent spread of egalitarian attitudes, explaining: 'there is a certain cult of inarticulateness. … What the "likes" and "you knows" do is make the speaker sound less emphatic and less dominant. They both bring you down to the same level as everyone else'.

In sociolinguistic terms, the second part of Pinker's explanation is accurate: *like* and *y'know* can function as hedges (though they have other functions too – see note 5). Hedges are expressions that reduce the force of an utterance, conveying lack of certainty or commitment. Hedging is often used for reasons to do with face, and as Pinker notes, one face-related consideration is the need to appear 'at the same level as everyone else'. But it is not clear what that has to do with 'a cult of inarticulateness'. If *like* is not redundant or meaningless, but functional, if it tells the hearer something that would not otherwise be apparent, why would using it be a mark of *inarticulacy*, a term that suggests a lack of expressiveness and precision?

The most likely answer takes us back to the point that writing rather than speech has dominated the language attitudes and practices of élite educational institutions. The definition of 'articulate' speech that seems to be operative for those quoted in the *Globe* article (and indeed for its author) is essentially 'speech that resembles writing': speech with the spoken language features, the pauses and 'fillers', edited out. The characterization of high rising terminals as 'declaratives [that] end in a question mark' shows just how far the bias to writing extends. (Elsewhere, the article refers to students 'replac[ing] commas with "you knows"'.) Speech, to state the obvious, does not have punctuation marks; punctuation marks in writing are necessitated by the unavailability of prosodic and paralinguistic devices for structuring information or conveying attitudes to propositions. Conceptualizing a rising intonation contour as a spoken representation of a question mark and *y'know* as a 'replacement' for a comma is possible only in a framework where written language is taken as the prototype for language itself. Though any reasonable person would immediately concede that speech comes before writing, both in the history of humankind and in the life-history of individual humans, most literate, educated people find it extremely difficult to think about language without using the written form as a reference point. But the result of judging speech on the same criteria that are applied to writing (an activity whose product teachers are more used to evaluating against well-established standards) is a rather trivial kind of verbal hygiene. Eliminating stigmatized 'mallspeak' features from students' speech is like correcting misplaced apostrophes in their writing – it concentrates on something symbolically significant but linguistically superficial.[6] In the terms I introduced in Chapter 3, this is 'styling' the students rather than 'skilling' them.

The spoken language instruction offered at places like MIT, Mount Holyoke and Smith is reminiscent in other ways of the service sector styling practices I examined in Chapters 3 and 4. For example, the college speaking centers make use of technology in a way that recalls the practice of 'counselling' in call centres. Like call centre operators and their supervisors, students and their tutors are able systematically to critique small details of performance by recording speech on tape, which they then play back repeatedly. In both cases, technology makes possible a kind of attention to the minutiae of speech that was not feasible in the 'olden days'.

This raises a point of more general significance. Linguists who are interested in the structure of spoken discourse have called attention to the *descriptive* advances made possible by technological innovations – first audio and video recording, then more recently large on-line corpora of spontaneous speech data (see for instance Cheshire, 1999). It is seldom pointed out, however, that the same innovations have prescriptive applications too. Just as technology provides more powerful tools for describing 'normal' linguistic behaviour, so it offers new possibilities for regulating that behaviour – and potentially, therefore, for changing what is 'normal' in certain contexts.

Whatever the similarities between the two cases, it is clear that the regulation of spoken discourse among élite college students differs from the styling of service employees in terms of its social meaning. What is ultimately at issue in the case of the college students is the association of 'articulacy' in speech with authority, status and power in the world. If one element in the anxiety about students' speech is concern about employability (*like* and *whatever* are credited with the same malign power as *aint* or multiple negation to scupper a candidate's chances at a job interview) another element is concern about the oratorical skills of future leaders. West Virginia Senator Robert Byrd is quoted in the *Globe* worrying that if Lincoln had been born in 1980 the Gettysburg address would have started: 'Four score and, like, seven years ago, you know, our forefathers, uh, brought forth, you know...'. A director of one of the college programmes says that while high oratory is not needed on every occasion, it should be in students' repertoires. Whereas customer service regimes use communication training to inculcate subservience, prescribing an informal, synthetically personalized style, the élite colleges use communication training to prepare their students for power by encouraging more formal and impersonal – indeed, 'rhetorical' – ways of talking. The communication skills acquired by students in élite colleges furnish a kind of cultural capital that can be converted not only to economic capital in the form of a high-paying job, but also to symbolic capital, a position of authority and influence in society. In my next example, the relationship between communication and power is rather different.

'Basic lessons for living': communication as a life skill

At the beginning of this chapter I quoted, once again, the BT Forum report *Communication: A Key Skill for Education*, which suggests that 'all children benefit from learning skills that make them better friends, better life-partners, better employees and better human beings' (Phillips, 1998: 7). The part of the report from which the quotation comes discusses an approach to communication that is now widely advocated in the UK and the US, albeit as yet less widely put into practice.[7] In this approach, communication is treated as a 'life skill', an aspect of 'social competence' that is relevant not just to young people's learning and their future employment prospects, but to their general ability to function both inside and outside the school. Where it has been taken up in schools, the life skills approach to talk tends to find its home in the non-academic areas of the curriculum, such as those dealing with personal, social, health and citizenship issues. Sometimes the goal is to address social problems like bullying and violence, substance abuse, teen pregnancy and sexually transmitted diseases. Improving young people's communication skills is thought to give them resources for resisting peer pressure and dealing with problems in more 'constructive' ways. In the US particularly, programmes with an overt 'prevention' agenda have proliferated in recent years (though doubts have begun to be expressed about their effectiveness, as I noted in Chapter 2).

The life skills approach has much in common with the quasi-therapeutic uses of communication training to be discussed in Chapter 6, and it might be asked whether there is any specifically educational rationale for it. One answer is given in the BT Forum report, where Angela Phillips links communication skills with educational achievement in the following way:

> At the bottom end of the educational pyramid are some 10–20% of children whose communication skills are so poor that they are virtually unable to access learning at all. Some are so withdrawn that they barely engage with their lessons and have difficulty making friends, others are so consumed with anger that they act up and spend most of their lessons outside the classroom, or outside the school altogether. …[W]ithout special help, [disruptive children's] inability to understand and articulate their feelings adequately or to empathize and to listen to others is liable to create problems for all. (Phillips, 1998: 7)

Communication is figured here as a kind of remedial subject for those at the 'bottom end of the educational pyramid'. Without communication skills, Phillips suggests, such children are unable to learn anything in school at all, and by implication they will enter the labour market severely lacking in cultural capital. Although this is an argument for the *educational* importance of communication skills, it will be evident that it differs markedly, not only from the arguments used to justify speech requirements in élite colleges, but also from the 'oracy' argument presented in, for example, the Kingman Report. The oracy model accords talk primarily intellectual functions ('thinking through problems, discussing assigned tasks and clarifying thought'), whereas in the life skills model the emphasis is more on self-discipline – the target skills include listening, concentrating, controlling anger and resisting the impulse to act in aggressive or antisocial ways.

Some arguments for the life skills approach are more explicit about its social agenda. The BT Forum report quotes a comment made by Marianne Talbot of the (UK) National Forum for Values in Education and the Community[8]: 'We need young people to be truly educated, not just to read and write but to be trustworthy and reliable. Communication is vital to teaching values and values must be at the heart of the curriculum' (Phillips, 1998: 7). This statement is made about 'young people' in general, but not all commentators on the subject are so inclusive. In his bestselling popular psychology book *Emotional Intelligence*, for instance, Daniel Goleman describes a number of 'social competence' or 'emotional literacy' programmes operating in schools in the US, and gives the following rationale for them:

> As family life no longer offers growing numbers of children a sure footing in life, schools are left as the one place communities can turn to for correctives to children's deficiencies in emotional and social competence. …[S]ince virtually every child goes to school…it offers a place to reach children with basic lessons for living that they may never get otherwise. Emotional literacy implies an expanded mandate for schools, taking up the slack for failing families in socializing children. (1995: 279)

Many of the 'basic lessons for living' that Goleman wants schools to teach turn out to be lessons in effective communication. Much of what is taught in the school 'social competence' or 'emotional literacy' programmes described in *Emotional Intelligence* echoes the content of the communication skills training materials for adults I reviewed in Chapter 2. For instance, the 'Self Science Curriculum' used at the Nueva Learning Center in California includes the following components (Goleman, 1995: 303):

- *Communications:* talking about feelings effectively; becoming a good listener and question-asker; distinguishing between what someone does or says and your own reactions or judgements about it; sending 'I' messages instead of blame.
- *Assertiveness:* stating your concerns and feelings without anger or passivity.
- *Group dynamics:* co-operation; knowing when and how to lead, when to follow.
- *Conflict resolution:* how to fight fair with other kids, with parents, with teachers; the win/win model for negotiating compromise.

Although only one of these components is actually labelled 'communication', all of them are clearly about particular ways of talking. The recommendations are highly reminiscent of texts aimed at an adult professional audience, such as Sandy McMillan's *How To Be A Better… Communicator* (1996). One specific point of resemblance is that 'assertiveness', a label which, again, is explicitly attached to only one item, is implicit in three out of the four. 'Sending "I" messages instead of blame' is a classic assertive strategy, while standard models for negotiation and conflict resolution usually suggest that a positive outcome depends on the parties adopting an assertive, rather than aggressive or passive, stance.

Another document reproduced by Goleman (1995: 301) is a list of the 'active ingredients of [effective] prevention programs' taken from the report of a consortium that evaluated a number of social competence initiatives in schools over a five-year period. 'Prevention' here refers to the agenda of most programmes, which was to prevent alcohol and drug abuse; but the evaluators recommended that the same 'key skills' should be covered in programmes of all kinds. Among their key skills are the following, relating to communication:

- Nonverbal – communicating through eye contact, facial expressiveness, tone of voice, gestures and so on.
- Verbal – making clear requests, responding effectively to criticism, resisting negative influences, listening to others, helping others, participating in positive peer groups.

Again, a number of features will seem familiar here from the discussion of workplace communication training in earlier chapters. The placing of nonverbal above verbal communication skills could conceivably be arbitrary, but it certainly recalls the order of priorities in the materials I discussed in Chapter 2, with their claim that nonverbal signals account for more than half of any message. The first four items in the verbal category are, once again, rather clearly related to the assertiveness paradigm (they could be paraphrased as make requests directly, don't be defensive, just say no, listen actively).

Some of the workplace and self-study materials I examined in Chapter 2 placed emphasis on developing a vocabulary of emotion words. This preoccupation is carried to remarkable lengths by school programmes in 'emotional literacy'. One of the 'active ingredients of prevention programs' listed in the document I quoted earlier is 'identifying and labeling feelings' (Goleman, 1995: 301); the Self Science Curriculum has as its first component 'observing yourself and recognizing your feelings; building a vocabulary for feelings' (1995: 303). Goleman gives an account of a fifth-grade social competence class in an inner city school in New Haven. The children have been asked to bring in a picture of a person's face from a magazine and name the emotion the face displays. The teacher makes a list of the emotion words students offer, including *sad, happy, worried, excited, frustrated, aggravated*. She goes on to distribute a worksheet depicting faces that express the six 'basic' emotions (happy, sad, angry, surprised, afraid, disgusted). What makes this an exercise in something more than just vocabulary building is the belief that people who behave antisocially often do so for one or both of two reasons: first, they are impulsive (they do not stop to think what they are feeling and why, but just act as nameless emotions surge up in them); second, they misread others' behaviour and facial expressions as hostile and threatening and retaliate against non-existent provocations.

Much earlier in the book, Goleman explains there is a clinical condition called *alexithymia*, 'not having words for feelings', which is thought to result from a 'disconnection between the limbic system [part of the brain that controls emotional reactions] and the neo-cortex [where the brain's language centres are]' (1995: 50). Alexithymics do not seem to know what they feel. 'Indeed', says Goleman, 'they seem to lack feelings altogether, although this may actually be because of their inability to express emotion rather than from an absence of emotion altogether' (1995: 51). This formulation is difficult to interpret (do alexithymics suffer from 'an absence of emotion altogether' or just an inability to communicate what they are feeling? If they suffer from both problems, does the first arise from the second or the second from the first?). It also glosses over some complicated questions familiar to philosophers and to ethnographers who study cultural variation in the expression of emotion.

A concrete example may help to make these issues clearer. In her book *The Trouble With Boys*, Angela Phillips (1994: 63) cites a study in which juvenile offenders detained in penal institutions were asked to describe how they felt. While both sexes reported a similar range of symptoms typically associated with depression (lack of motivation, disrupted sleep, feeling isolated), only the young women said they were 'depressed'; the young men said they were 'bored'. Phillips treats this as evidence of the lack of emotional self-awareness our culture imposes on males, and as an illustration of the damage it does (it is suggested that the young men's 'lack of a language' prevented them from alerting anyone to their real state of mind, thus increasing the risk they would attempt suicide). She assumes that the young men and the young women were actually experiencing the same thing, and that this would be accurately described as 'depression' rather than 'boredom' – in other words, when the young men reported their feelings they were making an error of fact. But there are other possibilities. It is possible that each sex might actually feel something different. It is possible that young men know what depression is as well as young women do, but think saying you are 'depressed' is incompatible with proper masculinity (in which case there may be a problem, but it is not a lack of either self-awareness or vocabulary).

Some linguists, psychologists and ethnographers have argued that emotions themselves are culturally and linguistically constructed (see, for instance, Harré, 1986; Lutz and Abu-Lughod, 1990). According to this argument, we all start off 'alexithymic': our pre-linguistic experience is of varying physiological states, and it is through contextualized learning, crucially including the acquisition of our culture's ways of speaking, that we learn that what we are feeling should be labelled 'anger' or 'depression'. In this account, as in the emotional literacy paradigm, words are all-important. The difference is, however, that Daniel Goleman and the authorities he cites regard emotions as a kind of universal code: emotional literacy consists in being able to name them *correctly*. In the constructivist approach, by contrast, feelings are brought into being *as feelings* (as opposed to 'raw' bodily events) by speaking and acting in particular, culturally ratified ways.

Emotion words are needed for making private experiences publicly accessible, but the question remains whether the labelling just verbalizes some objectively existing inner reality or whether it *constructs* an individual's experience in line with cultural norms of intelligibility and appropriateness. If one inclines to the latter view, then training in how to talk about one's feelings becomes, arguably, less a 'neutral' exercise in facilitating self-expression and more a matter of telling children how it is normal, acceptable or desirable for them to feel in various circumstances – which is to say, constructing for children a particular kind of self. Of course, this is something that is done in some fashion by socializing agents in any culture. To say it should not be done is equivalent to saying that children should not be socialized. But acknowledging that children need to be socialized to become competent members of their culture does not rule out critical examination of the particular values that define 'social competence' in a given programme of instruction. What and whose values are they?

Daniel Goleman himself offers an answer to the 'what' question:

> There is an old-fashioned world for the body of skills that emotional intelligence represents: *character*. ...The bedrock of character is self-discipline; the virtuous life...is based on self-control. A related keystone of character is being able to motivate and guide oneself, whether in doing homework, finishing a job, or getting up in the morning. ...[T]he ability to defer gratification and to control and channel one's urges to act is a basic emotional skill, one that in a former day was called will. (Goleman, 1995: 285)

As for the 'whose' question: although Goleman cites a range of Western thinkers from Aristotle to Amitai Etzioni in support of his description of 'character', it is surely not accidental that the virtues he emphasizes first – self-discipline, self-control, self-motivation – are ones that figure prominently in the rhetoric of enterprise culture.[9] Along with openness to risk and change, self-government (discipline, control) and self-motivation are the defining qualities of the enterprising individual.

Yet again I should point out here that there is nothing new in schools setting out to inculcate particular social dispositions and moral values in their students: that, as much as transmitting knowledge, has always been a function of education. What is more interesting about the kinds of initiatives I have been discussing in this section, however, is that they make what Anthony Giddens (1991) calls 'the reflexive project of the self' an explicit part of the remit of the school. 'Emotional literacy' programmes, in particular, involve the codification and systematic teaching of techniques (and language) for being self-reflexive: for understanding one's feelings and behaviour through introspection, disclosing feelings verbally to others and responding appropriately to others' disclosure of what they feel. Wanting children to develop these skills may not be new, but setting aside classroom time for formal instruction in them is.

Which children are felt to be most in need of this kind of instruction? Proponents of teaching communication as a life skill often assert that 'all children benefit', but when they come to discuss the benefits in more detail, the emphasis seems to fall sooner rather than later on children with social problems. Our attention is directed to the need to improve the communication skills of children whose educational attainment is low, whose behaviour at school is disruptive, whose families are 'failing', and who are seen to be at risk of falling into crime or drug abuse or premature sexual activity. At the same time, commentators tend to downplay the fact that the children who are talked about in these terms, and who are targeted in many social prevention programmes, are not randomly distributed across classes, races and ethnic groups. Daniel Goleman carefully does not specify a social location for 'failing families'; Angela Phillips talks about an 'educational pyramid' rather than a socio-economic hierarchy, and she does not point out that poor and Black children are overrepresented among the 'disruptive' pupils who 'spend most of their lessons outside the classroom'. To raise these issues would also be to raise the possibility that some children's problems have more to do with poverty and prejudice (including, some would argue, racism within the school system itself) than with deficiencies in their communication skills. If so, programmes of instruction in 'social competence' and 'emotional literacy' offer, at best, only a fraction of what those children need.

There is, however, one social difference that apparently does not need to be downplayed in discussions of this topic. Angela Phillips's silence about the race and class distribution of pupils who are excluded from school because of disruptive behaviour is in striking contrast with her loquacity about their gender. She notes that 80% of them are boys, juxtaposing this statistic with another: 'at [age] 11 boys are, on average, some nine months behind girls in the development of oracy' (1998: 7). For good measure she adds one of the findings of BT's National Communication Survey, conducted in 1996 with a sample of almost a thousand people: males aged between 16 and 30 'considered communication to be substantially less important' than their female peers. She could equally have cited the findings of a research report on 'effective communication in the teenage years', according to which adolescent boys are generally less positive than girls about communication (Catan, Dennison and Coleman, 1996: 6). Whenever communication is discussed from an educational standpoint, whether in relation to academic, vocational or social considerations, the difference between boys and girls is likely to crop up as a significant theme and an explicit cause for concern.

Boys and girls

The perception that girls and women are 'better' communicators than boys and men is not confined to the educational domain. We have already seen how it is used to justify sex discrimination in customer service-oriented workplaces like call centres, and in Chapter 6 we will see that it is also treated as common sense in advice on communication within personal relationships. I have chosen to focus on it in this chapter as a topic in its own right, however, because it is above all in relation to education, and especially to schooling, that the alleged inferiority of male communication skills has become a salient public issue.

In fact, the issue is not just communication skills: communication is one strand in a more complex discourse about 'underachievement'. During the last few years of the 1990s, boys' educational underachievement became a topic for extensive, anguished discussion among education professionals and in the media in many parts of the English-speaking world, including Australia, Britain, the Caribbean and the USA. In 1996 Her Majesty's Chief Inspector of Schools for England and Wales designated underachieving boys as one of the most significant problems facing the British education system. In 1997 educationalist Ted Wragg went further, writing in the *Times Educational Supplement* that 'as we enter the next millennium it is the under-achievement of boys that has become one of the biggest challenges facing *society* today' (16 May, my italics). By 1998 the idea of male underachievement as a serious problem was established not only in educational circles but in public discourse more generally. An editorial in *The Independent* newspaper on 5 January, 1998, for example, summarized what was fast becoming the orthodox view:

> The male backlash is here, and it has nothing to do with Robert Bly discovering the wild man banging bongos in American forests. We are talking about boys. They cannot read, write their own names or speak properly. They are physically and socially clumsy. …As a result…they are outnumbered in the work force and left to their own criminal devices. (Marshall, 1998: 95)

Significantly, the first charge made against boys here is that they are *linguistically* deficient: 'they cannot read, write their own names or speak properly'. The second charge makes reference to their being 'socially clumsy': this too is at least partly an issue about the way they communicate, or fail to communicate, using language. The consequences mentioned by the writer include boys being 'outnumbered in the work force' and 'left to their own criminal devices'. These images recur in discussions of 'the trouble with boys'. A great deal of current anxiety about male inability to communicate seems to express symbolically the fear that certain groups of men (in particular, working-class men) will be doomed to perpetual unemployment in a service economy that disdains their traditional assets (physical strength and stamina) and instead demands communication skills they do not possess.[10] Impoverished and marginalized, these men will express their frustration and resentment in violent, disorderly and criminal behaviour.

While this scenario may be extreme, it is not unreasonable to suggest that the shift to a service economy affects the prospects of working-class boys more adversely than it affects those of either girls or middle-class boys. Pat Mahony (1998) reports, for instance, on a study in which schoolchildren were asked about their career aspirations and their attitudes to particular school subjects. The research found that white working-class boys aspired to do 'tough' manual jobs of the kind that are now scarce, or else they hoped – unrealistically given their academic records – to enter professions such as architecture and medicine. Not a single working-class boy in the sample either wanted or expected to be employed in the service sector. The concern this raises is that working-class boys lack any motivation to acquire the kinds of skills – crucially including communication skills – that make school leavers employable in the new economy. As Mahony comments (1998: 47): 'If such employment as is available for groups of young working-class people exists largely in the service industries, then it has to be recognized that these require high levels of expertise in the expressive aspects of customer service'.

That most girls, by the time they leave school, have developed this 'expertise' to a higher degree than most boys is suggested not only by anecdote and folklore, but arguably also by statistics on gender and educational achievement. Girls' examination results at 16 are now generally better than boys'[11] (this recent reversal of an earlier tendency for boys to outperform girls is a major factor in current anxieties about boys' underachievement) but the gender gap is greatest in subjects like English and modern foreign languages, which foreground language and communication. Specific concern has been expressed about boys' approach to spoken interaction in the classroom. A 1993 report on *Boys and English* issued by the Office for Standards in Education (Ofsted) noted that boys behaved differently from girls in group discussion: 'They were more likely to interrupt one another, to argue openly and to voice opinions strongly. They were also less likely to listen carefully to and build upon one another's contributions' (Ofsted, 1993: 16). The paragraph in which these observations are made concludes: '*It is particularly important for boys to develop a clearer understanding of the importance of sympathetic listening as a central feature of successful group and class discussion'* (Ofsted, 1993: 16, emphasis in original). Joan Swann (1998) suggests that these comments have their roots in the belief discussed earlier in this chapter, that oracy is a crucial tool for learning. But it is not difficult to relate Ofsted's concerns to the issue of employability: the picture the report paints of boys interrupting, arguing and not listening just confirms the suspicion that they lack 'expertise in the expressive aspects of customer service'. 'Sympathetic listening' is as much a central feature of, say, a call centre operator's job as it is of a successful group discussion at school. Pat Mahony poses the obvious question (1998: 49): 'Does the future lie in the reskilling (and "feminization"?) of working-class boys...?'

While education professionals grapple with the question of whether and how to 'reskill' boys for a changing economy, other professionals are busy pathologizing boys, ascribing their communication skills deficit to biological or organic causes. In a revealing essay titled 'Law-and-Order Science', Philomena Mariani (1995) explains that increasing numbers of American children – four fifths of them boys – are being diagnosed with and treated for conditions like 'attention deficit/hyperactivity disorder', 'oppositional defiant disorder' and 'conduct disorder'. A *New York Times* editorial cited by Mariani glosses these 'disruptive disorders' in plain English as 'aggression, rowdiness, restlessness, loud-mouthedness, rebelliousness'. The *Times* sees such behaviours as features of normal boyhood, but they are seen by many experts as harbingers of 'antisocial personality disorder'. Decisive intervention is called for to prevent the disruptive child from becoming an antisocial and possibly criminal adult.

The phenomenon of 'disruptive disorders' may not seem on the face of things to be related to the issue of gender and communication skills, but closer examination reveals significant connections. Whether an individual is 'disruptive' or 'antisocial' is often assessed clinically using criteria that are partly or wholly to do with communicative behaviour. Thus among the disruptive disorder symptoms listed in the *Diagnostic and Statistical Manual of Mental Disorders* (DSM, the 'bible' of psychiatric medicine in the US) we find 'inattention', 'callousness', 'impatience', 'arguing' and 'bossiness'. All of these may be manifested in specifically verbal/communicative behaviour, while some (such as 'arguing') are exclusively and by definition linguistic. Indeed, it is striking that (with the possible exception of 'callousness'), the combination of symptoms just listed looks remarkably like the boys' group discussion behaviour described in the Ofsted report. But whereas Ofsted assumes that this behaviour is learnt and can be unlearnt, many scientists and clinicians view disruptive disorders as organic and permanent, though potentially controllable with drugs.[12] According to Philomena Mariani (1995: 135–6), these disorders have been theorized as the result of neurological impairments sustained at birth, less serious than full-blown brain damage but still capable of causing behavioural problems. They are said to be more prevalent in males because the embryonic male brain, 'hardwired *in utero* by exposure to testosterone', is less flexible than its female counterpart, and more vulnerable therefore to injury.

The pathologizing approach described by Mariani can lead in two directions. On one hand it may demonize boys as tomorrow's criminals, and legitimate extreme measures taken to control them. On the other hand, it may promote the idea of boys as pitiable victims of their sex's inherent biological frailty. In 1998, for example, the *New York Times* marked 'Take Our Daughters To Work Day' (an annual event sponsored by women's organizations) with a front-page report headed 'After Girls Get the Attention, Focus Shifts to Boys' Woes' (Goldberg, 1998: A1). Psychotherapist Michael Gurian told the *Times*:

> Four boys are diagnosed as emotionally disturbed to every one girl...two boys are learning-disabled for every one girl. In grades, our boys now get worse grades than our girls. If we go to brain-attention disorders, there are six boys with attention deficit disorder to every one girl. If we go to teen deaths, there are two teen boys dying for every one girl.

The kinds of clinical statistics Gurian adduces here can also lead discussion in two directions. The *Times* article, though written in the manner of 'balanced' or 'objective' comment, seems to favour the view expressed by some of the sources it quotes, that boys are being overdiagnosed with various clinical conditions because society no longer has any tolerance for normal boyishness. Elsewhere, however, statistics like these are seen as offering support for a new wave of biological essentialism: the evidence for superior female verbal, social and communication skills is allegedly so compelling as to require explanation in terms of natural selection and the genetically determined sex differences that result from it.

Along these lines, a 1997 study using girls with Turner's syndrome as subjects concluded that 'social cognition' – which was measured by observing interactional behaviour, for instance whether subjects listened without interrupting, and whether they demonstrated empathy – is controlled by a gene on the paternally derived X chromosome (Skuse et al., 1997). Turner's syndrome girls have only one X chromosome, whereas females normally have two; subjects who had got the X from their father scored higher on social cognition measures than those who had got it from their mother. This might imply that males (who invariably inherit their X chromosome from their mother) are genetically less verbally and socially skilled than females. Evolutionary psychologists have speculated copiously on why such an arrangement would have advantaged our distant ancestors, suggesting for instance that natural selection favoured males whose advanced spatial skills made them more effective hunters, and females whose advanced communication skills made them more effective social network builders.[13]

Whether females really do have an innate advantage in terms of verbal skills is inevitably a complex and controversial question, and here I do not want to digress too far into the arguments *pro* and *con*. However, it is worth noting that in the opinion of some researchers, both expert and popular *belief* in female verbal superiority (whether innate or acquired) is much stronger than the evidence supporting that position. The most recent meta-analysis of the relevant scientific literature reviewed 165 papers reporting research carried out on almost one and a half million subjects in North America, and found male-female differences in verbal ability so slight as to be statistically negligible. The authors comment: 'A gender difference of one tenth of a standard deviation is scarcely one that deserves continued attention in theory, research or textbooks' (Hyde and Linn, 1988: 62). More recent neuroscientific work using PET and MRI techniques[14] has suggested that language is more strongly lateralized (to the left hemisphere) in the male than the female brain. This may have implications for the recovery of language functions by men and women following injury to the left hemisphere, but not necessarily for the level of verbal skill found in non-brain-damaged individuals: it appears that male and females may use different parts of the brain to do essentially the same things (Jaeger, 1998). It should also be pointed out that experimental work on the hypothesis of female verbal superiority bears only marginally if at all on anything that might be defined as a 'communication skill'. Typical experimental tasks are decontextualized and asocial (common ones include generating synonyms, defining words, retrieving names for pictured objects, and solving anagrams). It is questionable whether findings about these 'verbal skills' tell us much about the sort of behaviour people have in mind when they assert that women are 'better communicators'.

Be that as it may, the renewed emphasis on male-female communicational differences as reflexes of innate dispositions seems to be seeping back into educational discourse. Traces of it can be discerned, for example, in a recent document produced by the Qualifications and Curriculum Authority (QCA), which examines (yet again) boys' underachievement in English. Titled *Can Do Better* (QCA, 1998), the document is intended to help English teachers help boys by designing classroom activities to suit their aptitudes better. It suggests for example that since boys have a greater tendency than girls to go 'off-task', teachers should provide more 'structured' classroom tasks. Since boys have more difficulty in 'talking about their feelings' it is important that they be given other things to talk about. This contrasts with the 1993 Ofsted report, which recommended helping boys understand the importance of sympathetic listening. The QCA document seems more disposed to take differences between girls and boys as given – boys just *are* better with structure and less good with feelings. Teachers whose goal is to raise boys' achievement have to work with the grain of a masculinity that is assumed to be fixed and immutable.

In all this discourse about boys and their inadequate communication skills, two things seem to be rather consistently overlooked. One is the question of masculine social privilege. Everyone agrees that boys' verbal disadvantage does not manifest itself in silence: on the contrary, as the Ofsted report points out, they often dominate discussion, albeit in ways their teachers do not consider constructive. Some researchers have suggested that boys (and men) do not lack understanding of 'the importance of sympathetic listening' and supportive verbal behaviour more generally, so much as they lack the motivation to do it themselves when girls and women are there to do it for them (Jenkins and Cheshire, 1990; Cheshire and Jenkins, 1991). It has also been suggested that if boys believe they will not be disadvantaged in the labour market by their failure to acquire 'high levels of expertise in the expressive aspects of customer service', they may well be right. A study carried out in Australia found that boys' relatively poorer literacy skills did not prevent them doing better economically than higher-achieving girls once out of school. 'Young men designated as having low and very low literacy levels were still able to earn more than young women who had very high levels of literacy achievement' (Gilbert, 1998: 28). While I know of no similar studies examining the effect of oral communication skills – at this stage it would be more difficult to find clear data on achievement levels – I would venture to predict a similar pattern. In the real world, economic outcomes are not straightforwardly a function of skills and qualifications. Consider the call centre manager quoted in Chapter 4, who admitted to hiring women because they were women, and not because of any skill they had actually demonstrated during the selection process. This apparent reliance on general preconceptions rather than concrete evidence about individual performance supports Bethan Marshall's contention that 'it is not at all clear that employers are even looking for the best qualified candidates' (Marshall, 1998: 102).

The other point that is consistently overlooked is even more fundamental. It is that the phrase 'communication skills' names a cultural construct, not a natural phenomenon with an objective existence in the world. Whether some person, or group of people, has good, bad or indifferent communication skills is entirely dependent on what 'communication' is taken to be, and what is thought to constitute 'skill' in it. The statement that 'women and girls have better communication skills than men and boys' might be better rendered as something like: 'the ways of speaking this community currently values are more often observed among women and girls than among men and boys' – or better still, 'are symbolically associated with the behaviour of women and girls rather than that of men and boys'; for it is by no means obvious that all women possess the array of verbal skills that are routinely attributed to them, nor that all men lack those skills.

The attribution of superior communication skills to women and girls has a number of real-world consequences, some of which are not especially positive for women. Being seen to have good communication skills may mean, for example, that you get channelled into certain kinds of work, especially routine service jobs whose pay and conditions make them far from enviable. The idea of women as good communicators also naturalizes the domestic division of labour whereby wives and mothers, rather than husbands and fathers, are made responsible for maintaining household harmony through talk (Fishman, 1983). In short, the postulate of female verbal superiority is part of the apparatus that maintains the current, unequal arrangement between the sexes. Maybe that is a reason why it is reiterated so frequently and enthusiastically; in my own view it is certainly a reason for feminists to treat it with the same scepticism as its opposite, female inferiority.

Conclusion

Because the issue of gender difference is so overtly, indeed obsessively, foregrounded in recent discussions of 'communication skills', commentary on this subject can be used to illuminate the more general question of how and why certain ways of talking come to be *defined* as 'skilful'. The interesting question about gender is not 'who has better communication skills, women or men?', but rather 'how and why has it come to be the case that the ways of speaking we think of as "feminine" are also the ways of speaking to which we accord the special value signalled by the juxtaposition of the words *communication* and *skill*?'

That this *has* come to be the case seems to me undeniable. Despite the efforts of people like Deborah Tannen (1991; 1995) to persuade us that women and men are communicationally 'different but equal', I suspect that most readers of the Ofsted report quoted above would find it natural to conclude that the boys who 'argue openly and voice opinions strongly' are less 'skilled' communicators than the girls who 'listen carefully and build upon one another's contributions'. That evaluation is not made overtly in the report, but it is suggested by the phrasing of the comparison: imagine how differently we might read the relevant passage if the writer had said that 'girls were less likely to assert themselves in talk or show commitment to their own opinions'. Fifteen or twenty years ago the author of a similar report might well have characterized the same observed differences between boys and girls in exactly those terms.

Yesterday's orthodoxy was that girls and women had 'communication problems', notably insecurity and lack of assertiveness.

Throughout this book, by contrast, the evidence has been accumulating that today, 'skill' in communication is strongly associated with such 'feminine' verbal behaviours as co-operation, rapport building, sympathetic listening, showing empathy and projecting emotion, and not – or at least, less – with such 'masculine' behaviours as verbal duelling, arguing, dominating the floor, being cool and reserved. Jenny Cheshire and Nancy Jenkins point out that this symbolically 'feminine' definition of skill is institutionalized in the assessment criteria for the GCSE English oral examination, in which credit is given for 'sensitivity and reciprocity' whereas 'competitiveness and point-scoring will not gain good marks' (Cheshire and Jenkins, 1991: 32). As they observe, both the assessed task itself (group discussion) and the criteria used to judge performance in it could not be more different from 'that traditional oral exercise in the English classroom, the formal debate' – a discourse genre which might be said to represent the *ne plus ultra* of competitiveness and point-scoring.

The shift in emphasis from competition to co-operation may well favour female students (though Cheshire and Jenkins argue that boys still do better in GCSE oral exams than they deserve to; the support provided by girls in group discussions makes up for boys' lack of interpersonal skills). Indeed, the whole discourse I have been examining in the section could be seen as doing boys an injustice by 'talking them down', fostering the tendency to view any and every boy as *a priori* communicationally inept. But the underlying reasons why so-called 'female' communicational styles are now valorized over 'male' ones have little to do with any conscious conspiracy to advantage girls and women relative to boys and men. Rather they reflect more general changes in our conception of the 'good person' (the flexible worker, the model spouse or parent, the responsible citizen). Contemporary economic and social conditions, we are repeatedly told by gurus from Tom Peters to Daniel Goleman, call for people – of both sexes – who are team players rather than maverick individualists, democrats rather than authoritarians, who prefer compromise to conflict and who are fully 'in touch with their feelings'.

This ideal of personhood also informs what is taught (and what is not taught) in 'life skills' and 'social competence' programmes. Consider the following description of 'Circle Time', an approach to teaching interpersonal and communication skills that is used in some British schools:

> The object is to provide a safe environment in which everyone has an equal opportunity to speak and to be listened to. ...Within the circles children are encouraged to talk about their feelings and about problems that may have arisen at school (or elsewhere). However, no child may use the circle as a means of shaming others. The emphasis is on expressing feelings rather than accusations. ...[I]f a child talks about having sweets stolen or being pushed

around by another child, the circle may...offer support and talk about their own experience of being victimized. ...[The circles] encourage the very complex social skill of mirroring (reflecting mood in a way which displays empathy). (Phillips, 1998: 13)

The norms of Circle Time talk as described or implied in this passage are evidently designed to promote discourse which is egalitarian, emotionally 'literate', nonjudgemental, supportive and empathetic. Conversely, they are intended to discourage more confrontational or adversarial forms of discourse. Thus a child who has been the victim of stealing or bullying may seek support from others in the circle, but s/he is specifically prohibited from confronting the thief or bully.

Whatever one thinks of the discoursal (and moral) preferences embodied in the practice of Circle Time, it clearly operates with a selective notion of what constitutes 'skill' in interactive spoken discourse. ('Mirroring' is encouraged; arguing, accusing and name-calling are not.[15]) Of course, the same general observation about selectivity could equally be made about the practices of the classical rhetoricians or the eighteenth-century salons: different aspects of spoken language-use may be privileged in different cultural and historical traditions, but all traditions are necessarily selective. What is striking in contemporary English-speaking cultures, however, is the degree to which the preferences exemplified in approaches like Circle Time have come to define 'communication skills' across institutions, contexts and domains. The same preferences can be found not only in the educational settings considered in this chapter (the only exception being the élite colleges, whose approach retains links with older traditions of rhetorical training), but also in many of the workplaces whose training and regulatory practices were discussed in the two preceding chapters.

Though education may take its cue from developments in the wider world – in the case we have been examining, for instance, some important changes have clearly been driven by the demands of the new capitalism – education systems ultimately play a key role in 'establishing the...hierarchy of linguistic practices' (Bourdieu, 1991: 49), not least because they oversee the distribution of qualifications which have national (and in some cases international) currency. The more institutionalized certain attitudes, values and practices relating to communication become in educational settings, the more important it is to remind ourselves that there is nothing timeless, universal, natural or unchallengeable about the way the category of 'communication skills' is presently defined. In the next chapter I will continue this line of argument, considering 'communication' in those domains where talk is treated as a privileged means for achieving personal happiness and individual self-fulfilment.

6

COMMUNICATION AND THE PURSUIT OF HAPPINESS

The main field of morality, the part of ourselves which is most relevant for morality, is our feelings

— *Michel Foucault, 'On the Genealogy of Ethics', 1983*

Unless you're able to recognize your own feelings, you won't be able to express them clearly and be open with other people. If you're not able to recognize other people's feelings, you'll only ever understand part of their picture

— TalkWorks: How to Get More Out of Life through Better Conversations, *British Telecom, 1997*

In 1995 British Telecom set up the BT Forum 'to help BT learn more about the human side of communication'. In 1996 the Forum commissioned market researchers to carry out the first of a projected series of National Communication Surveys. The researchers interviewed a random sample of 993 respondents. The four 'headline findings' presented in the executive summary of their report (BT n.d.) were: 'good communicators lead happier lives' (endorsed by 83% of those questioned); 'making the effort to communicate is the key to happy relationships with people' (73%); 'the best way to resolve a disagreement between two people is to get them talking' (78%) and 'many arguments would be resolved if people communicated better' (71%).

As significant as the fact that so many people agreed with them is the fact that these particular statements were presented for their consideration in the first place. Respondents were not asked, for example, whether they agreed that 'good communicators can more easily manipulate people and get their own way', or that 'many arguments would never happen if people talked less'. Communication is axiomatically a good thing, a vital ingredient in a happy, harmonious existence.

Tamar Katriel and Gerry Philipsen (1981) made a detailed investigation of the term *communication* in the usage of two women in the American Pacific Northwest, who were asked to keep a log of communicative events they engaged in over a period of time, and were also observed and interviewed. Both informants distinguished 'communication' (sometimes, '*real* communication') from 'mere talk', 'small talk' or 'normal chit-chat'. What made mere talk into 'communication' was a combination of three main factors. First, it had to be *close* – conducted either in a context of existing intimacy or in order to create intimacy. Second, it had to be *supportive* – not agonistic or simply neutral. Katriel and Philipsen suggest that supportiveness is marked by one party's self-disclosure and the other's 'empathic listening, nonjudgemental comments and non-inquisitiveness' in response to what is disclosed (1981: 312). Third, it had to be *flexible* – the parties had to be open to each other, receptive to feedback and to the possibility of change occurring (the informants often referred to this change as 'growth').

This notion of 'communication' was articulated alongside a particular view of the self and its relationships with others. The informants were of the opinion that each person has a unique individual self, which is capable of some change but retains a continuous core. This core self however needs validation from other people if it is to remain strong and healthy. In an observation that might seem to prefigure Anthony Giddens's (1991) arguments about the reflexive construction of self-identity and the importance of 'pure' relationships in late modern societies, Katriel and Philipsen note that, viewed from this perspective, 'communication' becomes

> …both vitally important and highly problematic. If people are unique, the kind of mutual disclosure and acknowledgement entailed in communication provide a necessary bridge from self to others. But if people are unique, they also lack the mutuality necessary for achieving interpersonal meaning and co-ordination. (1981: 304)

Another interesting finding of Katriel and Philipsen's study is that the informants persistently talked about 'communication' as a kind of *work*. They spoke of 'working' both on their relationships and on themselves, and of making 'efforts' to communicate. They represented personal life as an endless round of problem-solving: 'in this orientational system, not having a problem is interpreted as suppression or reluctance to face the problems one "must have" by virtue of being "alive" in the world today' (Katriel and Philipsen, 1981: 312). The kinds of talk informants identified as 'communication' or 'real communication' invariably revolved around the airing and the sharing of problems. As the researchers remark (1981: 311), if Hamlet had lived in late 20th century America he 'would have tried to sit down and talk things over with his family'.

The idea that communication is work (not recreation) and that it is part of the 'job' of constructing both personal identity and interpersonal relationships is one point of contact between the rhetoric of 'personal growth' and the culture of 'enterprise'. It might be suggested that the private pursuit of happiness takes on such significance in contemporary societies because people look to their private lives to compensate them for the stress and alienation that prevail elsewhere. Alternatively it could be argued that 'working' towards the goal of personal happiness is just another way of being enterprising: private life is not a refuge from the demands of enterprise culture but is increasingly subject to those same demands itself. It is seen, like working or learning, to require a particular set of 'skills': texts in the 'personal growth' mode (such as Daniel Goleman's *Emotional Intelligence* (1995), which I referred to in Chapter 5, and BT's *TalkWorks* materials (1997), discussed below) often refer to communication as a 'life skill'.

Katriel and Philipsen's study invites the objection that two informants constitute a very small sample on which to base conclusions about '"communication" as a cultural term in some American speech' (the subtitle of their article). However, their observations are supported by a study of a much larger corpus, consisting of over a year's output of a US television talk show, *Donahue*, which was carried out by Donal Carbaugh and published in his book *Talking American* (Carbaugh, 1988). Carbaugh argues that talk shows are a particularly rich source of insight into two culturally salient, and connected, discourses: a discourse of personhood, and a discourse on ways of speaking.

Thank you for sharing: 'communication' on talk shows

Donahue (named after the show's host Phil Donahue) belongs to the 'issue' subgenre of talk shows; at the time of Carbaugh's research it was the outstanding example of this type. The 'issue' format contrasts with an older 'personality' format in which the host interviews one or more celebrity guests.[1] Guests on 'issue' shows are not celebrities but people who can talk about a given topic on the basis of either personal experience or professional expertise. As Carbaugh notes, there is a preference for persons with somewhat unusual experiences – in his *Donahue* corpus we encounter born-again strippers, gay atheists, children who have 'divorced' their parents, and nurses who abused drugs on the job. The other characteristic element is a studio audience of 'ordinary' people who are invited to express their views on what is said by the guests, whether as individuals or collectively through co-ordinated joint responses like applause. The host frames, facilitates and referees the discussion.

Carbaugh argues that three ways of speaking are treated as normative in the world of the issue-based talk show: 'being honest', 'sharing' and 'communication'. In fact, his analysis suggests that 'communication' subsumes the other two rather than being distinct from them. It is that highly valued kind of interpersonal exchange in which people are 'honest' and in which they 'share' themselves – they are open *with* others and also open *to* others. That this is regarded as, in BT's words, 'the key to happy relationships with people' is attested by many remarks made on *Donahue*. 'The only thing that saved Craig and me is the communication', comments one woman on her marriage, while a new stepfather describes his difficult relationship with his stepchildren by saying 'I'm working at it. We're communicating better'. There is however one sense in which 'communication' does seem to be distinct from 'being honest' and 'sharing'. Carbaugh finds (as did Katriel and Philipsen) that 'communication' is conceptualized as something that occurs in private between intimates. Thus talk show participants often *refer* to it (as in the remarks quoted above), but it is not what they take themselves to be doing in the (public, non-intimate) context of the talk show itself.[2] By contrast, 'being honest' and 'sharing' are important norms within talk-show discourse. Since they are also components of 'communication' in more intimate contexts, Carbaugh's analysis of what they are taken to mean on *Donahue* sheds light on the overall meaning of *communication*, and especially on its relationship to a particular concept of personhood.

On *Donahue*, and also, according to Carbaugh, in mainstream US culture more broadly, persons are understood to be unique individuals who are endowed with inalienable rights, crucially including the right to free speech. The communicational imperative that follows is 'self-expression': to speak is to make public those ideas, beliefs and feelings that belong (uniquely) to the individual. Individuals are not just permitted but actively encouraged to 'say what they have to say'. But Carbaugh points out that when everyone is taken to have the *same* right to free self-expression, a tension or contradiction is set up: some opinions are not freely expressible because they infringe the rights of others to say and believe what they like. 'A speaker does not have a right to any opinion which extends beyond the individual, that is stated for another or is, in a sense, of social concern. Opinions stated as such are heard to violate the rights of others by "imposing" on them' (Carbaugh, 1988: 30). On *Donahue* a norm which Carbaugh labels 'righteous tolerance' is strictly enforced. People who 'impose' their views on others are negatively sanctioned, while people who share their honest opinions, but on the basis that they speak only for themselves, may be applauded without regard to the actual substance of what they say. The individual who expresses a view generally felt to be repulsive, or insane, nevertheless deserves credit for 'sharing' and/or 'being honest'. Where the audience is inclined to withhold that credit (from criminals or obvious bigots, for instance), Phil Donahue often intervenes to remind them of their obligation.

Donahue also regularly makes the move of sanctioning participants who appear to be advancing their own opinions as universally valid truths. For example, on one show a woman spoke forcefully against open adoption (that is, adoption arrangements in which children have ongoing contact with their natural parents) arguing that this was bad for the children involved and should therefore be outlawed. Donahue responded: 'no one is going to deny you your position but the question is why do you impose it on others?' (Carbaugh, 1988: 30). It is not only the host who can appeal to this principle of non-imposition. In another striking example, a young Christian fundamentalist expressed his resentment about having been taught evolutionary science in school by suggesting that those responsible had 'imposed' their own views and denied him the 'choice' to learn creationist doctrine. Invoking the norm of righteous tolerance is a highly effective rhetorical strategy on *Donahue* and can usually be relied upon to elicit applause. Carbaugh quotes another instance where a man who was 'married' to both a man and a woman responded to criticism from an audience member by exclaiming: 'I respect your views of morality and I would expect you to respect mine'. This remark sits uneasily with the conventional view of 'morality' as a domain of collective judgements on right and wrong – agreeing to respect any and every 'view of morality' arguably means abandoning moral judgement as such – but the comment was nevertheless greeted with approbation.

The research of Katriel and Philipsen (1981) and of Carbaugh (1988) suggests that *communication* in mainstream US usage denotes that form of talk in which people 'work' towards self-understanding, personal growth and intimacy with others. This talk is characterized by honesty, sincerity, openness and supportiveness; it is governed by a norm of 'righteous tolerance' according to which everyone has a right to their opinion, but it is not legitimate to impose your opinions on others or to judge them. These particularities of 'communication' also reflect more general convictions about persons and what is due to them: in particular that each person is unique, and is individually endowed with inalienable rights. Carbaugh, Katriel and Philipsen treat the meanings they uncover as peculiarly 'American', but as the findings of the (British) National Communication Survey suggest, similar attitudes to 'communication' can also be found outside the US. No doubt the cultural influence of the US (exerted not least through its popular television) is one relevant consideration here. More fundamentally, it seems likely that the liberal individualism and preoccupation with self which are so apparent in *Donahue* will be characteristic generally of late modern cultures, where the individual's biography and identity are not determined by tradition or social role but must be reflexively constructed.[3]

But one might also suggest a more specific source for the norms and beliefs discussed by Carbaugh and Katriel and Philipsen. Though these researchers analyse 'communication' as a 'ritual' whose main function is to reaffirm the status of a 'sacred object', namely the self, rather surprisingly they do not consider its possible relationship to another form of ritualized self-examination conducted through talk: *therapy*.

Talk as therapy

I use *therapy* here as an umbrella term covering not only prototypical cases involving a 'therapist' and one or more 'clients' in some sort of clinical setting, but also counselling, self-help enterprises like the meetings which support people 'in recovery'[4], and the discourse of popular psychology, both print and broadcast. Though it might seem cavalier to put such diverse phenomena together, for the purposes of this discussion they are linked, to each other and to 'communication', in two important ways. They are concerned with the self and its relationships with others; and they assume the efficacy of *talking* for solving personal and interpersonal problems.

The father of the 'talking cure', Freud, famously said that it was not intended to make people happy, but only to put ordinary unhappiness in place of neurotic illness. But while some of those who seek therapy today are, indeed, ill and their goal is simply relief, many more do not have mental health problems. They may be unhappy or dissatisfied with themselves and their lives, or they may be using therapy as a means to the self-knowledge and understanding that underpins the reflexive construction of self-identity. Just as some people maintain their bodily fitness by going regularly to the gym, so going to a therapist or a self-help group or 'recovery' meeting may be treated as a kind of 'self-maintenance'. The forms of therapy I will be most concerned with here are those which, while they may on occasion be undertaken in a clinical context, are widely used by (or, as we will see, *on*) people who have no official clinical diagnosis.

In Chapter 2 I suggested that 'therapy' is the source – albeit not always explicitly acknowledged as such – of a significant proportion of the knowledge and advice found in communication training texts, and in particular, it often provides the overarching framework in which general principles of interaction are presented. Thus in a sample of materials produced either for workplace training purposes or for general public consumption under the heading of 'self-improvement', I noted that recommendations drawn from the theory and practice of 'assertiveness' appeared in every item, while the conceptual apparatus and terminology of 'transactional analysis' appeared in several items. Below I will also draw attention to the close resemblance that exists between the norms of therapeutic talk and the norms of the TV talk show as described by Donal Carbaugh. The appearance of identifiably 'therapeutic' rules for speaking in such disparate contexts tends to support the argument made by Norman Fairclough (1989; 1992) that 'therapy' has become what he calls a 'discourse technology', a way of talking which, although originally developed for one purpose (the 'talking cure'), has come to be regarded as useful for many others. Therapeutic discourse strategies are seen as useful for encouraging self-disclosure and reflexivity, whether in job interviews or on television or, as we will see, in ordinary casual conversation.

The process of 'technologizing' encourages the use of therapeutic paradigms in ways that are simultaneously eclectic (putting different systems together) and selective (taking from each of them only what seems immediately relevant to the purpose at hand). This entails ignoring what are, in the therapeutic milieu, significant theoretical differences. For instance, assertiveness comes out of a behaviourist tradition, explicitly opposed to classical psychoanalysis (Rakos, 1991), whereas transactional analysis is more indebted to the analytic tradition and places emphasis on reading clients' current behaviour with reference to their experiences in early childhood (Berne, 1975). But in non-therapeutic contexts such differences need not signify. Assertiveness and TA become just 'tools' for helping people communicate more effectively. There is no reason why bits of both approaches should not be presented in the same training course or text.

The 'technologizing' of therapy goes along with the shift away from treating talk as 'polite social intercourse' and towards treating it as a means to 'the intimate meeting of minds and sympathies' (Zeldin, 1998: 94). But it is possible to be more specific about what it is that therapy offers. Susan Gal reminds us that beliefs about what is desirable in the speech of this or that group of people always go along with more wide-ranging beliefs about 'the nature of persons, of power and of a desirable moral order' (Gal, 1995: 171). These are precisely the concerns which are foregrounded in various practices of therapy. In therapeutic settings, moreover, beliefs about what persons are and how they should act are often encapsulated in norms that are specifically *linguistic*.

Consider the following extract from a group therapy session, recorded and transcribed by Cathryn Houghton (1995: 123–4). This session took place in a therapeutic institution in the US whose inmates were young, mainly Latina women. They had been involuntarily removed from their own communities and institutionalized as a result of their socially 'deviant' behaviour, which consisted in most cases of having had children they could not support economically through waged labour. Single mothers dependent on welfare, they were perceived as 'irresponsible' in their attitudes to sex, parenthood and work. The institution sought to inculcate more 'responsible' attitudes through group therapy, as well as to prepare the women for the labour market through vocational training. In this extract from a group session, one young woman, Mirna, is talking about wanting to have a baby, when the therapist intervenes:

Mirna:	You know how that is,
	when you just want to have a baby,
	just something that is yours
	and belongs to you…
Therapist:	No Mirna
	we don't know how it is
	please tell us
	but don't say 'you'
	it is your experience not ours
	so you need to say 'I' instead of 'you'
	this is how *I* feel when *I* see a baby.
Mirna:	OK. I.
Therapist:	So how does it feel to say 'I'?

What is most immediately striking in this extract is the explicitness with which the therapist invokes a particular rule of speaking – that in talking about one's own experiences and feelings, it is obligatory to use the pronoun 'I'. This could be seen as a more overt version of the precept Donal Carbaugh identified as salient for talk show participants, namely that one should share one's own experiences but not presume to speak for/about others. As Houghton points out, by invoking this rule the therapist is denying something Mirna's own choice of pronoun asserts, or presupposes, namely that the experience of 'just wanting to have a baby' is *not* Mirna's alone, it is shared by (at least) the people she is addressing. The therapist has no hesitation in using a collective pronoun, *we*, to invalidate this presupposition: 'no Mirna we don't know how it is…it is your experience not ours'. In the context of this interaction, it is possible and even likely that most participants would in fact claim to 'know how it is', since they have made similar choices in similar circumstances themselves. However, the therapist is using her institutional authority to remind them that one of the rules of therapy talk is to present oneself as an autonomous individual subject whose experiences and feelings are unique, and to make the same assumption about the subjectivities of other people. (In some therapeutic approaches, there is a technical term for failure or refusal to accept the postulate of autonomy and separateness from others: 'co-dependency'.)

Houghton analyses the therapist's intervention as an attempt to impose on Mirna the mainstream US cultural norm of individualism. In other words, saying *I* is not just a stylistic detail but the linguistic instantiation of a particular ideological conception of 'the nature of persons'. It also implies a 'desirable moral order', one in which individuals act autonomously and take responsibility for their own behaviour (in therapy this is sometimes called 'owning' your problems or feelings). Individualism is, as Houghton says, a mainstream cultural norm, not confined to therapeutic institutions. But what is different about the therapeutic institution is that here, to a much greater degree than in everyday life, or even on talk shows, the axiom 'everyone is a unique and autonomous individual' is translated into a *discourse norm*, namely 'saying *I*'. In ordinary conversation it would be extremely marked behaviour to correct someone's choice of pronoun in the way the therapist corrects Mirna's.

Even more marked, from the point of view of ordinary interaction, is the therapist's question: 'so how does it feel to say *I*?' Not only this question but the extract as a whole illustrates another respect in which therapeutic discourse norms formalize certain beliefs and values as norms of talk: it is considered important that feelings should not merely be felt, but actively verbalized. Again, this is not exclusively a therapeutic principle. A cliché of ordinary talk (also enacted in the 'sharing' of talk-show talk) is, 'don't bottle things up': that is, don't keep feelings inside yourself, let them out by talking (and perhaps other kinds of communicative behaviour, like crying). This expression draws on one of Lakoff and Johnson's 'metaphors we live by' (1980), the common metaphor of the human body as a container and emotions as its liquid contents. To 'bottle up' feelings is to prevent them finding an outlet, and the result is likely to be a sudden uncontrollable explosion. Talking is good because it 'defuses' explosive inner states. But in therapy, typically, the goal is not only to provide an outlet for 'bottled up' feelings, it is also to make those feelings available to therapist and client(s) for inspection and reflection – to speak them so that they may subsequently be spoken *about*.

In the case studied by Cathryn Houghton, the ultimate object is to *change* the feelings of inmates. The point of sending people like Mirna to institutions whose regimes are (at least in the view of the authorities) therapeutic rather than merely punitive is that changing their outward behaviour is believed to depend on changing deeper-rooted attitudes and desires. Houghton comments: 'It is a firmly held tenet of clinical practice that internal change and ideological reorientation cannot be motivated by coercive measures alone...To capture the words that reverberate throughout the therapeutic milieu, "you have to want to change"' (1995: 123). Yet again, though, it bears pointing out that the therapeutic milieu is not the only one in which this sentiment, if not the mantra itself, 'reverberates'. The preference for persuasion over pure coercion, and for self-direction over direction by others, pervades many of the disciplinary institutions of late modern societies. Although it continues to be contested in some areas (such as the treatment of criminals) it has basically prevailed in relation to child-rearing practices, education, employment (where the philosophy of 'empowerment' very obviously instantiates it) and such state-sponsored practices as health and sex education, social work and probation services. The preference for persuasion goes along with an assumption that almost every person is educable, capable of improvement if properly motivated. And this also assumes that people direct their own actions; they are not just fated to be unhappy or destined to do evil. Similar ideas are expressed in the 'conversion narrative' which is a staple of talk shows ('I was a stripper until I found Jesus', or 'I used to beat my wife, but I've learnt to manage my anger'), and in the concept of 'personal growth' which loomed large in the talk of Katriel and Philipsen's informants.

I am suggesting, then, that 'therapy' is significant, not because it stands apart from other cultural practices, but on the contrary, because it is an activity in which many of the themes of modern Western commonsense discourse come together. In therapy, commonplace presuppositions about the self and about moral conduct are made particularly explicit (because the self is the overt focus of therapeutic discourse), and these presuppositions are also quite often embodied in explicit rules for speaking. This is why therapy is a good candidate for 'technologization'. Because its discourse norms are based on beliefs that are also widely held outside the therapeutic context, it is easy to adapt the same norms to different settings and purposes.

The concept of the self as unique, autonomous, endowed with rights, capable of 'growth' but possessed of what one of Katriel and Philipsen's informants called a 'core', an essential personality formed early in life and unchanging thereafter – is found in many or most forms of therapeutic practice. Freud may have challenged the idea of stable, unified, rational and autonomous selves with his concept of the unconscious, but as some of his post-structuralist interpreters have pointed out, many therapists who locate themselves in the psychoanalytic tradition have in practice continued to idealize autonomy, unity, rationality and stability. The same tendency is also evident in therapeutic practices which are not, or are only tenuously, in the Freudian tradition, and in most of the products of self-help and popular psychology. The idea of therapy as a means to 'self-knowledge, 'self-discovery' and 'self-realization' assumes the prior existence of a stable self for the individual to know, discover or realize. In the field of communication, as noted above, the analogue of therapy's 'self-discovery' is 'self-expression'. Communication is conceptualized, implicitly if not explicitly, as the expression of thoughts, experiences and feelings by one unique autonomous self to other similarly constituted selves. Subjectivity is not constructed *in talk*, nor are experiences and feelings jointly constructed by the participants in an interaction; they are 'inside' the individual waiting to be communicated to other individuals through verbal, vocal and visual behaviour.

This model has consequences for what comes to be defined as a 'communication problem' or a 'communication skill'. One type of 'communication problem' arises when an individual does not try to communicate what is inside (is not open, does not 'share'), misrepresents what is inside (is not 'honest') or fails to represent what is inside intelligibly because s/he does not possess sufficient skill. Another type of problem arises when the individual in the role of listener is inattentive or unskilled, and so fails to grasp what other speakers are communicating about themselves ('their *selves*'). These are the problems implicitly or explicitly addressed in guidance texts under headings like 'being direct', 'making messages consistent', 'talking about feelings', listening 'actively' or 'sensitively' and 'avoiding misunderstandings'.

Other 'communication problems' arise from the tension Carbaugh notes between individuals' right to free expression and their obligation not to impose on others or judge others. This contradiction is at the heart of advice on assertive communication, defined succinctly in one of the training texts I examined in Chapter 2 as 'standing up for your own rights while respecting the rights of others'. Assertiveness is supposed to represent a golden mean in between two more problematic positions: submissiveness (failing to stand up for one's own rights) and aggressiveness (showing insufficient respect for others' rights). The framework of rights also motivates a number of more specific principles governing assertive interaction. For instance, it is commonly stated that 'everyone has a right to their feelings', which would be a redundant banality if it did not also imply that everyone has an obligation to acknowledge, without judging, the feelings expressed by others. The prohibition on judging others – not only their feelings but also their beliefs and goals – is a key discourse norm in all kinds of therapeutic and quasi-therapeutic enterprises (not only assertiveness training but also, for instance, counselling and twelve-step programs). Richard Rakos remarks in a discussion of the history and philosophical underpinnings of assertiveness training that one of the things that helped to popularize it in the 1960s and early 1970s was 'the rejection of absolute standards of morality, which was, in reality, a corollary of the discreditation of societal establishments...Ethical relativism emerged as an explicit characteristic of behavior therapy' (Rakos, 1991: 4). The same observation could equally be made about other therapeutic paradigms that became popular during the same period (such as transactional analysis).

On reflection it might be asked, though, whether the observation is not a little disingenuous. We have already encountered one instance – the therapeutic regime imposed on Mirna and her peers – to which the description 'ethical relativism' is scarcely applicable. Even if we were to exclude cases like this on the grounds that they are 'abuses' of therapy rather than examples of good practice, it could still be argued that therapy has a moral agenda. As Donal Carbaugh remarks about the talk-show norm of 'righteous tolerance', the emphasis placed on 'relativism' – on the fact that talk-show participants or participants in therapy have *differing* opinions, values or moral standards – plays down what, at a more fundamental level, is a matter of *consensus*; to wit, that the only acceptable response to these differences is *tolerance*. The speaker who says 'I respect your views of morality and I would expect you to respect mine' is at one level making a 'relativist' statement ('there is no single moral code that everyone must subscribe to'). At the same time, his formulation 'I would expect you to...' suggests there *is*, in fact, at least one moral principle that applies absolutely ('don't assume the right to judge other people'). This is not an ideologically neutral principle; rather it belongs to the ideology of liberalism. What Richard Rakos calls therapy's 'ethical relativism' is actually an expression of liberal beliefs about what constitutes a 'desirable moral order'. To the extent that therapeutic practices embody liberal values, they cannot be said to be 'value free'. Nor, as I will argue in more detail below, can advice on communication that draws on therapeutic models.

In this section I have argued that the assumptions underlying the concept of 'communication' which researchers have found attested in folk and popular culture (here I include both academic researchers, such as Carbaugh, Katriel and Philipsen, and market researchers, such as those responsible for BT's National Communication Survey) are very similar, indeed in some cases identical, to the assumptions underlying numerous variants of the 'talking cure'. Indeed, it does not seem unreasonable to suggest that therapeutic discourse and practice may be the main source for contemporary folk-beliefs on the subject. This is not to say that most people have first-hand experience of being 'in therapy' (even in America![5]). But there are many other channels through which therapeutic precepts are made available to a wider public. They include popular psychology and self-help literature, women's magazines, print and broadcast interviews in which celebrities discuss addiction and recovery, talk shows of the *Donahue* type (many of which employ a counsellor or therapist in an advisory role, as well as inviting therapists to appear as guest experts), educational programmes of the 'life-skills' variety, and public health information on subjects like childcare, sex, drugs, bereavement.

If therapy exerts a particularly strong influence over prevailing expert and lay definitions of 'communication', of the 'problems' it poses and the 'skills' it demands, what are the implications of that influence? It may be that for the purposes of therapy itself, norms like 'being honest' and 'not judging' are well motivated; but what does it mean when the same norms are recommended and taught as the standard for all kinds of other activities done in talk? In the following section I will consider how particular ideological presuppositions and moral value judgements come to shape definitions of 'good communication' in ways that are socially and politically consequential.

Problems of conflict and power

Contemporary guidance on communication values co-operation and consensus over competition and conflict. At the beginning of this chapter, for instance, I quoted some of the statements presented to respondents in the UK National Communication Survey, among them 'the best way to resolve a disagreement between two people is to get them talking', and 'many arguments would be resolved if people communicated better'. These statements imply or presuppose that argument and disagreement are negative, while conflict resolution is positive. Such an evaluation is in line with mainstream liberal assumptions about the 'desirable moral order', and it also has a particular relationship to the goals and methods of at least some forms of therapy.

Therapy has come to play an important role in attempts to change the attitudes and behaviour of aggressive and violent individuals: disruptive children, abusive parents, wife beaters and rapists may all be regarded as suitable cases for treatment rather than just punishment, and the treatment very often includes some form of communication skills training. Teaching 'anger management' and conflict resolution techniques is a therapeutic strategy quite commonly recommended in cases of 'family violence'[6], for instance, on the grounds that, as one commentator summarizes the research literature, 'abusers (and often [their] victims) manifest few constructive communication, social, negotiation, problem solving and argumentation skills' (Cahn, 1996: 12). This sentence renders in expert language a proposition that by now commands widespread popular agreement too, that violence is generally resorted to by inadequate, 'inarticulate' people who cannot use words to express themselves. Thus one team of researchers report that 'the inability to express oneself verbally was cited as a cause of a violent dating episode by about a third of a sample of victims and one quarter of the perpetrators' (cited in Roloff, 1996: 29).

Therapeutic interventions aim not only to substitute conflict *talk* for physical conflict but also to encourage 'constructive' forms of talk, while discouraging the 'coercive' verbal acts – such as threats and insults – that are thought to be a 'catalyst' for violence (Roloff, 1996). It is assumed that coercive communication occurs because of what Roloff glosses as 'an individual's inability to competently perform non-coercive techniques' (1996: 29). This is implicitly a causal account: *because* certain individuals are incompetent in using language persuasively, they resort to coercive strategies, and *because* these are not helpful in resolving the underlying conflict, the encounter quickly escalates to physical violence. Among the alternatives this account rules out is the possibility that some individuals in some situations do not have conflict resolution as their primary goal. It is surely conceivable that some people gain satisfaction from engaging in arguments or verbal abuse; that they do it because they want to or because it satisfies a need they feel at the time, and not simply because they are incapable of behaving in a more 'constructive' way.

The belief that there is something pathological about ways of talking which do not aim to establish or re-establish consensus derives, arguably, from a taboo on verbal aggression that is associated in particular with the social mores of white bourgeois liberal society. Reviewing the literature on conflict talk across cultures, the anthropologist Don Kulick (1993: 510–11) concludes that ethnographers who belong to or have been educated in that milieu have a tendency to assume that conflict in any culture must signal some kind of breakdown in normal social relations. Kulick considers this assumption unwarranted and ethnocentric, and he goes on to discuss an instance that calls it into question: the *kros* (a Tok Pisin word related to English *cross*, or 'angry'), which is a common speech event in the New Guinea village where he carried out fieldwork. In a *kros*, participants shout abuse at one another (or indeed, past one another) for lengthy periods. The goal is to display grievances against others publicly, but it is not to resolve them by talking. On the contrary, if the object of abuse tries to reason with the abuser or address the causes of conflict in the approved Western manner, the result is likely to be escalation and ultimately a brawl involving the whole village. In this case, Kulick argues, it makes no sense to see verbal conflict as portending social breakdown; nor, one might add, is it reasonable to portray participants as resorting to abuse because they lack more sophisticated communication skills. In this society verbal abuse *is* a communication skill.[7]

Verbal abuse may never have enjoyed high status in Western traditions of teaching talk, but Western communication experts have not always been so disapproving of all forms of conflictual or agonistic interchange. Indeed, the emphasis they currently place on conflict resolution might seem like a notable break with tradition if we recall that for many centuries in the West, the ability to argue well was regarded as the quintessential communication skill. The classical rhetorical tradition was agonistic first and last: argument was central to it, and was accorded a clear moral function – one argued not simply to win, but to arrive at a clearer understanding of the truth, which was thought more likely to emerge from a kind of discourse where propositions are not merely asserted but routinely challenged and defended. Argument also functioned as a form of entertainment, enjoyed by both participants and onlookers. In contemporary advice literature by contrast, argument is usually represented as trivial, futile, dysfunctional and distressing. It is acknowledged that people may *disagree* with one another; but there is a difference between disagreement and argument. The latter challenges the validity of others' opinions, and seeks to persuade them to change. In plainer language, arguments are won and lost. The 'I win, you lose' approach, however, is now often regarded as illegitimate – a point well made in Donal Carbaugh's analysis of talk-shows, whose participants, as we saw above, are free to disagree but not to 'impose their views on others'. Advice on communication, whether in personal or professional contexts (for an example of the latter, see McMillan, 1996), stresses that the best outcome is the one beloved of negotiators and conflict resolution experts: everyone wins.

It is undeniable that negotiation and conflict resolution are skills, and that in certain situations those skills are valuable. In other situations, however, negotiation may not be the best strategy. The general devaluation of argument as a communication skill has some potentially worrying implications. Taken to its logical conclusion it would undermine the belief – in fact, the classically liberal belief – in the value of rational discourse for revealing truth and correcting error. The 'best' answer to someone who asserts that the Earth is flat (or who wants school science books to teach that God created the world in six days) surely cannot be 'that's your opinion and you're entitled to it'. Donal Carbaugh expresses a comparable anxiety about the consequences of 'righteous tolerance' in his discussion of talk-shows (Carbaugh, 1988). A society which conducts its discourse on the principle that 'everyone has a right to their opinion, but no one's opinion is preferable to anyone else's' is in one sense 'democratic', but how can it move towards any collective notion of what might constitute the common good?

One might also worry that if people do not develop the skill of arguing effectively – if they are taught how to support but not dissent from others' contributions in talk – they will be disempowered: insufficiently confident to argue at all, or insufficiently accomplished in argument to make their case successfully. The emphasis placed by so many communication experts on negotiation, conflict resolution, co-operation and agreement suggests that they are teaching communication skills for a world in which people's relationships are basically egalitarian, their intentions toward one another are basically good and their interests are basically shared. If those conditions are fulfilled, co-operation may well be rational and rewarding. If they are not fulfilled, however, the norm of co-operation is likely, in practice, to favour the more powerful party.

As many commentators have noted, the existence of systemic power inequalities is difficult to accommodate within a liberal individualist framework. The liberal axiom that we are all positioned similarly and possessed of 'equal rights' leads to a view of conflict as essentially a local disturbance of the ideal, harmonious relation between individuals rather than as one instance of some more global contest between social collectivities over power. This view is one of the elements underpinning the idea that all kinds of conflicts can be resolved by helping the parties to communicate with one another better. Lack of consensus is taken to imply a failure of mutual understanding; conversely, it is often supposed that if people truly understood one another they would not find themselves in conflict. During the 1990s this line of reasoning was embodied in a whole subgenre of self-help books about male-female 'miscommunication', including the highly successful *You Just Don't Understand* (Tannen, 1991), and the even more popular *Men are from Mars, Women are from Venus* (Gray, 1992). The idea that many every-day conflicts between men and women arise from their inability to retrieve one another's true intentions fits well with a worldview in which people are equal, mean well, and share the same interests, so that any conflict between them must be local rather than global, 'surface' rather than 'deep' and remediable without major structural change. Far less reassuring is the argument made by feminist critics of the 'Mars/Venus' genre, that many conflicts between individual men and women arise from more fundamental conflicts of interest between the two groups. One critic, the linguist Alice Freed, chose to register her differences with Tannen under the title *We Understand Perfectly* (Freed, 1992). This neatly makes the point that comprehension is not the same as consensus. It is possible to be aware of what someone wants and still refuse to give it to them; to follow their argument without difficulty and still not accept it as valid. But if the source of conflict is not just misunderstanding then it cannot be resolved simply by more and better communication.

Better conversations?

At this point I want to consider how liberal assumptions about selfhood, conflict and power, and the 'therapeutic' discourse norms in which those assumptions are embodied, are taken up concretely in advice on communication. The example I will discuss in detail is a set of multi-media learning materials produced on behalf of the telephone company BT and bearing the exemplary title *TalkWorks: How to Get More Out of Life through Better Conversations* (BT, 1997). The materials consist of a 94-page booklet supplemented by a set of twelve audiotapes, which readers are invited to access by calling Freefone (0800) numbers.[8] (Though the tapes are described (BT, 1997: 2) as 'recordings of ordinary people talking to each other', they are in fact scripted and performed by actors. This is obvious when you listen to them, and it was also confirmed for me by BT sources.) In principle, the target audience was the entire British population: the materials were offered free of charge to any UK resident who requested them. In the first 18 months of the project, two million copies of the booklet were requested, while the 12 tapes collectively attracted around 600,000 calls.

The booklet and tapes were produced as part of a broader initiative under the aegis of Britain's 'Millennium Project' (a scheme in which companies in partnership with government undertake community service projects in the run-up to the year 2000). According to BT, the overall aim of the *TalkWorks* initiative is 'to help people become more effective communicators by providing a range of publications and learning materials'. *TalkWorks: How to Get More Out of Life through Better Conversations* was the first of these quasi-educational publications to be offered to the public at large. BT invested considerable resources in advertising its existence and publicizing its aims. It was launched, for instance, in a special 'infomercial' segment of a popular daytime TV magazine programme, *This Morning with Richard and Judy*. While the infomercial is a common phenomenon on US television, it is rarer in Britain, and BT's use of it was reported in the national press as a news story. Subsequently BT included information on *TalkWorks* in telephone bills and other promotional material sent out to its millions of customers.

We are dealing, then, with a text that consciously sets out to address a large, 'mainstream' audience. Its intended user is a 'normal', average sort of person, whose general social competence is not in doubt but who nevertheless could 'get more out of life' if his or her everyday conversations were 'better'. On the inside cover we learn that the advice contained in the booklet is based not only on 'the work of leading international experts' but also on 'discussions with hundreds of ordinary people throughout the country'. Yet in spite of the rhetorical emphasis placed on the ordinary commonsense of ordinary conversationalists, closer inspection makes clear that the BT materials embody an expert perspective on what makes conversation 'better' – more precisely, they embody the therapeutic assumptions discussed earlier in this chapter. (The main author, Andrew Bailey, is a freelance consultant who described himself to me as having no special expertise in interpersonal communication, but he was extensively advised by the American clinical and organizational psychologist Gerard Egan, author of a widely used text on counselling.) Like the talk-shows examined by Donal Carbaugh, these materials are an example of the kind of popularizing discourse through which expert understandings come to *be* part of lay common sense. In this discussion I will focus particularly on the way 'therapeutic' understandings shape the notion of 'better conversation' presented in *How to Get More Out of Life through Better Conversations* (hereafter, *Better Conversations*).

To begin with, *Better Conversations* appears to define conversation functionally in much the same way as the informants studied by Katriel and Philipsen (1981) and the talk-show participants recorded by Carbaugh (1988) defined 'communication', which is to say, as a means of coming to know oneself and others more intimately. Here for instance is part of the text of a section in the booklet entitled 'The importance of being open':

> Just as we can only get to know about another person's 'real self' through their words, we can only become familiar with our own real self by communicating openly and fully with other people. Conversation, it turns out, is the best way we have of exploring the full range and diversity of our own thoughts, memories and emotions...talking candidly about ourselves not only helps other people get to know us, it also helps us to get to know ourselves and be more genuine. (BT, 1997: 17–18)

The section goes on to warn of the negative consequences of failure to be open:

> Some people actively struggle to avoid becoming known by other people. We now know that this struggle can lead to a form of stress which is capable of producing a whole set of physical and emotional problems...As a rule, women are more comfortable with talking about their real selves than men. Women also live longer than men. This may not be a coincidence. (1997: 18)

In this passage the booklet's therapeutic orientation is more obvious. The 'we' who 'now know' that lack of openness causes stress is not an inclusive 'we' (the population at large, including readers), but points to some body of expert knowers. The subsequent reference to 'physical and emotional problems' suggests that these knowers' expertise is quasi-medical.

The norms of 'better conversation' are spelled out most clearly in a summary section at the end of the booklet (BT, 1997: 91–4), which offers '25 Top Tips'. Below is a full listing of these 'tips' (the italicized portions are direct quotes from the text; for the sake of brevity I have glossed the supporting explanations in my own words, with occasional quotations which are signalled by quote marks).

1. *Devote the time.* Talk with others is important and should not be rushed.
2. *Share the airtime.* Neither party in conversation should dominate.
3. *Stay in touch.* Talk with valued others should take place regularly.
4. *Value difference.* Talk is a means to learn about experiences and feelings that differ from our own, and this is a source of enrichment.
5. *Know your reputation.* Communication is influenced by how the parties see one another. If you have a 'negative' reputation you should work on the features perceived as negative.
6. *Own your thoughts and feelings.* Use 'I' statements and do not blame others.
7. *Recognize and respect feelings.* Be aware of what you are feeling and be open about it with others; conversely, be open to the feelings others are expressing.
8. *Don't assume.* Say what you mean and don't hint; encourage others to do the same.
9. *Accept responsibility.* Don't blame others for failures of understanding. 'While you can't be responsible for the other person's efforts, you can for your own'.
10. *Choose the right moment.* Bring up important issues when there is time to deal with them.
11. *Set the stage.* When initiating talk, make clear what you want to talk about and what your main point is.
12. *Be concrete and specific.* Talk about 'real' things, experiences and feelings. 'Be the main character of your stories'.
13. *Say what's on your mind.* Don't leave things unsaid.
14. *Summarize.* Regularly summarize what you have said so far.
15. *Listen on all channels.* Pay attention to tone and body language as well as words.
16. *Keep an open mind.* Avoid judging and making responses that are 'criticisms in disguise'.
17. *Show you understand.* Demonstrate 'empathy' by mirroring and paraphrasing others' meanings.
18. *Say when you don't understand.*
19. *Work hard at clarity.* If understanding appears imperfect, keep trying.
20. *Check your understanding.* Periodically feed back what you think someone means, to confirm you have understood them.
21. *Spare the advice.* If someone has a problem, be supportive rather than telling them what they should do. 'The best decisions are those people reach for themselves'.
22. *Deal with negative feelings separately.* If conversation isn't working because of negative feelings on either side, that should become the subject of a conversation specifically to deal with the issue.
23. *Respect small talk.* Gossip and chit-chat help people stay close and connected.
24. *Base your feedback on facts.* Give descriptions rather than evaluations of people's behaviour.
25. *Be yourself.* 'Being genuine is at the heart of all worthwhile communication'.

A number of things are of interest in this lengthy list of dos and don'ts. Some points reiterate advice which, as we have seen in previous chapters, has a 'generic' status in communication training materials: for instance that one should pay attention to vocal and visual as well as verbal messages (15); summarize and paraphrase (14, 20); request clarification and strive for clarity oneself (18, 19). The influence of the 'assertiveness' model is evident in prescriptions about making 'I' statements (6) and being direct rather than assuming or hinting (8). Though this model is in its origins therapeutic, we have seen that it is appealed to in all kinds of materials about effective communication. Many other 'top tips', however, carry stronger echoes of the talk-as-therapy ideology discussed in this chapter. For instance, the norm glossed by Richard Rakos (1991) as 'ethical relativism' and by Donal Carbaugh as 'righteous tolerance' receives emphasis in several tips: about valuing difference (4); keeping an open mind and not judging (16); supporting people in reaching their own decisions rather than giving advice (21); and describing rather than evaluating their behaviour when giving feedback (24). The maxim that one can only be responsible for one's own behaviour is explicitly stated in (9). Open and honest 'sharing' are recommended in (7), 'recognizing and respecting feelings'; (12), which urges the reader to talk about 'real' experiences and feelings and to 'be the main character of your stories'; and (13), which recommends leaving nothing unsaid. Tip (17) emphasizes that others' self-disclosures should be received with a display of empathy.

Finally, the idea of communication as the expression of an individual's essential self is asserted in the last item (25) commanding the reader, 'be yourself'. The appearance of this platitude at the very end of the list brings out a contradiction which has been noted regularly throughout this book. Is 'communication' an expression of people's 'authentic' selves and 'natural' personality traits, or is it a practice of self-fashioning that requires art and technical skill, not to mention expert assistance? Since any absolute endorsement of the former alternative would call into question the status of the advice text in which it appeared (if conversation is just natural self-expression, who needs 94 pages of advice telling them how to do it better?) the contradiction is usually dealt with by fudging the issue. Thus a list of 24 tips which are basically exhortations to construct a 'better' self (one which is, for example, open, nonjudgemental and empathetic as opposed to evasive, prejudiced and brusque), are followed by the observation that 'being genuine is at the heart of all worthwhile communication'.

The attitudes towards talk which I have illustrated from the booklet are also evident in the supporting audio material. Echoing the definition of 'real communication' given by Katriel and Philipsen's informants, the 12 tapes focus on talk which takes place in private settings between intimates, and is primarily about sharing and resolving *problems*. Although one of the booklet's '25 Top Tips' is 'respect small talk', conversation of this kind is conspicuous by its absence. In all dialogic sequences without exception[9], the topic is a problem faced by one of the participants. Problems range from the grave (a child's illness, the breakdown of a relationship) to the relatively trivial (a dispute with a neighbour about a fence), but there are no instances in which talk does not revolve around some kind of problem. Thus there are no examples of narratives performed simply to entertain, of joking, idle chat or gossip. It is clear from contextual information that the participants in dialogues are meant to be intimates – heterosexual partners, family members or close friends – and that they are talking in a private or domestic setting. They may talk *about* work, or a visit to the doctor, for example, but it is evident they are not talking *at* work or *to* the doctor.

When I inquired about the rationale for these choices it was explained to me that they reflected people's own perceptions of what kinds of talk they needed help with. If so, this strikes me as interesting in itself, for it is probably an effect of the pervasiveness of the notion of 'communication' analysed by Katriel and Philipsen. No doubt few people feel the need for instruction in how to gossip, but some might aspire to become more entertaining storytellers, and 'asymmetrical' encounters (with doctors and bosses for instance) are an area in which many of us might feel we have some degree of difficulty. These, however, may not be the kinds of issues that people raise when a researcher asks them to reflect on 'communication problems' they encounter in their personal lives, because of the strong connection 'communication' in that context has with intimacy and 'sharing'.

Bad talk, good talk

Some of the BT tapes exemplify a particular didactic format, to which I will give the label 'bad talk, good talk', and which I will use to explore in more detail the moral universe that is constructed linguistically in *Better Conversations*.[10] In these instances the 'same' interaction (or monologue, though this is rarer) is performed in two variant versions: in the first version something goes 'wrong'; in the second it is 'corrected'. Comparing the two versions makes it very clear what norms listeners are being exhorted to orient to, and what is taken to be a good or bad outcome. Additional evidence on this point is provided by the surrounding commentary, supplied by what I will call the 'framing voice', which is heard on all 12 tapes introducing the topic and linking segments together (each tape has only one topic, but it may be illustrated by anything from one to six talk sequences). The framing voice belongs to a woman, whose low pitch and advanced received pronunciation marks hers as a voice of authority[11]. She specializes in unambiguously evaluative or judgemental comments like 'not much progress there!' and 'that was a much better outcome!' producing an effect which is not just didactic but strikingly moralistic.

The example I have selected for extended analysis comes from tape 2, on which there are three 'bad talk, good talk' sequences. The topic of this tape is responding appropriately when someone initiates talk on a 'difficult' subject: the framing voice introduces it by saying: 'Conversations can be quite fragile when they're just starting out, especially if they involve difficult subjects. Making an unhelpful response can kill them stone dead, as these examples illustrate'. In this example, the second of the three scenarios, the difficult subject – the first speaker's unsatisfactory relationship with an aggressive, bullying boss – is broached by a woman to a male friend. Below I reproduce a transcript[12] of the 'bad talk' sequence, followed by the comments of the framing voice, then the 'good talk' sequence and the framing voice's assessment of it. ('W', 'M' and 'FV' stand for 'woman', 'man' and 'framing voice'.)

W:	I hate that creep
M:	which one in particular
W:	Turner
	he winds me up all the time
	just for the fun of it
M:	he's not winding you up
	he's just doing his job
	you can't let that affect you
W:	it does affect me
	every day
	every day I see him
	and I want to hit him
M:	rubbish
	you're just getting it out of proportion
	calm down
W:	that's what he said this afternoon when we were talking about bonuses
	you're just as patronizing as he is
	forget it
FV:	everyone has the right to their feelings, and failing to recognize them isn't the best way of getting a conversation off the ground. It's better to let the other person know you recognize and respect how they feel.
W:	I hate that creep
M:	hey what's going on
W:	it's Turner
	he winds me up all the time just for the fun of it
M:	you've mentioned him before
	he really must get to you
W:	it's his attitude
	he's just so aggressive
M:	oh is he singling you out
W:	no he has a go at everyone
	you get to resent it so much in the end that it's totally counterproductive
M:	yeah I can see that
W:	I guess I've got to learn not to let him wind me up so much
	but I reckon he's the one with the problem
	he should be learning how to handle his staff better
FV:	That was a much better outcome, which resulted from someone being allowed to explain the situation in their own way.

The comments of the framing voice make clear what the overall point of the sequence is supposed to be: conversations on difficult subjects are more successful where participants show respect for others' feelings (everyone has a right to their feelings) and permit others to 'explain things in their own way' (listen but don't judge). In the 'bad talk' sequence the man clearly flouts the relevant norms. He contradicts the woman directly ('he's not winding you up'; 'rubbish') and refuses to accept her definition of what the situation is ('he's just doing his job'). He also criticizes her emotional reactions ('you can't let that affect you'; 'you're just getting it out of proportion'; 'calm down'). As a result, two negative outcomes occur. The presenting problem between the woman and her boss is not solved, and the actual interaction between the woman and the man becomes increasingly conflictual, eventually breaking down completely.

In the 'good talk' sequence things go very differently. The man produces utterances that function to acknowledge the woman's previous contribution and prompt her to continue ('hey, what's going on'; 'you've mentioned him before, he must really get to you') and 'neutral' – that is, nonjudgemental – displays of understanding ('yeah, I can see that'). He also produces a question which works as a 'probe', and whose significance I will return to below: 'oh is he singling you out'. This behaviour on the part of the man enables what the framing voice calls 'a much better outcome'. The interaction itself does not break down, and the woman succeeds in generating her own constructive solution to the original problem: 'I guess I've got to learn not to let him wind me up so much'.

Yet one could argue that in crucial respects these two versions are not as different as they might appear. Particularly puzzling is the framing voice's comment that the 'better outcome' of the second version 'resulted from someone being allowed to explain the situation in their own way'. It is hard to see that the woman explains the situation any more elaborately or any more 'in her own way' in the second version. Arguably what happens is rather that, by behaving less aggressively and less overtly judgementally, the man persuades the woman to accept *his* interpretation of the situation. This is the same interpretation he offered in the 'bad talk' sequence – that the woman is overstating the problem, which is not a case of victimization, but a case of personal ineptitude leading the boss to behave aggressively towards all his employees. The woman comes up with a solution very similar to what the man came up with in the 'bad talk' sequence. He said: 'you can't let that affect you...calm down'. She says: 'I guess I've got to learn not to let him wind me up so much'. These utterances project identical practical consequences: the boss's behaviour does not change, but the woman changes her response to it.

A pivotal utterance in the 'good talk' sequence is the 'probe' I mentioned above: 'oh is he singling you out'. This elicits the answer 'no he has a go at everyone', after which the woman begins to focus less on the boss's behaviour than on her own reactions to it ('you get to resent it so much in the end that it's totally counterproductive'). It is this shift in focus from the boss's behaviour to her own that enables the woman to generate a solution; and what brings the shift about is the man's probe. The probe is crucial, then, but *not* because it allows the woman to 'explain the situation in her own way'. On the contrary, discourse analysis suggests that 'oh is he singling you out' is not an exploratory question but a *challenge*.

The classic question posed in any kind of micro-analysis of discourse is 'why this now?'. Why does the man ask just this question at just this point, and what work does it do? First of all, the item 'oh' is a 'discourse marker' often analysed as a 'change of state' token: that is, it marks the receipt of new information, especially information that is in some way unexpected or surprising to the recipient (Schiffrin, 1987). So the production of 'oh' here acknowledges the woman's prior turn, 'he's just so aggressive', but also suggests the man has had some doubt or question about it. A question then follows about whether the boss is singling the woman out. The asking of a question implies that the answer – whatever it is – is somehow relevant to the assessment of the situation. So in asking just this question the man is suggesting that it *matters* whether or not the woman is being individually victimized. If she is, presumably, it is 'worse' than if she is not. Earlier she has described what is happening in the words 'he winds *me* up all the time'. The man is now *challenging* what he took her implicitly to be claiming – that the boss's aggression is directed against her personally – by putting her in a position interactionally where she must either commit to that account 'on record', or else admit that she is not being individually victimized. Of course, it is open to her to challenge the presupposition in his question; she could say, for instance, 'what does that matter?' (a question that certainly occurred to me as I listened). But in fact she answers the question negatively ('no he has a go at everyone'). In doing so, she tacitly accepts his presupposition and downgrades the strength of her complaint. It is at that point that she begins to redefine the problem as essentially her own reaction to the boss's behaviour.

What is accomplished in the 'good talk' sequence, then, is not that the woman's initial account is accepted without question ('someone being allowed to explain the situation in their own way'). Rather, the interactional skills of the man are deployed to help the woman to *change* her understanding of the situation. She may have a right to her feelings of anger and resentment, but she needs to be brought to the realization that they are, as she later puts it, 'totally counterproductive'. The sequence is in some ways like a textbook piece of therapeutic discourse, with the man behaving like a good therapist (he does not contradict or criticize; he listens, acknowledges and prompts; but also and importantly he probes where he sees a gap or a problem in the woman's account) and the woman behaving like a good client (for instance, she answers the question 'is he singling you out' honestly, though her answer will undermine her implied position as an individual victim; she then 'takes ownership' of the problem and generates her own solution to it).

The solution produced by talking – 'I guess I've got to learn not to let him wind me up so much' – is 'constructive' in therapeutic terms. It follows the rule stated in the list of 'Top Tips' as, 'the best decisions are those people reach for themselves': here it is the woman who proposes the solution, whereas in the 'bad talk' it was the man who proposed 'not letting it affect you'. It gives due weight to the preference for conflict resolution over conflict (whereas the only course of action alluded to by the woman in the 'bad talk' was the conflict-escalating 'I want to hit him'). It is also in line with the statement that 'while you can't be responsible for the other person's efforts, you can for your own'. Although the boss is not represented as blameless, his behaviour is defined as his own problem ('I reckon he's the one with the problem'). The woman cannot solve the problem of the boss being unable to handle his staff, but she can learn to control the feelings his behaviour produces in her. It appears then that the kind of talk which is preferred in the 'I hate that creep!' scenario is 'good' in virtue of orienting to certain norms, which bear a strong resemblance to the norms that regulate therapy-talk. From that standpoint, the 'good talk' sequence may be judged to have a satisfactory outcome. There are, however, alternative standpoints from which the solution the woman arrives at would not seem particularly constructive. A feminist or labour activist, for example, might ask why learning not to let a bullying boss 'wind you up' is 'better' than confronting him, or making an official complaint against him, or looking for another job.

I suggested above that co-operation and consensus-building are strategies that work best in a context of basically egalitarian social relations; where relations are unequal, however, the norm of co-operation may in practice serve the interests of the more powerful party – in other words, reproduce the status quo. That suggestion is borne out by analysis of the gender dynamics in 'I hate that creep!'. Not only can the 'good talk' sequence be read as a woman learning to tolerate being bullied by a male superordinate, the actual exchange seems covertly to re-establish masculine authority, by casting the man as 'therapist' and the woman as 'client'. This is in contrast to the stance taken overtly on gender in *Better Conversations*, which is that women have superior communication skills (witness the quotation above on women living longer than men, and the choice, which must have been deliberate, to make the framing voice female). In fact, this inconsistency between overt and covert ideologies of gender appears quite consistently in male-female 'bad talk, good talk' sequences. In 'bad talk' the man is usually marked as the 'guilty party' (that is, the party whose inept or unsupportive behaviour makes 'bad talk' bad). A logical corollary of that choice, however, is that in the corresponding 'good talk' sequence the man plays the supportive 'therapist' role;

consequently it is his communication skills that are foregrounded, not the woman's. Across the 12 tapes, there is a persistent tendency to show men and women playing stereotypical roles in mixed-sex conversation: either male expert with female acolyte or boorishly insensitive male with put-upon female (the one deviation from this pattern is an even hoarier stereotype, namely henpecked husband with nagging wife).

There is another interesting sequence on tape 2 in which two women are *jointly* blamed for what goes wrong in a 'bad talk' sequence. This is both a rare example of women being 'guilty parties' at all, and the only example in which blame falls on more than one party. The scenario has two women friends talking about that perennial problem, their men. The first initiates talk with the utterance 'I'm really worried about Pete'. The problem is that Pete has been staying out late with his male friends and giving her no satisfactory explanation; she fears he may not be committed to their relationship. The second woman responds by bringing up similar problems she has experienced in her own relationship with 'Steve'. The framing voice comments: 'What we had there was two people not really listening to each other at all. For conversation to work, one person must play the role of the listener'. In the following 'good talk' the second woman allows the first to 'talk through' her worries about Pete and refrains from introducing the subject of Steve.

It is not clear why the framing voice chooses to castigate both parties for 'not really listening' rather than attributing blame exclusively to the second woman, who should logically have 'played the role of the listener' (as indeed she does in the 'good talk' sequence). But what is most striking here is the confident pronouncement that conversation can only work if there is a clear division of roles between speaker and listener. Most researchers who have worked on naturally occurring conversational data would dispute that such tidy role-divisions are either typical or necessary. In the specific case of talk between women friends (of which 'I'm really worried about Pete' is meant to be an example) the behaviour disparaged by the framing voice – responding to someone's account of a problem by producing 'matching troubles' – appears to be extremely common (Coates, 1996). Far from being evidence that someone is 'not really listening', the production of personal anecdotes that echo stories already told signals both attentive listening and a sympathetic attitude to prior contributions. If one asks in what context of talk about troubles it would be inappropriate to behave in this manner, though, one of the answers that most readily comes to mind is, 'in a therapy or counselling session'. In therapy there is, indeed, a division of roles: clients speak about themselves, and therapists, while they need not be wholly silent, must 'play the role of the listener' insofar as it would be inappropriate for them to start talking about their own troubles. What we see in 'I'm really worried about Pete', then, is the transfer of a rule which has an obvious motivation in therapy-talk into a context where it has no compelling motivation at all.

Conclusion

In this chapter I have tried to show how advice on spoken interaction aimed at ordinary people in their 'personal' capacities as friends, spouses, lovers, parents and so on is pervaded by general assumptions and specific recommendations that originate in the practice of the 'talking cure'. My intention is not to disparage therapy in all its forms and in every context, but rather to question its incorporation into regimes of verbal hygiene whose objects are people suffering from no illness or disability, but either trying to deal with the kinds of unhappiness and conflict that will always be a part of any normal existence, or else confronting more serious problems which, however, have little to do with the way they talk and are unlikely to be cured by a dose of communication training.

I have also tried to show that the institutional practices of therapy, and their realization in rules specifically for speaking, embody various ideological/moral presuppositions about the attitudes and conduct of the 'good person'. An obvious question this raises is the question of social or cultural difference. Do the values promoted under the banner of 'better' or more 'effective' communication have the status of universal desiderata, or does good communication mean no more than speaking in those ways that are deemed acceptable/conventional/desirable by a particular class of people in a particular society? On what grounds, for example, are the individualistic values promoted by the therapist whom Cathryn Houghton observed preferable to the collectivist values of Mirna and her fellow inmates? On what criteria could one judge the man who says on *Donahue*, 'I respect your views of morality and I would expect you to respect mine' a more 'skilled' communicator than the woman 'having a *kros*' in the New Guinea village studied by Don Kulick? Why is the second woman in 'I'm really worried about Pete' being a better friend when she 'takes the role of the listener' than when she takes up the first woman's theme of complaining about men by offering 'Steve' up for criticism? Such questions are seldom broached, let alone answered convincingly, in advice literature on communication.

One might also raise the issue of *contextual* differences. 'Better conversations' are even more difficult to make general rules about than 'better negotiations', 'better business presentations', 'better service encounters', and so on, because of the great variety of purposes for which people may converse and the range of social roles and relationships they may enact in conversation. One of the oddest pieces of advice in the BT booklet is the following (1997: 16): 'It's a good idea to understand the reasons why a conversation is taking place. Only then can you have a clear idea of what role you can play to fulfil the conversation's purpose'. On a first reading, this appears to be one of those pointless statements of the obvious in which certain social scientists specialize. Read it again, though, and it dawns on you that it is nonsense. As numerous discourse and conversation analysts have observed, talk is both context-dependent and context-renewing. It is in the course of conversing (as opposed to in some 'pre-conversational agreement') that participants negotiate their purposes and their roles. In many cases, the primary purpose of having a conversation is to have a conversation.

In BT's universe, however, any worthwhile conversation must have some 'constructive' end in view. *Better Conversations* includes a section reporting the results of an exercise in which people were asked how they recognize a 'good conversation'. Their responses are boiled down to 'four key things' (BT, 1997: 6): both parties should be equally involved; there should be a 'willingness on both sides to be open'; the atmosphere should be comfortable 'so even if what you are talking about is difficult, the important things get said'; and the conversation should 'make a difference', producing some useful result. At the bottom of the page there appears, beneath a drawing of a dog chasing its tail, the statement 'some conversations go round in circles and fail to reach a satisfying conclusion'. The reason why dogs chase their tails – for fun – is also a reason why human beings have conversations, but apparently it is not a good enough reason. Even the injunction 'respect small talk', one of the '25 Top Tips', is followed by this explanation of why small talk deserves respect: 'It's an important way to establish and demonstrate our closeness to people. Also, gossiping is good for you. It helps you stay in touch with the details that make daily life easier to organize' (BT, 1997: 94). Small talk, it appears, can be justified on both interpersonal grounds (it establishes 'closeness') and instrumental ones (it enhances efficiency). Its legitimacy is established by finding reasons why it is 'good for you'. But why should talking be placed on a par with eating your greens, as a matter of duty rather than enjoyment? Why is the expression 'talking for the sake of it' invariably pejorative?

The belief that our capacity to talk finds its highest and most satisfying expression in the kind of serious, quasi-therapeutic problem-solving exchanges that Katriel and Philipsen's informants labelled 'communication' is logical enough within the framework of assumptions I have examined in this chapter. It also makes sense, more generally, in terms of Anthony Giddens's (1991) account of the construction of self-identity and of intimacy or trust in late modern societies. For all that it embodies a cultural logic, though, the kind of guidance discussed above, and throughout this book, seems to me a depressing phenomenon. Partly this is because of the reductive (and sometimes plain misguided) quality of the advice itself; the talk people produce without any 'expert' help is immeasurably richer, more complex and more varied, than anything appearing in the advice texts I have surveyed. But contemporary discourse on communication is also depressing (to me, at least) for other reasons. In the epilogue I will briefly revisit what I consider to be the most significant shortcomings of the discourse and practices I have been examining in these pages. I will also consider how we might move towards a more positive and less reductive view of spoken interaction and its place in social life.

EPILOGUE

In New York City in the spring of 1999, Mayor Rudolph Giuliani and his police chief Howard Safir made a well-publicized visit to a Harlem police station. The officers who had assembled for roll-call were presented with wallet-sized 'politeness cards' reminding them to address members of the public as 'Sir' or 'Ma'am', and to say 'hello' and 'thank you'. Mayor Giuliani explained to the officers: 'we want you to go the extra mile to act nicer; we want you to go the extra mile to act more respectful' (*New York Times*, 8 April, 1999).

The timing of this initiative was not coincidental. In February 1999, NYPD officers had shot dead an unarmed West African immigrant named Amadou Diallo; they claimed that he looked like a rape suspect they were seeking, and that he appeared to be reaching for a weapon. Critics challenged this account, charging that Diallo was a victim of police racism and brutality. During March 1999, more than 1,000 people were arrested during daily protests at Police Plaza. Against this background, Giuliani and Safir followed the example of countless businesspeople, politicians and self-help pundits, by defining the problem as a 'communication problem', a question of the way officers interacted with the public. They then addressed this supposed problem using the 'customer care' approach. Specifically, they adopted the verbal hygiene strategy I have labelled 'styling', instructing officers to 'act nicer...act more respectful' and prescribing linguistic markers ('Sir', 'Ma'am', 'hello', 'thank you', and so on) to function as tokens of niceness and respect. Officers in Harlem appeared unimpressed. One told the *Times*'s reporter, 'Anybody who has got to carry a card to deal with the public shouldn't be on the job'. Another commented sarcastically, 'You mean I can't say "hey, mope, get over here!" any more?'

The NYPD politeness initiative exemplifies two tendencies that we have encountered repeatedly in this book. The first is the tendency to treat all sorts of problems as being caused by poor communication and/or resolvable through better communication, even when – as in the Diallo case – this is patently a superficial analysis. The second is the resort to scripting, styling and other forms of linguistic regulation which assume that every speaker in every situation should follow the same procedures, and that speakers cannot be trusted to communicate without exhaustive guidance on even the most elementary points. This approach does not produce 'better communication', nor does it produce more 'skilled' and 'empowered' communicators. It cannot produce those things, because it negates the single most important ability of a truly skilled communicator: the ability to assess what is going on in a situation and choose strategies that are likely to be effective in that situation. Let me expand on that argument by briefly revisiting two of the keywords of enterprise culture and its discourse on communication: *empowerment* and *skill*.

Empowerment revisited

A central argument in favour of 'better communication' and the verbal hygiene practices intended to produce it is that the ability to talk in certain ways *empowers* people. Developing their communication skills enables them to realize their goals and take charge of their own destinies. In principle this is an argument calculated to appeal not only to enthusiasts of the new capitalism but also to many of its critics. Liberation movements of all kinds have long affirmed the importance of language and communication, both in collective struggles and for the individuals involved in them. But what is *called* 'empowerment' in the discourse I have examined has little to do with liberating people from existing constraints on their agency or freedom. In many cases it has more to do with teaching them to discipline themselves so they can operate more easily within those constraints: become more flexible, more team-oriented, better at resolving the conflicts and controlling the emotions that threaten to disrupt business as usual.

I have remarked on the narrowing of the term 'communication' so that in both expert and popular usage it is frequently equated with just those speech genres that foreground self-disclosure and collaborative problem-solving. Communication training tends to valorize the speech styles that facilitate those activities (egalitarian, co-operative, nonjudgemental) and to teach the associated discourse strategies (for instance 'mirroring', asking open questions, giving verbal reinforcement). It would be wrong to suggest that those styles and strategies have no value, but it might well be argued that their value is most limited in the contexts and activity types where the connection between language and power is most obvious. They are not calculated to 'empower' speakers in a legal contest or political debate, for instance, or in any kind of confrontation with authority. These are cases in which the goal of using language is not to produce self-knowledge and intimacy (real or simulated) with others, but to *influence* others, and thus to shape the course of events in the world. To realize that goal requires forensic or rhetorical skills – the ability to argue, to challenge, to persuade – which are, as we have seen, neglected in most texts and training courses. If power is, as some theorists have suggested, the ability to get things done, then one might have concerns about what *cannot* be done using only the techniques that receive most attention from today's communication experts.

Skill revisited

It could also be argued that communication training does not empower people on the grounds that people are never empowered by being denied the opportunity to exercise choice and judgement. That is in effect what many regimes of communication training do, even as they claim to be developing 'communication skills' – a paradox that arises because the prevailing notion of 'skill' is mechanical and decontextualized. To appreciate the point, it is instructive to compare 'communication skills' with what sociolinguists and ethnographers of speaking, following Dell Hymes (1972), call 'communicative competence'. 'Competence' in Hymes's sense involves more than just mastering a set of mechanical rules for speaking in this or that situation: it means understanding what *choices* you have and being able to assess their implications. As Carol Myers Scotton observes, language-using has 'a grammar of consequences. Speakers are free to make any choices, but how their choices will be interpreted is not free' (1988: 155).[1] A 'competent' speaker is one who understands the 'grammar of consequences' and can judge which of the available choices will come closest to producing the desired interpretation in a particular set of circumstances.

In the 'skills' approach by contrast, the term *competence* is often equated with the demonstration of discrete 'competencies' of the kind that can be ticked off on a checklist: 'does the member of staff answer the phone with a smile?' 'Does s/he greet customers whenever they come within 10 feet?' This approach does not require the communicator to make judgements about the contextual meaning and appropriateness of smiling or greeting, only to perform the relevant action 'correctly'. It belongs to the rationalizing tendency that 'allows individuals little choice of means to ends' (Ritzer, 1996: 19). The ability to choose means to ends (and to choose *between* ends) is the essence of Hymesian communicative competence. When that ability is negated, the outcome is unlikely to be 'better communication': recall Safeway's apparent belief that the best communicators are those who greet customers every time the opportunity presents itself, whereas those who use their judgement get 'written up' for poor service.

If on one hand the skills approach may be criticized for 'dumbing down' the communicatively competent speakers to whom it is applied, on the other it is open to more serious objections. Our choices about speaking are one important aspect of our self-presentation, of the identities we construct for public display. But some of the more restrictive practices described in this book deny individuals the freedom to make choices about how they present themselves, while obliging them to deal with the interpersonal consequences of choices made for them by others. Supermarket workers and flight attendants, for instance, may be well aware that in the local 'grammar of consequences' their behaviour is likely to be interpreted as signalling sexual availability, but they are not free to choose an alternative way of communicating which does not have that consequence. Practices of this kind are more than just restrictive: they are oppressive.

Communication inflation?

Nothing I have written in these pages is meant to imply that communication does not matter. However, as I suggested in relation to Mayor Giuliani's politeness initiative, there is a problematic cultural tendency to inflate problems of language and communication to the point where the larger social landscape is completely obscured. Communication matters, but it does not always matter in the same way or to the same extent; and it is almost never the *only* thing that matters. The case of Amadou Diallo provides an obvious illustration. It is probably true that a prompt apology from the NYPD would have improved matters, and conversely that the department's failure to communicate regret or self-criticism made things worse. But 'better communication' would not have placated the department's critics, who would rightly have pointed out that an innocent man was still dead. Apologizing does not bring the officers responsible to justice nor ensure that other officers behave differently in future.[2]

One could cite many other instances of the same obsession with 'communication problems' when other and arguably more pressing problems cry out for attention. Proposals to address various kinds of anti-social behaviour through communication skills training often seem to suggest that lack of communication skills 'causes' the problem: that domestic violence, for instance, or disruptive behaviour at school, occur because people cannot express their feelings and resolve their problems verbally. This is problematic to the degree that it elides the question of what gives rise to the feelings themselves. Would it not be pertinent to ask, for instance, what is making a child angry enough to throw classroom furniture, and try to do something about that? Obviously, 'communication' has some part to play here: you cannot help a child with a problem if s/he is unable or unwilling to tell you what it is. I do not dispute, either, what is frequently attested by people suffering various kinds of distress – that talking can make you feel better. Talking on its own, however, will not solve the problems of children suffering abuse, neglect or economic deprivation. What troubles me is not the suggestion that such children could benefit from talking about their problems, it is the emphasis placed on improving their communication skills as opposed to ameliorating their life circumstances. 'Communication problems' need to be kept in proportion, which means seeing them as part of a bigger picture rather than inflating them so they take up the whole frame.

Another kind of 'inflation' occurs when the everyday activity of talking is imbued by experts with an air of extraordinary difficulty, paving the way for language-users to be (mis)represented as extraordinarily incompetent. (One advice text, titled *Difficult Conversations* (Patton and Stone, 1999), reportedly emerged from 15 years' research by a Harvard think-tank; this might prompt the question, how difficult could a conversation be?) In previous chapters I have quoted assertions that suggest a massive communication skills deficit affecting great swathes of the population. We are told, for instance, that the average person listens at only a quarter of the optimum capacity, and that anything up to a fifth of the school population cannot learn because their communication skills are so poor. Here we see the 'falling standards' argument, so familiar in relation to reading, grammar and spelling, being extended to spoken discourse as well.

Liberating communication

I would like to see the subject of communication 'liberated' from the rationalizing apparatus of scripts and checklists, and from the inflationary discourse that represents it as the cause and the remedy for all the world's problems. I would also like to see the *subjects* of communication – individual language-users – given more opportunities to study and to practise ways of using spoken discourse that are 'liberating' rather than limiting and oppressive.

This requires, among other things, that the teaching of spoken language must go beyond narrowly utilitarian definitions of 'skill', embracing a much wider range of discourse functions, genres and styles. Once upon a time, even the most earnest of advice writers did not regard talking only as a way to transact life's business and solve life's problems. Conversation was an 'art'; like music, dancing and good food, good talk was counted among life's pleasures. The aesthetic and ludic qualities of spoken discourse are particularly neglected in most current approaches to communication. Why should schoolchildren not study – and practise – the oral performance arts of storytelling, stand-up comedy, advocacy and oratory? Why should less attention be given to formal and public speech than to quasi-therapeutic small group discussion?

I am arguing, in sum, that a more positive approach to 'communication' would celebrate the rich variety of spoken discourse, and acknowledge the complexity of the skills it demands. The discourse and practice I have examined in this book does not celebrate variety and complexity; in some cases it does not even tolerate them. Is it not ironic that a culture so overtly concerned about communication, so willing to expend thought, time and money on the subject, should have such limited and limiting ideas about what makes it good to talk?

APPENDIX: RESEARCH METHODS AND RESEARCH ETHICS

In this project I used a combination of textual analysis, interviewing and observation to investigate normative practices relating to 'communication' in a number of different social domains. Here I want to provide an overview of the data collection process (more detailed information appears in the notes to individual chapters) and to discuss some of the general issues and problems raised by it.

The ultimate object of investigation in this case was spoken language; but as I suggested in Chapter 2, the institutional regulation of spoken discourse is quite strikingly a literate practice, which could not be carried on in the forms this book describes without the aid of writing. For that reason, a significant proportion of the information I collected and analysed came from written texts. Sources I used included workplace communication training materials, employee manuals and appraisal checklists, educational policy documents, examination syllabi and assessment criteria, and self-help and advice literature. Much of this textual material is in the public domain and is readily available to anyone; some of it, however, is not publicly accessible, and I will explain below how I came by it.

I did examine some texts in media other than (just) writing. An example is the BT TalkWorks materials discussed in Chapter 6, which combine written text with recorded speech accessed via the telephone (there is also a TalkWorks website). In some settings videotape is an important adjunct to communication training, and some self-help materials are now available in audiotape form (typically they are intended to be listened to while driving). In general, however, I found that the most important and/or most detailed prescriptions appeared in written form.

In addition to analysing texts, where possible I observed and interviewed people engaged in the practices under investigation. Obviously, it cannot be assumed that the everyday reality of work or schooling is an exact reflection of what is written in the company manual or the examination syllabus. Interviewing and observation are methods for building up a more detailed picture of practice. Interviewing is also a method for investigating the important question of how particular practices are experienced, understood and evaluated by practitioners.

I should point out that my opportunities to observe normal routines, and more particularly to record them, were restricted. I had decided to concentrate my fieldwork efforts on 'new' (restructured, service-oriented) workplaces, since it seemed to me that far less was known about them from a sociolinguistic point of view than was known about, say, classroom discourse. I was especially interested in call centres, because of the extent to which communication is foregrounded in operators' work. But gaining access on acceptable terms was not easy. At the time of my research there had recently been a number of critical press reports about working conditions in British call centres, and some managers were wary of my approaches. Often they were eager to show me their centres, which they felt had been unfairly criticized, but reluctant to let me talk to their staff unchaperoned, and insistent on approving what I wrote in advance of publication (a condition I was not prepared to consider). The call centre from which I received most assistance (where I was able to observe, interview, gather written materials and listen in on, though not record, calls) had a fairly 'relaxed' work regime, with little of the petty regulation I found to be common elsewhere. That is unlikely to be a coincidence: in general, it has to be remembered that companies prepared to co-operate with an independent researcher may well be an unrepresentative sample, in the sense of being more open and more 'enlightened' than those which refuse co-operation.

Because of constraints on access, this study cannot match either the quantity or the quality of the observational data presented in the work of Robin Leidner (1993), Paul du Gay (1996), Stuart Tannock (1997), Joyce et al. (1995) and Whalen and Vinkhuyzen (in press). All these researchers spent extended periods in a single workplace or a small number of them, with the blessing of the organizations concerned. Then again, it was never my intention to focus exclusively on a small number of individual cases. Case studies are extremely valuable, but they require a serious investment of time to negotiate terms, build rapport and maintain relations of mutual trust, and this inevitably limits the number of sites a single researcher can hope to investigate during a finite period of fieldwork. Since my aim was to map practices relating to 'communication' across a range of institutions and domains, I needed a larger and more varied sample.

The case study approach has another potential drawback, assuming that the researcher obtains formal permission from the institution(s) concerned. In hierarchical institutions, that means enlisting the co-operation of people near the top of the hierarchy, and this may affect what you can learn from and about those lower down. Even where you are free to approach staff, their knowledge that you are there by courtesy of the management may influence what they say to you. Given the 'critical' nature of my interest in 'new' workplaces, this was a particular concern for me, which I addressed by making not only 'official' approaches to companies through their management, but also 'unofficial' approaches directly to employees, who were contacted and subsequently interviewed outside their places of work. I recruited these informants initially through mutual acquaintances: many university students work in service occupations, and I was able to ask students I knew to put me in touch with colleagues who might be willing to help me. Later on, some informants approached me after hearing about my work or reading a piece I wrote about 'smiley talk' (the language of customer care) for the [Glasgow] *Herald* newspaper in 1998.

Obviously, the organizations I approached 'officially' could not be the same ones whose staff I recruited 'unofficially'. The whole point of the dual approach was to be able to talk to employees in a context where I had no relationship with the organization they worked for, and no personal contact with their superiors. But the consequence was that I ended up with different kinds of information about different workplaces. For instance, I could only carry out on-site observations in workplaces accessed through 'official' contacts; ordinary employees were not in a position to facilitate access. Both kinds of contacts provided opportunities to interview individuals, but since in practice it was easier to interview people when they were not trying to do their jobs at the same time, I collected more interview data from 'unofficial' than 'official' sources. (In all cases I asked permission to tape-record interviews, and if the informant refused I made written notes; I did no clandestine recording. For more details on interviewing procedures, see the notes to Chapter 4.) Perhaps surprisingly, 'unofficial' contacts were my best source for textual materials not in the public domain, such as the manuals that set out standard operating procedures, the materials given out during training and the performance criteria used in appraisal. Managers sometimes showed me these materials, but they were seldom willing to let me reproduce them. The reason they usually gave was that scripts, training materials and appraisal procedures are among a company's commercial assets, and that reproducing them publicly threatens 'competitive advantage' by giving inside information to the company's competitors.

Whatever their reasons, many companies are obviously very anxious to keep details of workplace routine confidential. (An early pilot study I tried to conduct collapsed instantly because the workers I had chosen to approach were strictly forbidden to talk to outsiders about *any* aspect of their work. The rule was to refer all inquirers to the public relations office, which suggests the motive was to avoid bad publicity.) Almost all the employees who supplied me with material told me they knew, or strongly suspected, that they could face disciplinary action or even dismissal if their employers found out. As I noted in my acknowledgements, the vast majority of these informants asked me to withhold their names, conceal or disguise the identity of the organizations they worked for, and alter small details of the texts I reproduced where their content might make the source recognizable. I have complied with all such requests. Where I reproduce 'confidential' materials I usually identify the source in generic terms only, and most of the company names I do use are pseudonyms. Real names of organizations (like Wal-Mart, Safeway or McDonald's) occur only in the context of discussions based on information that is already in the public domain.

Some of the data I draw on in discussing workplace practices was collected by other people. A team of sociologists researching aesthetic labour in service industries generously allowed me to see transcripts of focus group discussions they had conducted, and I have made occasional use of this material. I have drawn more extensively on data collected by four of my own students at Strathclyde University, who carried out participant observation in their own workplaces while preparing written assignments for a course I was then teaching (they chose the assignment topic themselves). The students collected written materials – including noting down the contents of texts such as notices that could not be physically removed from the workplace – described the training and work routines they participated in (as well as the forms of resistance that were part of employees' culture) and in two cases interviewed a sample of their co-workers. I use their work with their permission; specific acknowledgement is made at the relevant point in the text or notes.

Obviously it could be asked whether it was ethical for me to encourage employees (including the students) to reveal information they were not supposed to reveal, especially when this exposed them to the risk of disciplinary sanctions. Ethical issues – both the issue of personal risk and the issue of betrayal of an employer's trust – were discussed in some detail with all individuals who offered me information. Though most, as I noted above, were concerned to secure guarantees of anonymity in order to protect themselves, they were less concerned about betrayal of trust. They felt that it would be unethical to breach the duty of confidentiality enjoined on professionals such as doctors and lawyers, but passing a researcher your customer care manual or telephone sales script was not seen to have the same implications, since the duty of confidentiality was motivated by purely commercial considerations. The question is whether the commercial interests of capitalist organizations should override any public interest in scrutinizing workplace practices. It will be evident that I believe they should not, and fortunately this view was shared by my informants.

That said, I should make clear that few of my informants (including those who approached me themselves) fell into the category of 'disgruntled employees'. Though my sampling methods do not permit me to treat them as a 'representative' group, they did represent some range of experience and opinion. With only one or two exceptions they were keen to impress on me that their jobs had positive features as well as negative ones; some explicitly expressed a desire to be 'fair' to their employers. I should also say that some employers were unmoved by the prospect of a researcher scrutinizing their practices critically. One of the students mentioned above told his boss in general terms what he was doing: not only did this man have no objection to the student collecting internal documents and interviewing people 'for college', he offered to be interviewed himself. Confident that he knew what was best for his company, he regarded academic analysis not as a threat, but as an irrelevance.

That observation brings me to a point that should always be considered in relation to research: who benefits, and how? In this case, not the capitalist organizations I had dealings with: I think I can say that I left my research sites exactly as I found them. This had at least as much to do with my informants' attitudes to me as with mine to them. As the anthropologist Penelope Harvey (1992) has pointed out, discussing the relationship of Western ethnographers to the people they study, it is foolish to think of yourself as either exploiting or empowering people who privately regard you as a naïve, incompetent child. That seems to be how many businesspeople regard the inhabitants of the 'ivory tower', a place they contrast unfavourably with their own 'real world'. Unlike some of the researchers cited above (Joyce et al.; Whalen and Vinkhuyzen), I did not take on the role of a consultant, paid to help a company or an industry develop better training or more efficient procedures. Occasionally such a role was proposed to me (I declined), but far more often the assumption I encountered was that I had nothing useful to offer.

My 'unofficial' informants sometimes told me, by contrast, that they had found our discussions useful as well as interesting. I took them to be endorsing the widespread belief that verbalizing your experiences to a sympathetic listener promotes self-awareness and reflection – in other words, 'it's good to talk'. While the irony of that response is not lost on me, given my view that too much attention is paid to the quasi-therapeutic functions of verbal interaction, I certainly do not wish to deny its validity altogether. Social research using interactive methods may indeed have some of the benefits that are claimed for 'communication' in general (see Cameron et al., 1992). If people did not enjoy talking about themselves, and if they did not find the experience in some way illuminating, it would be far more difficult to recruit unpaid informants for research projects. That said, however, I think the value of the research reported here – if it has any – will ultimately lie less in the immediate effects on those who took part in it, and more in the discussions which I hope this book will generate.

NOTES

Prologue

1   In the discourse that is my subject in this book, the word *communication* almost invariably refers exclusively or primarily to talk, rather than to writing, mass media or the use of new electronic communication technologies. These are also salient cultural concerns, but they are usually discussed under other headings (such as 'literacy', 'media literacy', 'computer literacy'/ 'IT skills'). The point is discussed further in Chapter 1. See also Mattelart and Mattelart (1998) for an account of how 'communication' in its various senses has been theorized.

2   The source is an interview conducted in 1998 with Andrew Bailey, a freelance consultant who was responsible for the BT booklet and supporting materials.

3   Readers may perceive a problem or a contradiction here: I am concerned with globalization, which by definition is an international, cross-cultural and cross-linguistic phenomenon, but I focus exclusively on English-speaking societies (mainly, in fact, on the UK and the US). Certainly it is a serious limitation that I have not been able to consider the questions raised by the diffusion (less neutrally, the imposition) of communication styles and verbal hygiene regimes from the heartlands of consumer capitalism to other parts of the world (such as Eastern Europe and Asia). This process has implications for the status of English *vis-à-vis* local languages (as Sharon Goodman (1996) observes, 'Market Forces Speak English'), as well as for the texture of interaction in various contexts. I have neither the space nor the research evidence to discuss those implications in detail here, but I hope people who are interested in taking up the subject will find insights they can bring to bear on that task.

Chapter I

1   British Telecom was originally part of Britain's General Post Office (GPO), and as such was a publicly-owned monopoly. It was separated from other GPO functions such as the Royal Mail, and eventually privatized, since when it has become a major player in the global telecommunications industry (for that reason it now prefers to be known by the acronym 'BT').

2   Statistics are taken from *Listening to the Nation: Executive Summary;* the quote is taken from *Communication at the Heart of the Nation: Implications for Building a Communicating Society.* These documents, available from BT, are unattributed, undated and unpaginated. The full report on the National Communication Survey is Smith and Turner, 1997.

3   At this point, a caveat is necessary. Anyone familiar with recent management theory will recognize the account offered below of 'new ways of managing' as one

in which differing approaches, originated by different people at different times, and in some cases contradicting one another, are blended together and presented under the umbrella of 'new managerial approaches' or simply 'enterprise', as if they were a single thing. This theoretical simplification may not be good scholarly practice, but it does reflect the way the ideas in question are often used in real organizations. As Micklethwait and Wooldridge (1997) point out, the most important change in managerial approaches over the last decade is not the adoption of any one model, but the more general willingness of organizations to continually remake themselves using new 'management tools' developed by theorists and applied by consultants. However, according to Micklethwait and Wooldridge, organizations' response to management theory tends to be *ad hoc* and uncritical. This produces 'contradictory organizations', committed simultaneously to ideas that do not go together (for instance, that a successful organization streamlines its workforce to minimize costs, and at the same time seeks to maximize the loyalty and trust of its employees). What follows, then, is a brief account of some key ideas that have influenced many organizations today, but it should not be taken as a rigorous account of management theory itself (on the history and status of this discourse, see Micklethwait and Wooldridge (1997), also Jacques (1996)).

4   This vision statement is written as if it were a collective utterance by all the company's employees: the pronoun in 'our work environment will value our ideas and our entire life experience' can only mean 'the workforce's'. My source confirmed that the statement was in fact written by senior managers with some assistance from an outside consultant; employees were not consulted.

Chapter 2

1   'Speech communication' is a disciplinary label more commonly found in the US than Britain. It denotes a multi-disciplinary social science approach, which may draw on, for example, psychology, linguistics and semiotics. 'Communication studies' is a commoner label in Britain, and there is some tendency for it to refer in particular to the study of mass communication media.

2   A comparative survey covering several ancient rhetorical traditions, Eastern (for example, India and China) as well as Western (for example, Greece and Rome) is Kennedy, 1998. Ethnographic discussions of metalinguistic discourse and instruction in speaking skills among traditional indigenous peoples include Stross, 1974 and Sherzer, 1987.

3   I owe this point to Mel Wininger (p.c.), who is currently doing archival research on the literacy practices of one midwestern college.

4   'Politeness' and its French analogue *politesse* had a particular and complex meaning during this period, related but not exactly equivalent to the meaning of *politeness* in present-day English. Writers on the subject of politeness often defined it in terms of the ability to be at ease in company and to make oneself agreeable to others. It also implied 'polish' or refinement. Something of the flavour of the concept, as well as the difficulty of pinning it down precisely, is conveyed by the words of Lord Chesterfield in his *Letters to his Son* (written between 1737 and 1768): 'The look, the tone of voice, the manner of speaking, the gestures, must all conspire to form that *Je ne sais quoi* that everybody feels, though nobody can exactly describe' (quoted in Cohen, 1996: 45).

5   I am aware that talking about 'psychology and therapy' in this way might be considered imprecise and misleading, so let me attempt to be more specific. First,

they are not the same thing (therapists need have very little background in academic psychology; psychologists need not engage in therapeutic or clinical enterprises). Second, each term is an umbrella for a wide range of differing concerns. In the case of psychology, the academic discipline should be distinguished from the genre known as 'popular psychology'; though it should be noted that popular psychology may draw on academic psychology. The subfields of academic psychology that are most often invoked (for example, their empirical findings are cited or their prominent figures mentioned) in literature about communication (pop psychological or otherwise) are: clinical; social; organizational. In the case of 'therapy', Anthony Giddens (1991) has warned against treating it as an 'expert system' on the grounds that it takes a bewildering number of different forms, none of which commands universal respect or even acceptance. In the literature of communication it is clear that certain therapeutic practices are the ultimate source of many specific recommendations, though the immediate source may be a work of popular psychology. Therapeutic paradigms that are influential in this regard include transactional analysis, the theory and practice of 'assertiveness' and approaches that have developed out of 12-step programs on the model of AA and the associated 'recovery movement'. I discuss the relationship between communication training and 'therapy' in more detail in Chapter 6.

6   The exact provenance of the materials is difficult to determine. The copy in my possession was obtained in the mid-1980s by responding to a newspaper advertisement. The advertisement was placed and the material supplied by a publishing company based in northwest England. However, the copyright notice suggests that this company had merely purchased the right to republish material produced almost three decades previously, probably in the USA. The notice reads: '©1951 Career Institute, Inc.', and then '1978 Career Institute, Inc (English Edition).' Whether significant revisions were made for a British readership is not clear, though it is evident that some additional material has been added in the form of a preface to each lesson headed 'a personal chat with your tutor'. These 'chats' are signed by an individual who is identified in the introduction to the course as the 'Director of Studies' for the UK company. It is not specified who will answer any letters students might write in search of tutorial guidance, but one assumes it will not be the people named as authors of the 12 lessons, most of whom must be retired or dead by now.

7   Again I am indebted to Mel Wininger, historian of literacy practices and assiduous frequenter of junk shops, for unearthing *A New Self-Teaching Course* and allowing me to examine it. Obviously my observations on this text as a product of its time, and similar observations made about *Effective Speaking and Writing*, must be treated with some caution. Although I have no reason to doubt the two texts are 'representative', generalizations about the genre they belong to would ideally be based on analysis of a much larger corpus of examples, and on proper historical investigation of their production and reception.

8   I will be returning to the items included in this sample throughout the book, but I should make clear that my overall corpus contains other materials as well, which I have excluded from consideration in this particular discussion. Here I focus on what I am calling 'instructional materials', i.e. materials supplied to participants in a training course or made available commercially for purposes of self-study. Typically such materials are quite voluminous, and are presented in the form of books, loose-leaf binders or folders, or in the case of some self-study materials, audiocassettes. Later on I will consider other kinds of materials, such as the scripts and prompt-sheets used to regulate workplace performance, the checklists used to appraise it, memos advising of changes in policy and practice, etc. These documents are not produced for training purposes, they are not comprehensive

in their coverage, and they do not aim to disseminate knowledge about communication, though some (for example, appraisal checklists) may be regarded as a supplementary tool for developing skills. They are therefore less relevant to the present discussion.

9   What is said about body language in communication training materials also seems to owe a (usually unacknowledged) debt to the work of Edward T. Hall, a pioneer in the field of intercultural communication and author of *The Silent Language* (1959). Hall was a member of the 'Palo Alto School' of communication scholars, an interdisciplinary grouping that came together in California in the 1940s and also included Erving Goffman and Gregory Bateson. The group opposed itself to then-current orthodoxies based on mathematical information theory and social scientific behaviourism. As will be noted below, however, communication training materials today remain strikingly indebted to these mid-century orthodoxies, even though they also make use of insights intended to refute them.

10 Inferential models, such as Gricean pragmatics or its development in relevance theory (Sperber and Wilson, 1986), assume that any instance of communicative behaviour is treated by the recipient, not as *containing* the producer's meaning, but as one source of *evidence* for the producer's meaning. The recipient must *infer* what is meant by putting that evidence together with other relevant knowledge. The weight given to any particular piece of evidence (such as body language as opposed to words) will depend on the whole configuration of circumstances in a given case. In any event, since the meaning is not 'in' the message, but emerges from what the recipient does with the message, it makes no sense in an inferential framework to claim that this or that constituent carries n% of the meaning.

11 In 1999 the trade journal *Training* conducted a survey on the subject of the evaluation of training by UK businesses. It found that 37% of organizations carried out no evaluation, and only 11% had ever produced a detailed case that training represented a good return on investment. (This survey was reported in the Management Plus section of *The Times*, June 24 1999.)

12 This charge was made in an editorial in the *New York Times* of April 27 1999, which criticized city and state authorities for wasting money on ineffective or unproven prevention programs.

Chapter 3

1   Wal-Mart is a chain of US out-of-town hypermarkets founded by Sam Walton – hence 'so help me Sam' – and in 1997 the *Wall Street Journal* reported it had taken over from General Motors as the largest private employer in the US. The 'oath' is cited by Micklethwait and Wooldridge (1997), who say that new employees are made to raise their right hand and recite it, as if taking the oath in court (see further, Ortega, 1998).

2   The Open University offers degree courses to adults by distance learning (or as the OU calls it, 'supported open learning'). Originally conceived as a 'university of the air', it makes extensive use of BBC radio and television broadcasts. The programme to which this section refers is titled 'Empowerment', and forms part of a course module on 'Managing in Organizations'.

3   This information comes from transcripts of focus group discussions conducted by Dennis Nickson, Chris Warhurst and Anne Witz with the assistance of Anne-Marie Cullen. Participants worked in banks, shops, hotels, bars and restaurants, and were recruited as part of a sociological study of 'aesthetic labour'.

All references below to focus group discussions are based on these materials; I am extremely grateful to Anne Witz and her colleagues for making them available to me.

4 These materials were obtained 'unofficially' from employees of the relevant organizations, among which I refer in particular to a non-profit arts organization ('City Arts'), a chain of shops selling electrical goods ('John Stephenson Ltd'), and two major supermarket chains. In all these cases I have participant-observation data as well as documentary materials, and in two cases I have interview data (my thanks to Raymond Bell, Gordon Graham, Samantha Houten and Karen MacGowan). I will also draw on information given in newspapers and on the internet about Safeway supermarkets in the USA.

5 I cannot resist quoting another, less felicitous example from the same materials: it is attributed to a manager from the British Harvester restaurant chain, who allegedly remarked: 'it's amazing how much better our meal tastes to the customer when the toilets are clean'.

6 'Caring, co-operating and communicating' appears to be a standard formula. It reappears in several different sets of training materials in my corpus, including the John Stephenson materials discussed in detail below.

7 The ethnomethodologist Harold Garfinkel used to set his students tasks designed to illustrate the complexity of ordinary social behaviour. For instance, he would instruct them to respond to utterances in casual conversation by asking 'what do you mean?' This was meant to demonstrate that there never comes a point when the meaning of an utterance has been exhausted: asked what they mean, people can always come up with a further layer of explanation. Students carrying out such 'Garfinkel experiments' very frequently found that they provoked a hostile response, until they explained to their baffled and furious interlocutors that they were only doing an assignment for college.

8 The source is an internet discussion group, 'Forced Smiles at Safeway'. For drawing my attention to the *Washington Post* report I am grateful to Scott Kiesling, and for additional assistance I thank Keith Nightenhelser.

9 The offence here may arise from two very different sources. On one hand there is a longstanding tradition of snobbish anti-Americanism in Britain, according to which American expressions are simply 'vulgar' and represent the 'corruption' of a language that originally belongs to 'us'. In complete ideological contrast, however, there is a critique of 'coca-colonialism' which is more concerned to preserve the distinctive linguistic and cultural traditions of other nations in the face of the global dominance of the USA.

10 For the examples given in this paragraph I thank Don Kulick (Swedish), Erika Sólyom (Hungarian), and two delegates to the 44th Annual Meeting of the International Linguistic Association in New York in April 1999, who made comments from the floor regarding post-apartheid South Africa and contemporary Japan.

11 I thank Amanda Harris for this anecdote. Although the issue did not come up in research I did in Britain, while visiting the US I was told more than once by workers in certain sectors (for example, clothes, cosmetics and toiletries retailing, waiting in upmarket restaurants) that male employees perceived the way they had to act as 'effeminate'. One woman reported men in her workplace receiving comments from other men present in the store to the effect that they were 'faggots'. Service scripts and style-rules are officially 'unisex', imposed without regard to the employee's gender, but it can be argued in many cases that they are more consonant with femininity as conventionally understood than with conventional (heterosexual) masculinity (this argument is made in detail in Cameron, 1999b).

12 From a feminist point of view, the same analysis could be made of most hetero-
    sexual partnerships: although these relationships are intimate, solidary and in
    theory egalitarian rather than hierarchical, emotional labour is not equally shared
    between women and men, but is disproportionately performed by women
    for men.

Chapter 4

1   For information relevant to this chapter I am grateful to the Bank of Scotland,
    BIFU (Banking, Insurance and Finance Union), USDAW (Union of Shop,
    Distributive and Allied Workers), and to those who provided data on several call
    centres, as follows. Centre A dealt with technical enquiries relating to telecommu-
    nications. Centre B belonged to a bank and Centre C to an insurance company.
    Centre D provided directory assistance to the subscribers of several telephone
    companies. Centre E belonged to a utility company and Centre F to a financial ser-
    vices (credit) company. Centres G and H belonged respectively to a cable/satellite
    TV company and a railway company. The types of data I obtained from these
    sources were reports and policy documents, employee manuals, training and per-
    formance appraisal materials, transcripts of interviews with managers, supervi-
    sors and operators, and notes from on-site observation. However, for reasons
    explained further in the Appendix, different centres provided different combina-
    tions of data-types.
2   Many call centres are open 24 hours, which means employees work a variety of
    shift patterns. For full-timers in the centres I discuss, shift lengths ranged between
    7.5 hours and 12 hours. Overtime working was common.
3   One manager I interviewed insisted that her organization, a large clearing bank,
    had not 'downsized' as a result of the shift to call centres. Instead she explained
    that the shift reflected a change in what branch staff were seen to be there for: not
    dealing with routine enquiries but selling additional services. 'Today', she told
    me, 'your branch is more of a shop'. A report compiled for the financial services
    union BIFU concedes that banks and insurance companies are not promoting tele-
    phone banking specifically in order to reduce the size of their workforce but
    'because it is the easiest way to centralize more information in a form that can be
    retrieved from anywhere'. However, the report notes that 3000 bank and building
    society branches closed between 1990 and 1996 (Reardon, 1996).
4   A special call centres supplement to the [Glasgow] *Herald* newspaper (March 9
    1999) advertised a large number of jobs for operators: the basic rate on offer in
    most cases was about £10,000 a year (around US $15,000), rising to about £15,000
    for supervisory positions.
5   It could be pointed out that other clerical jobs are just as repetitious – for example,
    working in a traditional typing pool or a contemporary data processing centre –
    while other service jobs equally impose on workers an externally dictated and
    relentless pace of work (for example, operating a supermarket checkout). In
    the supermarket case, however, there is usually more variation in pace over the
    course of a shift. No shop has a constant and unrelenting flow of customers. The
    data processing case is a better analogy (data processors also often have targets
    based on number of keystrokes, which are enforced, like call-handling targets in
    call centres, by hi-tech surveillance). Data processing is another kind of clerical
    production line; but I will explain later on what additional demands are made on
    call centre operators in virtue of the fact that their work involves primarily *spoken*
    language-use.

6   800 is a high number and 32 seconds an unusually short duration. These figures reflect the nature of the business of this particular centre – providing directory assistance. Other kinds of business are generally expected to take longer. For instance, an informant who sold rail tickets reported a target of four minutes (around 120 calls per eight-hour shift). Whalen and Vinkhuyzen report that customer service representatives logging faults in photocopying machines were expected to process 120–200 calls per shift. The lowest number I found was in Centre A, the telecom enquiries centre, where operators might process 80 calls.

7   The use of speech synthesis itself raises some interesting issues. According to the phonetician and speech synthesis expert Caroline Henton (p.c.), clients often want synthesized speech to simulate the same qualities (for example, 'warmth', 'softness') which are typically demanded of human operators in service environments. That this is an area of growing interest is confirmed by a *New York Times* report on the development of synthetic 'touchy-feely voices' (Eisenberg, 1999). See also note 9 below.

8   On 16 April 1999, a 'Lost and Found Sound' feature on US National Public Radio's news magazine programme *All Things Considered* focused on material from the archives of the phone company AT&T, and broadcast some examples of the early routines operators had to follow. One was a directory assistance call quite similar to the 1990s example reproduced below.

9   Eliza is an early instance of what is now known as a 'chatterbot', a machine that engages humans in 'conversation' with some degree of plausibility (something scientists have sought to achieve because indistinguishability from a human in conversation is the 'Turing Test' for artificial intelligence). It is predicted that chatterbots (the most recent models of which parrot less and 'understand' more) may in future be able to carry out customer service tasks that currently require human labour (Pescovitz, 1999).

10 Many call centres have guidelines which allow operators to terminate a call under extreme provocation, for example, if the caller uses obscene and abusive language. The manager who talked about 'being an Aunt Sally' ran a centre where this was not the case. His customers were usually calling about malfunctions in vital and extremely expensive equipment, and it was considered reasonable for them to express high levels of anxiety. Operators at this centre were expected to be able to cope with being sworn at, and the manager took account of this when recruiting staff.

11 Some call centres do require their employees to wear a uniform, despite the fact that the customer cannot see them. This is held to enhance performance by promoting the worker's identification with the corporate culture and image.

12 This survey was carried out by the Henley Centre on behalf of two corporate clients, and reported in *The Scottish Banker* (May 1998). Script-reading employees were not the top pet hate: what respondents disliked most was being greeted by an automated menu containing multiple options ('if you want to pay your bill, press 1', etc.). They also disliked systems that placed callers on hold but gave no indication of how long the wait time would be. Overall, the survey responses suggest that what most customers want is prompt attention from a *person* who will attend to their individual query. The more 'machine-like' an aspect of the service is, the more customers express dissatisfaction with it. But since in spite of their rhetoric managers have other aims besides delighting each individual customer (for example, processing the maximum number of calls in the minimum amount of time), this probably will not deter them from going further down the road of automation as better and cheaper technology becomes available.

13 A related consideration in call centres is that operators are not just talking, but typically also using a computer keyboard and mouse. Moves are often prompted by the computer, and it can take time for the next field to come up on the screen or for a search to be completed. The consequence is an accountably long pause, which the operator has to manage so that the caller knows the channel is still open and that something is happening. This is particularly difficult when, as one manager put it, 'you don't want your customers to think your computer equipment is crap'.

14 A similar effect is produced by scripted public announcements such as the ones that are now regularly made on British trains. A good example is: 'For customers wishing to smoke during the journey, smoking accommodation has been provided. Smoking accommodation is available in coach M for first-class ticket holders, which is located towards the front of the train, and in coach B for standard-class ticket holders, which is located towards the rear of the train. For the safety and comfort of all passengers, smoking is not permitted on any other part of the train'. For length, syntactic complexity, consistent preference for formal over everyday lexis, and needless repetition of noun phrases, this would be hard to beat.

15 The only scripts I have seen where this is seriously attempted are sales-talk scripts, which also have the peculiarity that they tend to script the customer's dialogue as well as the salesperson's. Sharon Goodman (1996) reproduces a pension-selling script which indicates the preferred manner of speech using 'stage directions' such as [*pause*] and [*softly*]. On sales routines see also Clark et al., 1994; Leidner, 1993.

16 My own contact with BIFU confirmed this: the union has taken a particular interest in the issue of occupational voice loss (and associated conditions of the vocal apparatus). Problems arise mainly from the working conditions of the call centre, in which it is not uncommon for operators to be speaking continuously without a break for five hours; since people all around them are doing the same, the environment is noisy and they may have to raise their voices. One occupational health researcher has noted that the voice most vulnerable to damage is 'the projected voice: the voice used with the deliberate intention of exercising an influence on others: appealing, commanding, trying to persuade, to win over the audience' (Dejonckere, quoted in BIFU, 1997). The same researcher notes that 'mental tenseness, stress and anxiety' (which as BIFU notes are common among call centre workers) promote 'functional disorder of the vocal apparatus'.

17 All references to interview data in this section come from a set of interviews conducted between May and December 1998. I interviewed four call centre managers, two supervisors and six operators, employed in different centres, located in central Scotland, northern England and London. All interviews were conducted individually, in most cases face to face but in two cases on the phone. They were 'semi-structured' – I had a schedule of questions, but I encouraged informants to respond at length where they had more to say, and did not demur when they introduced additional concerns. Each interview lasted at least 30 minutes. My main purpose in interviewing was to elicit facts about call centre regimes to supplement documentary information in my corpus. With one exception the managers had themselves been operators and they were also asked about their experiences on the phones. About half of all interviewees had worked in more than one centre and they were asked about the regimes operating in all centres they had worked in. I was thus able to elicit quite a lot of factual information from a small number of people. The data used in this section, however, come mainly from responses to a question dealing with the good and bad things about

working in a call centre. Here I was trying to elicit perceptions rather than facts, so it is important to bear in mind that my sample was small. Then again, although they did not know one another and were not interviewed together, these informants' reported perceptions were strikingly similar (for example, they all mentioned the same things as stressful).

18   I asked informants to say what kind of people they worked with (or employed, if they were managers). The categories most frequently mentioned were parents [meaning mainly mothers] of school-age children, students, young people taking a year out before university, and recent graduates. This is a typical profile for a form of so-called 'flexible' work, which is often done by people just joining the labour market or by those who have other commitments like studying, childcare or a second paid job (Dex and McCulloch, 1997). Graduates predominated in my own sample, almost certainly because they were more willing to give up time to be interviewed. In most centres the majority of operators were women, but subjects with some experience added that the gender imbalance was far less pronounced than it had been a few years before. Call centre work was also perceived as something done mainly by younger people. There are some workers over 40 whose experience has been in more traditional office and clerical jobs, but most are between 20 and 35. Many do not see their present job as permanent or as part of any long-term career plan. The graduate operators I interviewed had typically 'drifted into' call centre work after trying and failing to find jobs which required a degree. (According to one recent study (Shavit and Müller, 1998), about a quarter of UK graduates fail to find occupations of a status commensurate with their educational qualifications when they leave university.)

19   Some did not understand 'remote location' either: one of my Scottish informants reported that (English) callers sometimes reacted to her accent with astonishment: 'what are you doing in Scotland? This must be costing me a fortune!'. (In fact calls to most centres, regardless of distance, are charged at a special rate.)

20   The Chairperson of the Telecom Users' Association told the *Independent on Sunday* that in the association's view, many or most call centres are too understaffed to provide adequate customer service. The telephone systems in use at call centres typically have more lines than there are operators, so that queuing is common; but calls are charged from the moment the system picks up, not from when an operator takes the call. Both queuing itself and the cost callers incur because of it are the subject of many complaints.

21   For instance, the Communication Workers' Union has negotiated agreements with some employers covering the conditions under which calls will be monitored and in which tapes will be kept.

22   Stuart Tannock (1997) also cites a case where cannery workers have developed a sign language.

23   On workers' negative experiences of sex-line work see Danquah, 1993, and for an argument that the psychological effects of telephone sex work make it 'comparable to, if not more insidious than, being a flesh and blood prostitute', see Goldstein, 1991.

Chapter 5

1   A useful source on the history of oracy from the 1960s to the 1990s is Norman, 1992.

2   I call the approach 'enterprising' because there is a clear parallel between this model of education and the 'empowerment' model in management, which also

concentrates on specifying outcomes rather than giving employees step-by-step instructions (see Chapter 1).

3   In Britain, for example, competence-based National Vocational Qualifications were introduced in the late 1980s. A good explanatory (and critical) account of the NVQ competence-based model is given by Karen Evans (1995). A key skills curriculum which is intended to be followed by 16–18 year olds in addition to their academic studies is currently in preparation.

4   In fact it cannot be assumed that 'communication skills' are wholly unrelated to more traditional notions of 'correctness' and 'well-spokenness', i.e. competence in a high-status linguistic variety. Though in principle there is no necessary connection, in practice it appears that many employers who specify that their recruits should have 'good communication skills' are at least as concerned about accent and dialect as they are about things like active listening. In the course of research I was told a number of stories about employers, managers and examiners for vocational qualifications labelling people poor communicators because they used nonstandard grammar or had 'broad' accents. At present it appears that communication skills are supplementing rather than superseding more traditional forms of 'linguistic capital'.

5   A discourse marker is a syntactically detachable element used to 'bracket' a unit of talk. Examples are *oh, well, y'know, I mean*. An item of this type will mean something different as a discourse marker from its dictionary definition as an ordinary word. *Well* in 'well, I don't know about that' does not mean the same as *well* in 'are you well?' and *y'know* in 'it's difficult, y'know' does not mean the same as *'you know'* in 'If you know the city you won't have trouble finding the place'. Because their meaning is typically vague and only tenuously connected to the non-marker meaning, discourse markers are often disparaged in folk terms as 'meaningless' or 'fillers'. In fact, their function is to indicate something about the status of the preceding or following information and/or the attitude of the speaker to that information. For example, *y'know* marks what is being said as information the speaker assumes the hearer shares. *Well* often marks what the speaker is about to say as possibly not the 'right' answer from the hearer's point of view. So these apparently redundant, detachable items do important work in interaction, providing evidence for the state of each party's knowledge and their shifting orientations to that knowledge. (A detailed analysis of some common discourse markers in English is presented in Schiffrin, 1987.)

6   Here it should in fairness be acknowledged that the emphasis on 'cleaning up mallspeak' may well be more prominent in the *Globe* report than it is in the actual programmes being reported. Just as most college composition courses do not focus exclusively or primarily on mechanical errors in grammar or spelling, so their spoken language analogues probably have more, and more sophisticated, aims than just eliminating *like, y'know* and *whatever*. The interesting thing, however, is that features like these, which belong not merely to spoken rather than written language, but specifically to informal and interactive modes of speech, are being treated as educationally significant at all.

7   Angela Phillips (1998: 9) notes that in Britain, school-based initiatives of the 'life skills' variety are mostly undertaken by 'small voluntary projects or by inspired teachers in individual schools or LEAs [local education authorities]'. Many of the US projects discussed by Daniel Goleman are collaborations between schools and university education or psychology departments, which have underwritten programmes using research grants. Obstacles to putting the approach into practice more widely include a shortage of suitably trained teachers, problems fitting it into an already full school timetable and in some quarters, resistance to what one source quoted by Phillips (1998: 9) called 'mess[ing] with children's emotions'.

8   This body develops guidance for schools on promoting pupils' spiritual, moral, cultural and social development; it also takes up issues of specific concern to the government such as teenage pregnancy and parenthood. The Forum has been described to me as representing some range of views and interests, and as having a 'mixed' ideological agenda, neither straightforwardly conservative or traditionalist nor particularly radical.

9   Goleman's follow-up book *Working With Emotional Intelligence* (1998) is based on an explicit recognition of the resemblance between his notion of a 'socially competent' or 'emotionally intelligent' person and current definitions of an enterprising worker. He presents as a felicitous discovery the 'fact' that the most valuable workers in any company are not the smartest, best informed and most technically accomplished individuals but those with the best-developed 'character'. The discovery looks less remarkable, however, if Goleman's notion of character/competence/intelligence drew (consciously or unconciously) on an ideal constructed by capitalist institutions in the first place.

10   This anxiety plays out differently in Britain and the US, as was pointed out to me by a contributor from the floor at the Berkeley Women and Language conference in 1998, whom I thank. The difference reflects the much more pronounced concern with race, as opposed to social class, in the US: fears of a proliferating 'underclass' are strongly racialized. The conference participant who raised this issue suggested that young African-American men are not stereotyped as 'inarticulate' in the same way as white working-class men in the UK; their cultural milieu is thought to be a highly verbal one (though they are often stereotyped as verbally 'aggressive'). Where Black economic disadvantage is linked to some linguistic 'deficit' the argument is more likely to be couched in terms of low literacy levels or the use of a stigmatized language variety, AAVE, than in terms of 'inadequate communication skills'.

11   Limitations of space prevent me from rehearsing the many qualifications that need to be made to this generalization. A particularly important *caveat* is that statistics simply comparing 'girls' and 'boys' do not reveal significant differences between girls or boys of different classes and ethnicities, though more delicate analysis shows that such differences exist. For more detailed discussion of what the statistics show and how they might be explained, see Epstein et al., 1998; Marshall, 1998; on the (long) history of male underachievement, see Cohen, 1998.

12   Here it might be noted that the resort to pharmaceutical methods for controlling behaviour problems in children and young people is more common than either emotional literacy programmes or therapy. (This does not make criticism of the latter approaches otiose, but it does put it into a slightly different perspective.) It has been suggested to me informally that there is a class/race dimension to this issue (i.e. privileged kids get therapy while others get Ritalin). Philomena Mariani reports however that the majority of the children in the clinical populations used for the 'conduct disorder' studies she examined were white and middle class. The key demographic indicator for a CD diagnosis was gender, with boys outnumbering girls by four to one.

13   One book-length treatment of language behaviour from the perspective of evolutionary theory, which discusses sex/gender differences at length, is Dunbar, 1996.

14   PET and MRI stand for 'Positron Emission Tomography' and 'Magnetic Resonance Imaging'. Both are essentially techniques for making brain activity (its location and intensity) visible.

15   That not only arguing, but also accusing and name-calling, are valued as skills in some traditions will be illustrated in Chapter 6 below.

Chapter 6

1   It also contrasts with a newer 'tabloid' format, also issue-based but featuring more guests, shorter segments, and a more 'sensationalist' approach (see further Gamson, 1998).

2   Mel Wininger points out to me that on some of the newer 'tabloid' shows, private/intimate encounters are publicly staged, for example, warring couples reconcile on camera.

3   Here I should make clear that although I dispute that there is something uniquely 'American' about the cultural patterns described by Carbaugh, Katriel and Philipsen, I am not claiming that these patterns are universal or even consistent across advanced capitalist societies. I do not have sufficient evidence to make such claims (for I take it that the extent to which certain ideas are diffused across cultures, and the kind of influence they exert in different settings, is a question requiring empirical investigation). When discussing the meaning of the term *communication* it obviously needs to be remembered that we are dealing with an *English* word. It cannot be assumed that the equivalents which appear in bilingual dictionaries are used with the same range of meanings – though conversely I would not want to assume that the meanings of words in one language cannot be influenced by their usage in others. In sum, the observations made here are meant to apply primarily to societies in which English is the language of mainstream discourse, though without foreclosing on the possibility that they may apply more widely.

4   The 'recovery movement' is associated with the '12-step program' approach to addiction and dependency, pioneered by Alcoholics Anonymous. However, many groups today support people 'in recovery' from a wider range of afflictions, such as eating disorders, co-dependency, 'loving too much', and so on. A fuller account is given by Rapping, 1996.

5   This parenthetical comment is prompted by a minor scandal that took place in Britain in early 1999. The BBC launched an investigation and eventually disciplined researchers on a daytime TV talk show when it was revealed that they had been booking professional actors to appear as guests because they were unable to find suitable 'ordinary' people. One response made by media commentators to this revelation was that it had been bound to happen, because the talk show was an imported, American genre, which Britain was ill-equipped to imitate. Talk shows depended on a steady supply of ordinary people able and willing to talk about themselves in particular ways. In America, the argument went, large numbers of people had learned this 'skill' by being in therapy; in Britain on the other hand, almost no one had experienced therapy and so the supply of suitable talk-show guests for home-grown TV programmes had long since been exhausted.

6   The expert literature on this subject is full of abstract and euphemistic or misleading terms like 'family violence': usually it is only one person within a family who engages in violence (and usually this is an adult male). In a moment we will encounter the phrase 'violent dating episode', a piece of jargon which renders it unclear what (and whose) behaviour is being talked about.

7   The community studied by Kulick is not unique in this respect. Ethnographers in a number of cultures have reported instances where speech genres involving or consisting of inventive verbal abuse have high value, and where certain individuals are recognized as particularly skilled in the abusive arts. One example is discussed in Labov's well-known article on ritual insults among young African-American men in New York City (Labov, 1972).

8   At the time of writing the numbers are still in operation (0800 700 921–32), but new *TalkWorks* materials are in preparation and the original tapes are unlikely to be available much longer. Supplies of the original booklet have already been exhausted. I thank consultant Andrew Bailey for answering questions on this and many other aspects of the *TalkWorks* initiative.

9   Here I should clarify that the tapes include monologues (11 sequences, most of which also deal with problems) as well as dialogues (15 sequences). There are no sequences where more than two participants engage in talk – probably because this would be hard to follow on the telephone.

10 A more extended version of this discussion can be found in Cameron, 1999a.

11 Received pronunciation (RP) is an accent of British English that is not associated with any region of the country but is purely a marker of social class – it marks upper or upper middle-class status. RP is itself not entirely homogeneous, and some analysts use the designation 'advanced' for the kind of RP characteristically used by upper-class or aristocratic speakers. In tests designed to uncover the social evaluations people make on the basis of accent, RP speakers score highly on traits like authority and competence (but not friendliness or warmth). BT's choice of an advanced RP-speaker for the framing voice thus reinforces the authority that is already implied by the content and positioning of her scripted remarks.

12 Here it should be borne in mind that the tape records a spoken performance of a written script, and furthermore a rather artificial performance designed to meet callers' need for immediate intelligibility (thus there are no false starts, redundant repetitions, overlaps or simultaneous speech). With that in mind, I judged it unnecessary (and potentially distracting) to render features of the performance in detail. I have simply 'chunked' the scripted dialogue to reflect the prosodic organization actors give it; in the case of the framing voice's comments I have not even done that much, since whereas the dialogue shows some concern to simulate 'ordinary' talk, the framing voice makes no attempt whatever to disguise the fact she is reading a formal, written text aloud. The analysis I offer below does not depend on anything that is not actually in the script.

Epilogue

1   Scotton's observation is made in the context of a discussion of code-switching, but her point applies more generally.

2   I should point out here that the officers involved in the Diallo shooting had been indicted on second-degree murder charges shortly before Giuliani and Safir's visit to Harlem. They are still awaiting trial as I write.

BIBLIOGRAPHY

Bayliss, Valerie (1999) *Opening Minds: Education for the 21st Century.* London: Royal Society of Arts.

Berne, Eric (1966) *The Games People Play.* New York: Grove Press.

Berne, Eric (1975) *What do you say after you say hello?* London: Corgi Books.

BIFU [Banking, Insurance and Finance Union] (1997) *Occupational Voice Loss: A Negotiator's Guide.* BIFU Research Department.

Boden, Deirdre (1994) *The Business of Talk: Organizations in Action.* Cambridge: Polity.

Bourdieu, Pierre (1991) *Language and Symbolic Power* (ed. John B. Thompson; trans. Gino Raymond and Matthew Adamson). Cambridge: Polity.

Britton, James (1970) *Language and Learning.* London: Allen Lane.

Brown, Penelope and Levinson, Stephen (1987) *Politeness: Some Universals in Language Usage.* Cambridge: Cambridge University Press.

BT (1997) *TalkWorks: How to Get More Out of Life through Better Conversations.* London: British Telecommunications plc.

BT (n.d.) *The National Communication Survey: Executive Summary.* London: BT Forum.

BT (n.d.) *Communication at the Heart of the Nation: Implications for Building a Communicating Society.* London: BT Forum.

Burchell, Graham (1993) 'Liberal government and the techniques of the self', *Economy and Society,* 22 (3): 266–82.

Burke, Peter (1993) *The Art of Conversation.* Ithaca, NY: Cornell University Press.

Cahn, Dudley (1996) 'Family violence from a communication perspective', in Dudley Cahn and Sally Lloyd (eds), *Family Violence from a Communication Perspective.* Thousand Oaks, CA: Sage. pp. 1–19.

Cahn, Dudley and Lloyd, Sally (eds) (1996) *Family Violence from a Communication Perspective.* Thousand Oaks, CA: Sage Publications.

Cameron, Deborah (1995) *Verbal Hygiene.* London and New York: Routledge.

Cameron, Deborah (1999a) 'Better conversations: a morality play in twelve tapes'. *Feminism and Psychology,* 9 (3): 325–43.

Cameron, Deborah (1999b) 'Styling the worker: language, gender and emotional labor in new service workplaces (or, you don't have to be nice to work here but it helps to pretend)'. Paper presented to the 44th Annual Meeting of the International Linguistic Association, New York.

Cameron, Deborah, Frazer, Elizabeth, Harvey, Penelope, Rampton, M.B.H. and Richardson, Kay (1992) *Researching Language: Issues of Power and Method.* London: Routledge.

Carbaugh, Donal (1988) *Talking American: Cultural Discourses on Donahue.* Norwood, NJ: Ablex.

Career Institute, Inc. (1978 [1951]) *Effective Speaking and Writing.* Stockport, Cheshire: R.W. Heap Publishing.

Carnegie, Dale (1982) *How to Win Friends and Influence People.* Revised edn. New York: Pocket Books.

Carter, Meg (1998) 'Despite the palm trees, working in a call centre can be far from paradise'. *Independent on Sunday*, 17 May.

Catan, Liza, Dennison, Catherine and Coleman, John (1996) *Getting Through: Effective Communication in the Teenage Years*. London: BT Forum.

Cheshire, Jenny (1999) 'Standard spoken English', in Tony Bex and Richard Watts (eds), *Standard English: The Widening Debate*. London: Routledge. pp. 129–48.

Cheshire, Jenny and Jenkins, Nancy (1991) 'Gender issues in the GCSE oral English examination: Part II. *Language and Education*, 5 (1): 19–40.

Clark, Colin, Drew, Paul and Pinch, Trevor (1994) 'Managing customer "objections" during real-life sales negotiations', *Discourse & Society*, 5 (4): 437–62.

Clyne, Michael (1996) *Inter-cultural Communication at Work*. Cambridge: Cambridge University Press.

Coates, Jennifer (1996) *Women Talk: Conversation Between Women Friends*. Oxford: Blackwell.

Cohen, Michèle (1996) *Fashioning Masculinity: National Identity and Language in the Eighteenth Century*. London: Routledge.

Cohen, Michèle (1998) 'A habit of healthy idleness: boys' underachievement in historical perspective', in Debbie Epstein, Jannette Elwood, Valerie Hay and Janet Maw (eds), *Failing Boys: Issues in Gender and Achievement*. Buckingham: Open University Press. pp. 19–34.

Covey, Stephen (1989) *The Seven Habits of Highly Effective People*. New York: Simon & Schuster.

Czerniawska, Fiona (1998) *Corporate Speak: The Use of Language in Business*. London: Macmillan.

Danquah, Meri Nana-Ama (1993) 'Hanging up on phone sex', *Washington Post*, June 13: C1.

Department of Education and Science [DES] (1988) *Report of the Committee of Inquiry into the Teaching of English Language [the Kingman Report]*. London: HMSO.

Dex, Shirley, and McCulloch, Andrew (1997) *Flexible Employment: The Future of Britain's jobs*. London: Macmillan.

Dimmick, Sally (1995) *Successful Communication through Neurolinguistic Programming: A Trainer's Guide*. Aldershot: Gower.

Drew, Paul and Heritage, John (eds) (1992) *Talk at Work: Interaction in Institutional Settings*. Cambridge: Cambridge University Press.

Drew, Paul and Sorjonen, Marja-Leena (1997) 'Institutional dialogue', in Teun van Dijk (ed.), *Discourse as Social Interaction: Discourse Studies Vol. II*. Newbury Park: Sage. pp. 92–118.

Dunbar, Robin (1996) *Grooming, Gossip and the Evolution of Language*. London: Faber & Faber.

Eckert, Penelope (1996) 'Vowels and nail polish: the emergence of linguistic style in the pre-adolescent heterosexual marketplace', Stanford University/Institute for Research on Learning.

Eisenberg, Anne (1999) 'Text-to-speech programs with touchy-feely voices'. *New York Times*, 25 March.

Elliott, Larry and Atkinson, Dan (1998) *The Age of Insecurity*. London: Verso.

Epstein, Debbie, Elwood, Jannette, Hey, Valerie and Maw, Janet (eds) (1998) *Failing Boys: Issues in Gender and Achievement*. Buckingham: Open University Press.

Evans, Karen (1995) 'Competence-based education and training: the British experience'. Issues Paper 3, Office of Training and Further Education, Victoria [Australia] Department of Education. Victoria: TAFE.

Fairclough, Norman (1989) *Language and Power*. London: Longman.

Fairclough, Norman (1992) *Discourse and Social Change*. Cambridge: Polity.

Fairclough, Norman (1995) *Critical Discourse Analysis*. London: Longman.

Fishman, Pamela (1983) 'Interaction: the work women do', in Barrie Thorne, Cheris Kramarae and Nancy Henley (eds), *Language, Gender and Society*. Rowley, MA: Newbury House. pp. 89–102.

Foucault, Michel (1983) 'On the genealogy of ethics: an overview of work in progress', in H. Dreyfus and P. Rabinow (eds), *Beyond Structuralism and Hermeneutics*, 2nd edn. Chicago: University of Chicago Press. pp. 29–52.

Freed, Alice (1992) 'We understand perfectly: a critique of Tannen's view of cross sex communication', in Kira Hall, Mary Bucholtz and Birch Moonwomon (eds), *Locating Power*. Proceedings of the Second Berkeley Conference on Women and Language, Vol. I. Berkeley, CA: Berkeley Women and Language Group. pp. 144–52.

Freemantle, David (1998) *What Customers Like About You: Adding Emotional Value for Service Excellence and Competitive Advantage*. London & Santa Rosa, CA: Nicholas Brealey.

Gal, Susan (1995) 'Language, gender and power: an anthropological review', in Kira Hall and Mary Bucholtz (eds), *Gender Articulated: Language and the Socially Constructed Self*. London: Routledge. pp. 169–82.

Gamson, Joshua (1998) *Freaks Talk Back: Tabloid Talk Shows and Sexual Nonconformity*. Chicago: University of Chicago Press.

Gay, Paul du (1996) *Consumption and Identity at Work*. London: Sage.

Gee, James Paul, Hull, Glynda and Lankshear, Colin (1996) *The New Work Order*. St. Leonards, NSW: Allen & Unwin.

Gervasio, Amy and Crawford, Mary (1989) 'Social evaluations of assertiveness: a critique and speech act reformulation', *Psychology of Women Quarterly*, 13: 1–25.

Giddens, Anthony (1991) *Modernity and Self Identity: Self and Society in the Late Modern Age*. Cambridge: Polity.

Gilbert, Pam (1998) 'Gender and schooling in new times: the challenge of boys and literacy', *Australian Educational Researcher*, 25 (1): 15–36.

Goffman, Erving (1959) *The Presentation of Self in Everyday Life*. Garden City, NY: Doubleday.

Goldberg, Carey (1998) 'After Girls Get The Attention, Focus Shifts To Boys' Woes'. *New York Times*, 23 April: A1.

Goldstein, Harry (1991) 'The dial-ectic of desire: for women at the other end of the phone sex line, some fantasies ring painfully true', *Utne Reader*, March/April: 32–3.

Goleman, Daniel (1995) *Emotional Intelligence*. New York: Bantam Books.

Goleman, Daniel (1998) *Working with Emotional Intelligence*. New York: Bantam Books.

Goodman, Sharon (1996) 'Market forces speak English', in Sharon Goodman and David Graddol (eds), *Redesigning English: New Texts, New Identities*. London: Routledge. pp. 141–64.

Gray, John (1992) *Men are from Mars, Women are from Venus*. New York: HarperCollins.

Grimsley, Kirstin Downey (1998) 'Service with a forced smile: Safeway's courtesy campaign also elicits some frowns'. *Washington Post*, 18 October: A1.

Gumperz, John J. (1982a) *Discourse Strategies*. Cambridge: Cambridge University Press.

Gumperz, John J. (ed.) (1982b) *Language and Social Identity*. Cambridge: Cambridge University Press.

Gunnarsson, Britt-Louise, Linell, Per and Nordberg, Bengt (1997) *The Construction of Professional Discourse*. London: Longman.

Hall, Edward T. (1959) *The Silent Language*. New York: Doubleday.

Hall, Kira (1995) 'Lip service on the fantasy lines', in Kira Hall and Mary Bucholtz (eds), *Gender Articulated: Language and the Socially Constructed Self*. London: Routledge. pp. 183–216.

Handy, Charles (1996) *Beyond Certainty: The Changing World of Organizations*. London: Hutchinson.

Harré, Rom (ed.) (1986) *The Social Construction of Emotions*. Oxford: Blackwell.

Harris, Thomas (1969) *I'm OK, You're OK: A Practical Guide to Transactional Analysis*. New York: Harper & Row.

Harvey, Penelope (1992) 'Bilingualism in the Peruvian Andes', in Deborah Cameron, Elizabeth Frazer, Penelope Harvey, B.M.H. Rampton and Kay Richardson, *Researching Language: Issues of Power and Method*. London: Routledge. pp. 65–89.

Hochschild, Arlie (1983) *The Managed Heart: The Commercialization of Human Feeling*. Berkeley, CA: University of California Press.

Hollway, Wendy (1991) *Work Psychology and Organizational Behaviour: Managing the Individual at Work*. London: Sage.

Houghton, Cathryn (1995) 'Managing the body of labor: the treatment of reproduction and sexuality in a therapeutic institution', in Kira Hall and Mary Bucholtz (eds), *Gender Articulated: Language and the Socially Constructed Self*. London: Routledge. pp. 121–41.

Hunter, Estelle B. (1935) *A New Self-Teaching Course in Practical English and Effective Speaking: Comprising Vocabulary Development, Grammar, Pronunciation, Enunciation and the Fundamental Principles of Effective Oral Expression*. Chicago: The Better-Speech Institute of America.

Hutchby, Ian (1999) 'Frame alignment and footing in the organization of talk radio openings', *Journal of Sociolinguistics* 3 (1): 41–63.

Hyde, Janet Shibley and Linn, Marcia C. (1988) 'Gender differences in verbal ability: a meta-analysis', *Psychological Bulletin*, 104: 53–69.

Hymes, Dell (1972) 'On communicative competence', in J.B. Pride and Janet Holmes (eds), *Sociolinguistics*. Harmondsworth: Penguin. pp. 269–93.

Jacques, Roy (1996) *Manufacturing the Employee: Management Knowledge from the 19th to the 21st Centuries*. London and Thousand Oaks, CA: Sage.

Jaeger, Jeri (1998) 'Brains and language: does sex make a difference?' Paper presented at the Fifth Berkeley Women and Language Conference, Berkeley, California.

Jenkins, Nancy and Cheshire, Jenny (1990) 'Gender issues in the GCSE oral English examination, part I', *Language and Education*, 4 (4): 261–92.

Joyce, H., Nesbitt, C., Scheeres, H., Slade, D. and Solomon, N. (1995) *Effective Communication in the Restructured Workplace*. 2 vols. Victoria, Australia: National Food Industry Training Council.

Katriel, Tamar and Philipsen, Gerry (1981) '"What we need is communication": "communication" as a cultural term in some American speech', *Communication Monographs*, 48: 301–17.

Keiner, Judy (1992) 'A brief history of the origins of the National Oracy Project', in Kate Norman (ed.), *Thinking Voices: The Work of the National Oracy Project*. London: Hodder and Stoughton. pp. 247–55.

Kennedy, George (1998) *Comparative Rhetoric: An Historical and Cross-cultural Introduction*. London and New York: Oxford University Press.

Kjellerup, Niels (1998) 'Call centre productivity: a sustainable solution'. The coaching culture call center website, *www.callcentres.com.au*

Kulick, Don (1993) 'Speaking as a woman: structure and gender in domestic arguments in a New Guinea village', *Cultural Anthropology*, 8 (4): 510–41.

Labov, William (1997 [1972]) 'Rules for ritual insults', in Nikolas Coupland and Adam Jaworski (eds), *Sociolinguistics: A Reader and Coursebook*. London: Macmillan. pp. 472–86.

Lakoff, George and Johnson, Mark (1980) *Metaphors We Live By*. Chicago: University of Chicago Press.

Langford, Wendy (1998) 'All you need is love?' *Trouble & Strife*, 38: 60–8.

Leidner, Robin (1993) *Fast Food, Fast Talk: Service Work and the Routinization of Everyday Life*. Berkeley, CA: University of California Press.

Leonard, Mark (1997) *Britain*™: *Renewing Our Identity*. London: Demos.

Levinson, Stephen (1992) 'Activity types and language', in Paul Drew and John Heritage (eds), *Talk At Work*. Cambridge: Cambridge University Press. pp. 66–100.

Lutz, Catherine A. and Abu-Lughod, Lila (eds) (1990) *Language and the Politics of Emotion*. Cambridge and New York: Cambridge University Press.

McMillan, Sandy (1996) *How to be a Better…Communicator*. London: Industrial Society/Kogan Page.

Mahony, Pat (1998) 'Girls will be girls and boys will be first', in Debbie Epstein, Jannette Elwood, Valerie Hay and Janet Maw (eds), *Failing Boys: Issues in Gender and Achievement*. Buckingham: Open University Press. pp. 37–55.

Mariani, Philomena (1995) 'Law-and-order science', in Maurice Berger, Brian Wallis and Simon Watson (eds), *Constructing Masculinity*. New York: Routledge. pp. 135–56.

Marshall, Bethan (1998) 'Boys go to Jupiter to be more stupider, and girls go to Mars to be super-stars', *Critical Quarterly*, 40 (2): 95–103.

Mattelart, Armand and Mattelart, Michèle (1998) *Theories of Communication: A Short Introduction*. Trans. Susan Gruenheck Taponier and James A. Cohen. London and Thousand Oaks, CA: Sage Publications.

Micklethwait, John and Wooldridge, Adrian (1997) *The Witch Doctors: What the Management Gurus Are Saying, Why It Matters and How to Make Sense of It*. London: Mandarin Books.

Milroy, James and Milroy, Lesley (1991) *Authority in Language*, 2nd edn. London: Routledge.

Mumby, D. and Clair, R.D. (1997) 'Organizational Discourse', in Teun van Dijk (ed.), *Discourse as Social Interaction: Discourse Studies Vol II*. Newbury Park: Sage. pp. 181–205.

Mullen, John (1997) 'Graduates deficient in soft skills', *People Management*, November.

Norman, Kate (ed.) (1992) *Thinking Voices: The Work of the National Oracy Project*. London: Hodder and Stoughton.

Office for Standards in Education [Ofsted] (1993) *Boys and English*. London: Ofsted.

Ortega, Bob (1998) *In Sam We Trust: The Untold Story of Sam Walton and how Wal-Mart is Devouring America*. New York: Times Business.

Orwell, George (1989 [1949]) *Nineteen Eighty-four*. Harmondsworth: Penguin.

Owen, Marion (1983) *Apologies and Remedial Interchanges*. Berlin: Mouton.

Patton, Bruce and Stone, Douglas (1999) *Difficult Conversations*. London: Michael Joseph.

Pescovitz, David (1999) 'Sons and daughters of HAL go on line: with chatterbots on the web, conversation can be surprising, or surprisingly limited'. *New York Times*, 18 March: G1/8.

Peters, Tom (1990) 'The best new managers will listen, motivate, support: isn't that just like a woman?' *Working Woman*, September, pp. 216–17.

Phillips, Angela (1994) *The Trouble With Boys: A Wise and Sympathetic Guide to the Risky Business of Raising Sons*. New York: Basic Books.

Phillips, Angela (1998) *Communication: A Key Skill for Education*. London: BT Forum.

Post, Emily (1922) *Etiquette: The Blue Book of Social Usage*. New York: Funk and Wagnell.

Qualifications and Curriculum Authority [QCA] (1998) *Can Do Better: Raising Boys' Achievement in English*. Hayes, Middx: QCA Publications.

Rakos, Richard (1991) *Assertiveness: Theory, Training and Research*. London: Routledge.

Rapping, Elayne (1996) *The Culture of Recovery: Making Sense of the Self-help Movement in Women's Lives*. Boston: Beacon Press.

Reardon, Geraldine (1996) *Dialling the Future? Phone Banking and Insurance*. London: BIFU.

Ritzer, George (1996) *The McDonaldization of Society: An Investigation into the Changing Character of Contemporary Social Life*. Revised edn. Thousand Oaks, CA: Pine Forge Press.

Roberts, Celia, Davies, Evelyn and Jupp, Tom (1992) *Language and Discrimination: A Study of Communication in Multi-ethnic Workplaces*. London: Longman.

Roloff, Michael E. (1996) 'The catalyst hypothesis: conditions under which coercive communication leads to physical aggression', in Dudley Cahn and Sally Lloyd (eds), *Family Violence from a Communication Perspective*. Thousand Oaks, CA: Sage Publications. pp. 20–36.

Rose, Nikolas (1990) *Governing the Soul: The Shaping of the Private Self*. London: Routledge.

Scheeres, Hermine (1998) 'New workplaces: talk and teamwork'. Paper presented at Sociolinguistics Symposium 12, London.

Schiffrin, Deborah (1987) *Discourse Markers*. Cambridge: Cambridge University Press.

Scotton, Carol Myers (1988) 'Code switching as indexical of social negotiations', in Monica Heller (ed.), *Codeswitching: Anthropological and Sociolinguistic Perspectives*. Berlin: Mouton de Gruyter. pp. 151–86.

Sennett, Richard (1998) *The Corrosion of Character: The Personal Consequences of Work in the New Capitalism*. New York: W.W. Norton.

Sewell, G. and Wilkinson, B. (1992) 'Someone to watch over me: surveillance, discipline and the just-in-time labour process', *Sociology*, 26 (2): 271–89.

Shannon, C. and Weaver, W. (1949) *The Mathematical Theory of Communication*. Urbana-Champaign, IL: University of Illinois Press.

Shavit, Yossi and Müller, Walter (eds) (1998) *From School to Work: A Comparative Study of Educational Qualifications and Occupational Destinations*. Oxford: Clarendon Press.

Sherzer, Joel (1987) 'Women's and men's voices in ethnographic perspective', in Susan Phillips, Susan Steele and Christine Tanz (eds), *Language, Gender and Sex in Comparative Perspective*. New York: Cambridge University Press. pp. 95–120.

Skuse, D.H., James, R.S., Bishop, D.V.M., Coppin, B., Dalton, P., Aamodt-Leeper, G., Bacarese-Hamilton, M., Creswell, C., McGurk, R. and Jacobs, P.A. (1997) 'Evidence from Turner's syndrome of an imprinted X-linked locus affecting cognitive function', *Nature*, 387.6634: 705–8.

Smith, Patten and Turner, Rachel (1997) *Listening to the Nation*. London: BT Forum.

Sperber, Dan and Wilson, Deirdre (1986) *Relevance: Communication and Cognition*. Oxford: Blackwell.

Stross, Brian (1974) 'Speaking of speaking: Tenejapa Tzeltal metalinguistics', in Richard Bauman and Joel Sherzer (eds), *Explorations in the Ethnography of Speaking*. Cambridge: Cambridge University Press. pp. 213–39.

Stubbs, Michael (1997) 'Language and the mediation of experience: linguistic representation and cognitive orientation', in Florian Coulmas (ed.), *The Handbook of Sociolinguistics*. Oxford: Blackwell. pp. 344–57.

Swann, Joan (1998) 'Language and gender: who, if anyone, is disadvantaged by what?', in Debbie Epstein, Jannette Elwood, Valerie Hay and Janet Maw (eds), *Failing Boys: Issues in Gender and Achievement.* Buckingham: Open University Press. pp. 147–61.

Tannen, Deborah (1991) *You Just Don't Understand: Men and Women in Conversation.* London: Virago.

Tannen, Deborah (1995) *Talking from 9 to 5.* London: Virago.

Tannock, Stuart (1997) 'Positioning the worker: discursive practice in a workplace literacy program', *Discourse & Society,* 8 (1): 85–116.

Taylor, Frederick (1911) *The Principles of Scientific Management.* New York: Norton.

Taylor, Steve (1998) 'Emotional labour and the new workplace', in P. Thompson and C. Warhurst (eds), *Workplaces of the Future.* London: Macmillan. pp. 84–103.

Thorpe, Nick (1999) 'Airline pay offer wipes the smile off staff's faces'. *The Scotsman,* 7 January.

Tyler, Melissa and Taylor, Steve (1997) '"Come fly with us": emotional labour and the commodification of sexual difference in the airline industry'. Paper presented to the Annual International Labour Process Conference, Edinburgh.

Wernick, Andrew (1991) *Promotional Culture: Advertising, Ideology and Symbolic Expression.* London and Newbury Park, CA: Sage Publications.

Whalen, D. Joel (1996) *I See What You Mean: Persuasive Business Communication.* London and Thousand Oaks, CA: Sage Publications.

Whalen, Jack and Vinkhuyzen, Erik (in press) 'Expert systems in (inter)action: diagnosing document machine problems over the telephone', in Christian Heath, Jon Hindmarsh and Paul Luff (eds), *Workplace Studies: Recovering Work Practice and Informing Systems Design.* Cambridge: Cambridge University Press.

Witz, Anne, Warhurst, Chris, Nickson, Dennis and Cullen, Anne-Marie (1998) '"Human hardware"? Aesthetic labour, the labour of aesthetics and the aesthetics of organization'. Paper presented to the Work, Employment and Society conference, Cambridge.

Wodak, Ruth and Iedema, Rick (1999) 'Introduction: organizational discourses and practices'. Special Issue, 'Discourse in Organizations', *Discourse & Society,* 10 (1): 5–19.

Zeldin, Theodore (1998) *Conversation: How Talk Can Change Your Life.* London: Harvill Press.

Zernike, Kate (1999) 'Talk is like, you know, cheapened: colleges introduce classes to clean up campus "mallspeak"'. *Boston Globe,* 31 January: A1.

INDEX